PRIDE AND POWER

UNIVERSITY OF ILLINOIS PRESS, URBANA, 1964

PRIDE AND POWER

The Rationale of the Space Program

by Vernon Van Dyke

As I look back upon these two years of involvement in this exciting activity, I find myself wishing that we could have been operating in support of more clearly understood and nationally accepted goals or purposes. . . . How can we decide how important it is to spend, on an urgent basis, the very large sums of money required to put a man into orbit or to explore the atmosphere and surface of Mars or Venus unless we have a pretty firm grasp of what the purpose behind the whole space effort really is? And yet, who knows the answers to this and many similar questions today? Who is thinking about them and doing something about developing some answers?

—T. Keith Glennan, first NASA Administrator

We have given this program a high national priority, even though I realize that this is in some measure an act of faith and vision, for we do not now know what benefits await us.

—President John F. Kennedy

If the historians and the political scientists and the sociologists are keeping an alert eye and an open mind on this decade's space adventure, it may give them some fresh and startling ideas on the kinds of things that have motivated societies and nations.

—Robert Colborn, *International Science and Technology*

PREFACE

This book stems mainly from curiosity about the values and interests—the motives or reasons—that inspire political behavior, especially in the field of international relations. I began by asking to what extent the space program is motivated by a desire to enhance American prestige over the world, and this question quickly led to a number of others, both in and out of the international field. The result is an analysis of the general rationale—the why and how—of the space program.

I found that the most powerful motives—above all in political circles—are of a competitive sort. When people abroad compare our achievements in space with those of the Soviet Union, we want to come out on top. Even more important, when we ourselves make the comparison, we want to be able to credit ourselves with first place; to be second is bad, and to be second-rate is intolerable. Further, we are anxious lest the Soviet Union gain a military advantage in space, and so want to explore the military possibilities if only as a kind of contingency insurance. Motives such as the promotion of scientific, technological, and economic progress are less compelling in political circles, though in other circles one or another of them may be dominant.

As to the how of the space program, my concern is again with the political. I do not ask about the scientific and technological measures to implement the program, but about governmental measures. And in saying what the governmental measures are I also try to say why these measures were adopted or what purposes they serve.

In dwelling on motives and on actions taken in response to them, I am attempting explanation. The explanation is obviously not in terms of causal conditions that are beyond human control —though such explanation might be possible—but rather in terms of the conscious reasons that people entertain concerning the wisdom of this or that action. At the same time, I am either appraising or providing a basis for appraising the actions undertaken or proposed.

The book was made possible by a Senior Research Award in Governmental Affairs extended to me by the Social Science Research Council. The award permitted me to spend a year in Washington, D.C., where the Brookings Institution made me a Guest Scholar. In my research I chose to rely in the first instance on written sources, which turned out to be voluminous: the various kinds of congressional materials, the mimeographed releases of the National Aeronautics and Space Administration (NASA), the Department of Defense, and other executive agencies, numerous specialized journals (e.g., *Air Force/Space Digest*), scattered books and articles, and press reports. The NASA Historian, Dr. Eugene M. Emme, was kind enough to open his unclassified files to me, and they proved to be a rich source of data. To supplement these sources and to resolve doubts where I could, I interviewed persons in various governmental and nongovernmental offices and agencies; some of them also helped by reading portions of my manuscript. For the assistance given to me, my thanks go especially to the following: above all, to Dr. Charles S. Sheldon II, of the staff of the National Aeronautics and Space Council, who became a regular source of information and advice and who read most of the manuscript; to Major Richard C. Henry, USAF, whom I consulted particularly about the military potentialities of space; to Arnold W. Frutkin, Julian Scheer, O. B. Lloyd, Melvin Day, James Dean, Willson Hunter, Brian Duff, and Frank Anderson, all of NASA; to Dr. Hugh L. Dryden, Deputy Administrator of NASA; to Robert Packard, Chief of the Outer Space Section of the Office of International Scientific Affairs in the Department of State; to Lowell Bennett, Robert M. Evans, Harry Kendall, Irving R. Wechsler, Simon Bourgin, and Dr. Claude B. Cross, all of the U.S. Information Agency; to Dr. Glen P. Wilson and Philip B. Yeager of the staffs of the Senate and House space committees, respectively; to Robert G. Smith of the System Development Corporation; to Lambert L. Lind, Jr., of United Aircraft; to Dr. Martin L. Peller of the Johns Hopkins University Applied Physics Laboratory; and to Joel Orlen of the staff of the Space Science Board of the National Academy of Sciences. The Iowa senators, Bourke B. Hickenlooper and Jack Miller, and Representative Fred Schwengel were all helpful to me. Dr. David Hartman of Washington, D.C., and Professor Don Kash, now at Arizona State University, gave me valuable assistance in various ways. At the Brookings Institution I gained much from conversations that went on through the year, especially with Andrew Westwood and D. A. FitzGerald, both of whom have had rich experience in Washington; and Dr. Merton J. Peck helped me particularly with Chapter 7. Finally, my thanks go to my colleagues at Iowa, particularly to Professors Lane Davis and Samuel Patterson, for the comments and suggestions that they have made. The usual exoneration applies: those whom I have consulted are not to be blamed for the faults that the book may contain.

I deal mainly with the public arguments relating to various issues concerning the space program—the arguments that Congress and the voters have been asked to consider. In these terms, I believe that the sources that I have tapped are reasonably complete, though it would be foolish to claim that I have missed nothing. I also present some historical analysis, and for this purpose my data are obviously incomplete, for some are classified and some are no doubt still in the private files and memories of the persons who have played key roles in the development of the space program. When and if these data become available, they will no doubt call for a modification of this or that account or interpretation. Only the future will tell to what extent the modifications are supplements and to what extent they are corrections.

University of Iowa   Vernon Van Dyke
December 1, 1963

CONTENTS

PART IV. CONCLUSION

PART **I** INTRODUCTORY

INTRODUCTION

1

Though the space program is widely regarded as scientific and technological, it is also obviously political. It is implemented by government, partly for political reasons, and it involves both international competition and domestic controversy.

The controversy, at its core, is over the question what the reasons for the space program are and whether they justify the costs. Manned space flight is the chief issue, particularly the effort to get a man to the moon and back in this decade. How important is it that the trip occur and that it occur on so urgent a basis? How important is it that we beat the Russians or at least avoid being beaten? Apart from this issue, what other reasons for the space program operate, and how cogent are they? There is less controversy over governmental arrangements and activities for implementing the program, but enough to be significant nevertheless.

The fact of controversy over the rationale of the space program indicates a major purpose of the chapters that follow: to contribute to thought on the question why we have the program and on the basis of what principles it should be managed.

Other purposes can be served simultaneously. How decisions get made and to what extent the process is or can be rational are questions of universal application in political science. Decisions are central to political behavior—decisions by individual voters, by administrators or office holders, by governmental agencies of all sorts—and they can be studied in many different ways. In what follows I propose to study in a macroscopic way the major decisions that have been made relating to the American space program. I say macroscopic because I will not make a meticulous effort to determine precisely how much influence specific individuals have had on decisions and precisely what their personal thought processes have been; rather, I propose to engage in a more general analysis of the reasons given to explain or justify the decisions that have been made and to identify the categories of persons or groups endorsing or responding to the various reasons. I will pay special attention to attitudes in the Executive branch of government and in Congress. I do not expect to arrive at a definitive answer to the question whether major governmental decisions can be rational, or even whether decisions concerning space have been rational. But I hope to contribute to consideration of the problem. I have in mind Charles E. Lindblom's analysis of "The Science of 'Muddling Through,'" and will refer to it again in the concluding chapter.

Still another purpose relates to the general problem that can figuratively be described as the failure of the United States to know its own mind. Especially in connection with foreign policy, virtually every crisis that the country confronted from the time of the Spanish-American War to World War II found the President and his advisers without a well-thought-out conception of the purposes (the goals, values, interests, motives [1]) that ought to be pursued. Time and again, therefore, improvisation has occurred, and goals have been pursued that had little or nothing to do with those previously proclaimed. Each crisis, each surprise, has called up a new, or at least a different, conception of goals, and each new or different conception has later been superseded by another. The characteristic is illustrated by the space program. Sputnik I and its successors led the United States to adopt goals (to act for reasons) some of which had rarely been mentioned theretofore. In particular, the idea that we should act so as to maintain or enhance our national pride and that this requires us to beat the Russians in scientific and technological achievement is a new and different motive called up by Sputnik; and that it may go the way of former major objectives is suggested by the late President's proposal of September, 1963, that instead of racing the Russians to the moon we should join with them in a cooperative program.

---

[1] Vernon Van Dyke, "Values and Interests," *American Political Science Review*, 56 (September, 1962), 567-76.

I will suggest an explanation of the apparent inconstancy of American purposes in Chapter 11.

Reasons Commonly Cited for the Space Program

Though the reasons for the space program will be examined in detail in later chapters, it may be helpful at the outset to provide a sample of them. One of the early efforts to identify them coherently was made in 1958 in an "Introduction to Outer Space," prepared by President Eisenhower's Science Advisory Committee, under the chairmanship of Dr. James R. Killian, Jr. It describes four factors that give "importance, urgency, and inevitability to the advancement of space technology."

The first of these factors is the compelling urge of man to explore and to discover, the thrust of curiosity that leads men to try to go where no one has gone before. Most of the surface of the earth has now been explored and men now turn to the exploration of outer space as their next objective.

Second, there is the defense objective for the development of space technology. We wish to be sure that space is not used to endanger our security. If space is to be used for military purposes, we must be prepared to use space to defend ourselves.

Third, there is the factor of national prestige. To be strong and bold in space technology will enhance the prestige of the United States among the peoples of the world and create added confidence in our scientific, technological, industrial, and military strength.

Fourth, space technology affords new opportunities for scientific observation and experiment which will add to our knowledge and understanding of the earth, the solar system, and the universe.

In recommending the legislation that created NASA (the National Aeronautics and Space Administration), President Eisenhower listed the purposes of the organization. Among other things it was to contribute to "the preservation of the role of the United States as a leader in aeronautical and space science and technology." And this purpose is among those endorsed by Congress in the National Aeronautics and Space Act itself. Prior to taking office, President-elect Kennedy appointed an Ad Hoc Committee on Space, with Dr. Jerome B. Wiesner as Chairman, and its report included statements concerning the goals of a space program.

In addition to the need to develop ballistic missiles to provide for our military security, there are five principal motivations for desiring a vital, effective space program. . . .

First, there is the factor of national prestige. . . . During the next few years, the prestige of the United States will in part be determined by the leadership we demonstrate in space activities. . . .

Second, we believe that some space developments, in addition to missiles, can contribute much to our national security. . . .

Third, the development of space vehicles affords new opportunities for scientific observation and experiment—adding to our knowledge and understanding of the earth, the solar system, and the universe. . . .

Fourth, there are a number of important practical non-military applications of space technology—among them satellite communications and broadcasting, satellite navigation and geodesy, meteorological reconnaissance, and satellite mapping—which can make important contributions to our civilian efforts and to our economy.

Finally, space activities . . . offer exciting possibilities for international cooperation with all the nations of the world. The very ambitious and long-range space projects would prosper if they could be carried out in an atmosphere of cooperation as projects of all mankind instead of in the present atmosphere of national competition.

James E. Webb, Administrator of NASA, has made a number of statements of the rationale of the program that he directs. One of them is as follows, and others will be noted in subsequent chapters. "That is our objective—to develop superior competence in space which will be available for any national purpose which may be required, whether it be the peaceful utilization of space for the benefit of mankind, or to keep the peace and forestall its exploitation by any nation for aggressive purposes. . . . We will . . . occupy a position second to none." NASA's Deputy Administrator, Dr. Hugh L. Dryden, has spoken along the following lines: "The ultimate and practical purpose of these large expenditures is twofold: (1) insurance of the Nation against scientific and technological obsolescence in a time of explosive advances in science and technology; and (2) insurance against the hazard of military surprise in space."

Another commentator cites national pride as a justification of the space program. "It should be enough without all the other reasons and rationalizations that have been presented. It is the proper motivation of a prideful people with vitality, a sense of destiny, and confidence in their own ability." [2] Still another view is that we are engaged in "an effort with no practical, describable motive at all. An effort engaged in simply for its own sake. . . .

[2] Harold Leland Goodwin, *Space: Frontier Unlimited* (Princeton: Van Nostrand, 1962), p. 111.

Some will quarrel with the description of space exploration as a motiveless enterprise. And yet most of the motives advanced for it seem to me more like by-products than like major purposes." [3]

President Eisenhower never attempted a coherent statement of the rationale of the space program, and neither did President Kennedy. But some of Kennedy's statements might be cited, selected so as to suggest motives not brought out fully by the quotations already given. Once Kennedy referred to the congressional injunction that NASA should contribute to "the preservation of the role of the United States as a leader," and he said that it was "to meet that great responsibility that I have suggested a great national effort in the field of space for the American people." He thought that it was "time for this nation to take a clearly leading role in space achievement." According to him, the United States wishes "to demonstrate to a watching world that it is first in the field of technology and science. . . . I do not believe that we want to permit the Soviet Union to dominate space, with all that it might mean to our peace and security in the coming years." "If we can get to the moon before the Russians, we should." [4]

But why, some say, the moon? Why choose this as our goal? And they may well ask why climb the highest mountain. Why, thirty-five years ago, fly the Atlantic? Why does Rice play Texas?

We choose to go to the moon. We choose to go to the moon in this decade, and do the other things not because they are easy, but because they are hard, because that goal will serve to organize and measure the best of our energies and skills, because that challenge is one that we are willing to accept, one we are unwilling to postpone, and one we intend to win, and the others, too.

It is for these reasons that I regard the decision last year to shift our efforts in space from low to high gear as among the most important decisions that will be made during my incumbency in the office of the Presidency. [5]

A year later Kennedy's mood was quite different.

Why should man's first flight to the moon be a matter of national competition? Why should the United States and the Soviet Union, in preparing for such expeditions, become involved in immense duplications of research, construction, and expenditure? Surely we should explore

---

[3] Robert Colborn, "In Our Opinion," *International Science and Technology*, January, 1963, p. 19.

[4] U.S. President, *Public Papers of the Presidents of the United States*, John F. Kennedy . . . January 20 to December 31, 1961 (Washington, 1962), pp. 310, 403, 407, 734 (hereafter cited as *Public Papers of the Presidents*).

[5] *Public Papers of the Presidents*, Kennedy, 1962, p. 669.

whether the scientists and astronauts of our two countries—indeed of all the world—cannot work together in the conquest of space, sending someday in this decade to the moon, not the representatives of a single nation, but the representatives of all of our countries.

Now most of these statements of purpose can be fitted together; most of the motives cited may really be operating. Nevertheless there is enough variety and contradiction in the statements to arouse curiosity. What motives actually seem to operate? What differences are there in the motives endorsed by different persons and groups at different times? What unintended effects, if any, does the space program seem to be producing? Can a rational man find a rationale that permits him to support the program, or must he conclude that modifications of some sort are required? What does behavior relating to space tell us about our behavior—and about human behavior—in other realms?

THE HISTORICAL DEVELOPMENT OF THE SPACE PROGRAM

2

The American record pertaining to space is both miserable and impressive. We might argue about the reasons for the miserable aspects of the record. To some extent there was a failure to foresee certain scientific and technological possibilities. Even after these possibilities became reasonably well established, there was a failure to see their potential importance in a psychological and political sense; and coupled with this was a certain blindness to evidence of growing Soviet capacities. Perhaps these reasons should suffice as an explanation, but they fall short in that they do not tell us the why of the failures and the blindness. Implicitly they raise the question whether there was something about the outlook of those mainly responsible that dulled sensitivities, whether there was a lack of a clear and coherent set of values that might have made them alert to relevant possibilities and developments. When people do not know what matters to them—what their goals are—failures and frustrations are not surprising.

There is less room for argument about the assertion that the record is impressive. A program of great magnitude is under way, flowing from legislation, from organizational arrangements, and from an awakened sense of purpose—all worth noting. Moreover, the program is producing striking results in various areas, and more are yet to come. Whether they are worth the costs, whether the resources being devoted to space might produce still more desirable results if they were devoted to other undertakings, is another question.

Doubts About Missiles

Early doubts and hesitations about the feasibility of developing long-range missiles necessarily implied similar doubts about satellites. And such doubts existed. In December, 1945, Dr. Vannevar Bush, wartime Director of the Office of Scientific Research and Development, testified before a Senate committee on speculation concerning a "high-angle rocket" that might travel as far as 3,000 miles and be aimed accurately enough to hit a city with an atomic bomb. Dr. Bush found the speculation annoying. "I don't think anybody in the world knows how to do such a thing, and I feel confident it will not be done for a very long period of time to come." He wished that the American public "would leave that out of their thinking." [1]

In the same month an Army Air Force Scientific Advisory Group organized by Dr. Theodore von Karman made a report designed to identify the most promising lines of development for the Air Force. The report spoke of V-2–type rockets, saying that it might be possible to increase their range by 30 times, and it spoke of a satellite as a "definite possibility." But there was no development of either thought. Once mentioned, both thoughts were dropped in favor of a stress on what could be done within the atmosphere. [2]

From the spring of 1946 on the Air Force gave intermittent support, on a marginal basis, to studies pertaining to long-range missiles, but it was pessimistic. The A-bomb warhead was still very heavy, and the H-bomb had not been developed at all, which meant that the problem of developing a booster that would be adequate in terms of thrust and accuracy was very great. At the time, the manned bomber seemed preferable by far as a delivery vehicle, and even the projected unmanned Navaho—air-breathing and air-supported—seemed more promising than long-range missiles that would travel through the vacuum of space. It was not until 1951 that the Air Force got the Atlas project under way on

---

[1] U.S. Congress, Senate, Special Committee on Atomic Energy, *Atomic Energy*, Hearings . . . Pursuant to S. Res. 179, 79th Cong., 1st Sess., 1945, Part 1, p. 179.

[2] Theodore von Karman, *Toward New Horizons: Science the Key to Air Supremacy*, report to General of the Army H. H. Arnold . . . Hq., Army Air Forces, Washington, D.C., December 15, 1945, pp. ix, 4, 13, 25.

an enduring basis. In the early postwar years both the Army and the Navy confined themselves to relatively short-range missiles and sounding rockets. The Navy's program included the Viking, the stepping stone toward the Vanguard program. The Army brought Wernher von Braun and more than a hundred other Peenemünde scientists and engineers to this country after the war, but not until 1951 did it begin to give them more or less substantial support and not until 1955 were they authorized to develop an IRBM. For the whole Department of Defense, the 1953 fiscal year is the first one in which the obligational program for ICBM-IRBM missile systems exceeded $1 million.[3]

The situation changed strikingly after 1953, when it became clear that thermonuclear bombs could be developed light enough to be delivered by missiles, and when intelligence activities (mainly if not entirely the operation of radar devices in Turkey) revealed significant Soviet progress with missiles. The prospect was that within a few years Soviet missiles with nuclear warheads might be able to knock manned American bombers out of the sky, and longer-range missiles might be able to destroy air bases and cities within the United States. This prospect made the development of similar American capabilities imperative—a fact stressed in February, 1954, in the report of the Air Force's Strategic Missiles Evaluation Committee, headed by Dr. John von Neumann. The Air Force promptly assigned the ballistic missile program the highest priority, but it was not until the fall of 1955 that Secretary of Defense Wilson followed suit; he then made it a Department of Defense objective "to carry out research and development programs on the ICBM and IRBM at the maximum rate technology would permit." Even then, according to Trevor Gardner, Secretary Wilson "inexplicably issued instructions which tended to slow down the entire ballistic missile program. The real problem—how to maintain technical superiority over the U.S.S.R.—had unfortunately been sidetracked in favor of balancing the budget."[4]

Proposals for Satellites

Actions looking toward the launching of an earth satellite by

[3] U.S. Congress, Senate, Committee on Armed Services, Preparedness Investigating Subcommittee, *The United States Guided Missile Program*, prepared by Charles H. Donnelly, 86th Cong., 1st Sess., 1959, p. 99.

[4] Trevor Gardner, "How We Fell Behind in Guided Missiles," *Air Power Historian*, 5 (January, 1958), 10.

the U.S. government began at least as early as the spring of 1945. From hindsight, perhaps the most striking statement concerning the possibility was made in a RAND report of May, 1946, "Preliminary Design of an Experimental World-Circling Spaceship." [5]

Although the crystal ball is cloudy, two things seem clear:

1. A satellite vehicle with appropriate instrumentation can be expected to be one of the most potent scientific tools of the 20th century.

2. The achievement of a satellite craft by the United States would inflame the imagination of mankind, and would probably produce repercussions in the world comparable to the explosion of the atomic bomb. . . .

Since mastery of the elements is a reliable index of material progress, the nation which first makes significant achievements in space travel will be acknowledged as the world leader in both military and scientific techniques. To visualize the impact on the world, one can imagine the consternation and admiration that would be felt here if the U.S. were to discover suddenly that some other nation had already put up a successful satellite.

But the first proposals got nowhere. In 1948 a Technical Evaluation Group in the Department of Defense considered proposals submitted by the Navy and the Air Force, only to conclude that neither had "as yet established either a military or a scientific utility commensurate with the presently expected cost of a satellite vehicle." At the same time, the Group held that "the question of utility deserves further study and examination." [6]

In truth, this was a time when skepticism prevailed, variously based on doubts concerning the feasibility of placing satellites in orbit, or doubts about whether the returns would justify the costs, or doubts about whether Congress and the people could be induced to foot the bill. A House committee report indicates that in the Department of Defense "for a long time it was considered not quite respectable to talk in terms of space flight." [7] Lloyd V. Berkner says that "when a group of scientists, after a summer of study in 1952, advocated that the United States seriously undertake a

---

[5] Quoted by R. Cargill Hall, "Early U.S. Satellite Proposals," in *Congressional Record*, Vol. 109, No. 159 (October 7, 1963), A6279.

[6] Eugene M. Emme, *Aeronautics and Astronautics, an American Chronology of Science and Technology in the Exploration of Space 1915-1960* (Washington: NASA, GPO, 1961), p. 59.

[7] U.S. Congress, House, Committee on Science and Astronautics, *Military Astronautics* (Preliminary Report), H. Rpt. No. 360, 87th Cong., 1st Sess., 1961, p. 1.

space program, the idea was hooted down as outrageous." [8] The general air of conservatism and the stress on economy under Eisenhower and Secretary of Defense Wilson were not propitious to boldness pertaining to space or, for that matter, to imaginative research. Wilson thought of putting objects in orbit as a "nice scientific trick," a useless stunt, and told a press conference that he would not be alarmed if the Soviet Union did it first.[9] "Some top-level people [including Wilson] expressed the view they did not care what is on the other side of the moon or why the grass is green." [10]

Nevertheless, as developments pertaining to missiles made it seem more and more feasible to launch satellites, interest began to spread. By the end of 1954 several plans were under development in the Department of Defense, the two leading ones being Project Orbiter—an Army-Navy proposal calling for the use of the Redstone booster that the von Braun group was developing—and what became Vanguard, proposed by the Naval Research Laboratory. In the same general period, interest in satellites was developing outside government circles, especially in the American Rocket Society, among scientists planning for the International Geophysical Year (IGY), and more broadly in the National Science Foundation and the National Academy of Sciences. When the White House Press Secretary announced in July, 1955, that President Eisenhower had approved plans for launching a small unmanned earth-circling satellite as part of the U.S. participation in the IGY, he was flanked by the President of the National Academy of Sciences and the Director of the National Science Foundation; and "he stressed that the satellite would be constructed strictly for scientific purposes, and not with any war purpose in mind. . . ." [11] At the same time, Eisenhower placed responsibility for the launching in

[8] Lloyd V. Berkner, "Science and the World Tomorrow," lecture of January 19, 1962, Industrial College of the Armed Forces, mimeo., p. 1.

[9] Jay Holmes, *America on the Moon: The Enterprise of the Sixties* (Philadelphia: Lippincott, 1962), p. 49; *Newsweek,* 50 (October 21, 1957), 30.

[10] "Project Vanguard, a Scientific Earth Satellite Program for the IGY," report to the Committee on Appropriations, by Surveys and Investigations Staff, in U.S. Congress, House, Committee on Appropriations, Subcommittee on Department of Defense Appropriations, *Department of Defense Appropriations for 1960,* Hearings, 86th Cong., 1st Sess., 1959, Part 6, pp. 69-70 (hereafter cited as House Appropriations, "Project Vanguard").

[11] Erik Bergaust and William Beller, *Satellite* (Garden City: Hanover House, 1956), p. 37.

the Department of Defense, which meant that it had to decide which satellite project or projects to support.

The Department made a notoriously bad decision, after resorting to procedures and reasoning much too complex to trace here. It chose Vanguard rather than Orbiter. Probably the dominant fact is that few assigned much political importance or urgency to the matter. In pressing the case for Orbiter, the Army predicted that it could get a satellite in orbit by January, 1957, and said that "since this is the date by which the U.S.S.R. may well be ready to launch, U.S. prestige dictates that every effort should be made to launch the first U.S. satellite at that time." [12] But there is no evidence that this kind of consideration got much attention. As President Eisenhower later said, the Vanguard project was "deliberately separated from our ballistic missile efforts in order, first, to accent the scientific purposes of the satellite and, second, to avoid interference with top priority missile programs. . . . Our satellite program has never been conducted as a race with other nations." [13] Concern for national military security was thus interpreted to require not that space activities be got under way but that they be kept out of the way. Under the prevailing view, national prestige was not at stake, and no one thought of mentioning national pride, i.e., the importance to national self-esteem that the country should be first in space. The requirement was simply that one satellite be placed in orbit during the IGY (that is, by the end of 1958). Twenty to thirty million dollars was thought of as the probable cost. "The Vanguard program was conceived in presputnik 1955 in an aura of unwarranted, but nonetheless real, national complacency concerning the technical supremacy of the United States. It was planned as a comparatively low-level, economical effort and was not to interfere with the ballistic missile development." [14] Denials that we were in a race coupled with the selection of the name Vanguard do much to suggest the smugness of the time.[15]

Dr. Lloyd V. Berkner, former Chairman of the Space Science Board of the National Academy of Sciences, has suggested that "a little

[12] House Appropriations, "Project Vanguard," p. 59.

[13] U.S. President, *Public Papers of the Presidents of the United States,* Dwight D. Eisenhower . . . January 1 to December 31, 1957 (Washington, 1958), pp. 734-35 (hereafter cited as *Public Papers of the Presidents*).

[14] House Appropriations, "Project Vanguard," p. 54.

[15] Kurt R. Stehling, *Project Vanguard* (Garden City: Doubleday, 1961), p. 64.

timely scientific advice" was called for regarding the prospect that the Soviet Union would launch a satellite. "Our policy-makers seem to have had no appreciation of the international reaction that would follow the accomplishment of that scientific feat." [16] Whether it was "scientific" advice that was needed is perhaps a question of semantics. The truth is that there were relatively abundant and open reports concerning developing Soviet capacities, to say nothing of the reports that American secret intelligence was producing.[17] The question is why these reports (like those that should have given warning of Pearl Harbor) had so little effect. Perhaps those making the crucial decisions were really hearing only what was congenial to their ears. And perhaps they were not entirely self-conscious and articulate about the values that turned out to matter both to them and to the American people more generally. America's prestige, her leadership in the world, her place second to none may have been unconsciously assumed as a part of the natural order of things rather than consciously regarded as prized distinctions to be striven for and earned. Those who are unaware of their values are not likely to recognize developing threats.

For what was no doubt a mixture of reasons, the Army persisted in its effort to get a role for itself in the satellite effort. Twice in 1956 it formally sought approval for a launching attempt, only to be "specifically instructed not to use any part of the Jupiter or Redstone programs for scientific satellites." [18] Its Jupiter-C fired an inert fourth stage 3,300 miles down range in September, 1956, and both General Medaris and Wernher von Braun claim that if a solid propellant had been put into the fourth stage, it could have been placed in orbit at that time. A year later, on September 12, 1957, the Scientific Advisory Panel, attached to the Office of the Army Chief of Research and Development, estimated that a Soviet satellite would be launched within 30 days. On October 4, Sputnik I went up, and a month later Sputnik II. A Vanguard test vehicle not originally scheduled to attempt a satellite launching burned on its pad on December 6. Meantime, after Sputnik I, the

---

[16] Lloyd V. Berkner, "Earth Satellites and Foreign Policy," *Foreign Affairs*, 36 (January, 1958), 229.

[17] U.S. Congress, House, Select Committee on Astronautics and Space Exploration, *The National Space Program*, H. Rpt. No. 1758, 85th Cong., 2d Sess., 1958, pp. 204-8 (hereafter cited as H. Rpt. 1758, *The National Space Program*).

[18] House Appropriations, "Project Vanguard," p. 60.

Army finally got permission to launch, and on January 31, 1958, Explorer I went into orbit.

Actually, in terms of the original plans, Vanguard turned out to be a resounding success; but standards of judgment (thoughts concerning relevant instrumental and goal values) were so thoroughly transformed by Sputnik that it is usually remembered as an inglorious and shameful failure. We did not beat the Russians.

The Political Swing to Science

One of the most striking reactions to Sputnik is an enhancement of the status of natural scientists and an increase in their influence over national policy. Within two months President Eisenhower announced the establishment of a new office, the Office of Special Assistant to the President for Science and Technology, and transferred the Science Advisory Committee from the Office of Defense Mobilization to the White House, making it the President's Science Advisory Committee (PSAC). The first Special Assistant—also to become Chairman of PSAC—was James R. Killian, Jr., then President of MIT.

The purpose of the new office, said Eisenhower, "is to make it possible for me, personally, whenever there appears to be an unnecessary delay in our development system, to act promptly and decisively." [19] Now, whether there is unnecessary delay depends in part on knowing that you want to do something. In the absence of a goal, the question of a delay in achieving it does not arise. And the problem before Sputnik was much more in identifying goals than in prosecuting them. It is quite obvious that Eisenhower and Defense Secretary Wilson and very many others had failed to identify the goals that, as events proved, really turned out to matter to Congress and to a very substantial portion of the population. This will come out more clearly in subsequent chapters. Eisenhower evidently had some sense of the failure, for he brought the President's Commission on National Goals into existence; but for whatever reason, he did not seek federal funds to support the work of the Commission. It was a small-scale effort, privately financed. And the direct response to Sputnik was not a thorough inquiry into American values but the appointment of a Special Assistant to the President for Science and Technology.

[19] *Public Papers of the Presidents*, Eisenhower, 1957, p. 796.

From another point of view, this move was more logical. Science and technology have become increasingly important to productive activity within the country and over the world, and increasingly important to military power. In appointing Dr. Killian, President Eisenhower indicated that he "will have the active responsibility of helping me follow through on the program of scientific improvement of our defenses." This seemed to intimate—quite correctly —that both scientific inquiry and the potentialities revealed by it should be pursued more vigorously than in the past—in part, at least, for the purpose of contributing to American security. That Congress agreed is suggested by the fact that it increased appropriations for the National Science Foundation from $40 to $130 million.

Organizational Arrangements for the Space Age

Like the President, both the Department of Defense and Congress reacted to Sputnik with moves for organizational change. Within the Department of Defense, Secretary McElroy in February, 1958, established the Advanced Research Projects Agency (ARPA), to which he assigned responsibility for Vanguard and for other space activities. Congress cooperated by amending legislation restricting the Department to activities relating to weapons systems and military requirements; for a period of one year (pending a decision on how space activities should be managed on a more enduring basis) it authorized it "to engage in such advanced space projects as may be designated by the President."

Meantime the Preparedness Investigating Subcommittee of the Senate Armed Services Committee, under Lyndon B. Johnson, had launched into extensive hearings on missile and satellite programs, and in the first months of 1958 the Senate established a special committee and the House a select committee to deal specifically with problems associated with the exploration of space; in each case the members were the ranking majority and minority members from the most interested standing committees, e.g., the appropriations committees and the armed services committees, and the chairman was the majority leader—Johnson in the Senate, and McCormack in the House. In April President Eisenhower made his recommendations for space legislation, and in July Congress enacted the National Aeronautics and Space Act of 1958. Sharp struggles attended these developments, especially with regard to the role of the military in space activities, but on balance there was far more concord than discord.

President Eisenhower strongly urged that most space activities should be under civilian management, and the principle came to be almost universally endorsed.[20] Among the reasons that he cited in recommending this was the great importance of obtaining "the fullest cooperation of the scientific community at home and abroad." Moreover, he said "a civilian setting for the administration of space function [sic] will emphasize the concern of our nation that outer space be devoted to peaceful and scientific purposes." Nevertheless, the Space Act of 1958 does not endorse the principle of civilian management as strictly as did the Atomic Energy Act of 1946, which even assigned the development and production of weapons to the civilian commission. Instead of doing this, the Space Act, after stipulating that space activities shall be conducted by a civilian agency, goes on to state an exception: that activities peculiar to or primarily associated with weapons or defense shall be conducted by the Department of Defense. Inevitably the arrangement makes for persistent questions concerning the roles and the relationships of the two agencies.

The civilian agency provided for in the Act is the National Aeronautics and Space Administration (NASA). For its first Administrator, Eisenhower selected T. Keith Glennan, President of the Case Institute of Technology. Formally coming into existence on October 1, 1958, NASA incorporates and supersedes what was the National Advisory Committee for Aeronautics (NACA), which after its establishment during World War I built up an impressive record of research pertaining to aircraft, assisting the industry in scientific and technological developments of great significance. It was a research organization, with nothing in its record comparable to the extensive operations that the space program was to involve. NASA took over its responsibilities for research in aeronautics, together with its 8,000 scientists and other employees, located mainly at various research centers and stations outside Washington; its Director, Dr. Hugh L. Dryden, became NASA's Deputy Administrator. In addition to incorporating NACA, NASA took over the nonmilitary space activities, including Vanguard, that had been conducted by ARPA. And by transfer from the Army it assumed jurisdiction over the Jet Propulsion Laboratory, operated

[20] H. Rpt. 1758, *The National Space Program*, pp. 7, 37.

under contract by the California Institute of Technology. In time it also acquired the portion of the Army Ballistic Missile Agency at Huntsville that was especially concerned with large launching vehicles. Other NASA centers have subsequently been established, e.g., the Houston Manned Spacecraft Center.

The Space Act also provided for a National Aeronautics and Space Council over which the President was to preside. Eisenhower chose to make very little use of this body, and in 1960 recommended that it be abolished; but Lyndon B. Johnson, then majority leader of the Senate, favored a different course. In April, 1961, President Kennedy signed new legislation reviving the Council. The legislation removed the President from the membership and replaced him with the Vice President, i.e., with Johnson, who was designated Chairman. Other members of the Council are the Secretary of State, the Secretary of Defense, the Administrator of NASA, and the Chairman of the Atomic Energy Commission. The function of the Council is "to advise and assist the President, as he may request, with respect to the performance of functions in the aeronautics and space field." It is assisted by a small staff under an Executive Secretary.

Other agencies have come to be involved in space also. The Department of State is necessarily concerned with international cooperation in relation to space, which will be discussed in Chapter 14; and the U.S. Information Agency is concerned with the impact of space activities on the image of the United States abroad. The Department of Commerce, through the Weather Bureau, is heavily involved in the meteorological satellite program. The Atomic Energy Commission is responsible for the effort to develop nuclear sources of electrical energy and propulsive thrust. The Federal Communications Commission gets into the picture in connection with the assignment of frequencies for telemetering devices and in connection with the prospective global space communication system. And, of course, such different agencies as the Bureau of the Budget and the General Accounting Office are concerned with space agencies and activities as a part of their normal duties.

In Congress itself the special and select committees established in 1958 were temporary. To replace them Johnson and the Senate favored a joint committee, like the Joint Committee on Atomic Energy. Rayburn, the Speaker of the House, was very reluctant to add to the number of standing committees, and was hostile to the idea of a joint committee. In this situation, it is said, McCormack went along with the idea of a joint committee, and got the approval of his select committee for the principle, mainly to have a bargaining counter in dealing with Rayburn. McCormack would give up the demand for a joint committee if Rayburn would accept the proposal to create a new House standing committee; and it was to cover not only astronautics but also science. This arrangement was made, and when Johnson in the Senate asked about the earlier tentative understanding that there would be a joint committee, he was referred to Rayburn, his mentor from Texas. Thus, in the end, each house set up its own standing committee: the Committee on Aeronautical and Space Sciences in the Senate and the Committee on Science and Astronautics in the House. The difference in terminology has some significance, for the House committee deals with issues pertaining to science whether or not they relate to space. Once again it is interesting to note the identification of space with science, and not with such problems as national security and the determination of relevant values.

The Record Under Eisenhower

The early years of the space age were marked by a series of Soviet firsts of a spectacular sort. Sputnik I, of course, was spectacular by the very fact that it was a satellite. Sputniks II, III, and IV confirmed Soviet capabilities and emphasized them in terms of the weights placed in orbit. For Sputnik II the weight was estimated to be 11,000 pounds, of which 1,120 were due to scientific instrumentation; and for Sputnik IV over 14,000 pounds, of which 2,500 were due to scientific instrumentation. These weights for scientific instrumentation compare to 18 pounds for Explorer I, 3 for Vanguard I, and 19 for Explorer III. Another Soviet shot, Cosmic Rocket I, sent 800 pounds of instruments beyond the earth's gravity and into orbit around the sun. Cosmic Rocket II impacted on the surface of the moon, and Cosmic Rocket III took pictures of the hidden side of the moon. There followed a series of shots carrying biological payloads and other items into orbit, in part in preparation for manned space flight. Two dogs were recovered from space after one of the Soviet shots, and one dog and other animals after each of two others. One Sputnik went into orbit around the earth, and then was boosted into an interplanetary flight with Venus as the goal, only to be prematurely lost to radio contact. Finally, on April

12, 1961, came Vostok I and the first manned orbital flight, with Major Yuri Gagarin as the astronaut.

In the period of the above shots, the United States was active too. While the Soviet Union was launching 13 satellites and escape payloads, the United States (through the calendar year 1960) launched 33 rated as successful.[21] And these efforts included some notable firsts, e.g., the discovery of the Van Allen radiation belts. A number of Americans, including President Kennedy, have claimed that the United States took an early lead and has retained it in terms of the scientific knowledge gained from experiments in space, despite the much greater weight of scientific instruments that the Soviet Union has orbited.

But aside from the fact of putting payloads into orbit, the American accomplishments down to the inauguration of Kennedy were mainly of an esoteric sort, in contrast to Soviet spectaculars; and this meant that American prestige and pride were not recouped as fast as they might have been. The contrast was made all the greater by the fact that the Soviet Union did its best—and its best was very good, especially since it got a kind of cooperation from the U.S. intelligence services—to conceal failures from the outside world while the United States followed a policy of openness with respect to Vanguard and NASA launchings. The failure of the launching vehicle that was supposed to put Vanguard I in orbit on December 6, 1957, was a deeply mortifying response to Sputniks I and II, and by the end of 1960 34 additional attempts to launch satellites or escape payloads had failed. A few vehicles were destroyed for safety's sake; some broke up in flight; the second or third stage sometimes failed to ignite, or malfunctioned in another way; moon shots failed to reach the moon. Following the first orbital flight by Gagarin, the best the United States could do (on May 5, 1961) was to boost Astronaut Shepard up to an altitude of 116 miles and then recover him 302 miles down range.

As the number of American launches suggests, the U.S. space program achieved considerable magnitude under Eisenhower. Total budgets for space activities went up from $179 million in FY1957 (the fiscal year ending June 30, 1957) to the $1.2 billion that Eisenhower planned for FY1961—a sevenfold increase. The development of much more powerful boosters (e.g., the Saturn) was initiated,

---

[21] U.S. President, Report to the Congress, *United States Aeronautics and Space Activities, 1962* (Washington: National Aeronautics and Space Council, 1963), p. 107.

and the Mercury program (of which Shepard's suborbital flight was a part) was got under way. Nevertheless, in comparison with the demands that many were making and in comparison with what happened under Kennedy, the Eisenhower Administration followed a policy of calm conservatism. Eisenhower shared the view expressed by Deputy Secretary of Defense Donald Q. Quarles in November, 1957: "I find in the existence of the first satellites no cause for national alarm. In this respect I am disagreeing with many people who have been saying 'Let's beat them'; 'Let's put up a bigger satellite'; 'Let's hit the moon with a rocket.' . . . We must not be talked into 'hitting the moon with a rocket' just to be first, unless by so doing we stand to gain something of real scientific or military significance." [22]

The statement acknowledges the existence of contrary views and, in fact, many disagreed. The words *shock, panic*, and *hysteria* are commonly used to describe the reaction of the time. For good reasons or bad, Sputnik aroused fears for American security; it reduced American prestige and wounded American pride. Representatives and senators who were vocal on the subject (admittedly a small proportion of the total) were overwhelmingly for a more aggressive space effort. Members of the House space committee in particular were much more inclined to press money onto NASA than to make cuts. Repeatedly they asked Glennan and other witnesses whether they were really asking for enough. "How much money would you need to get us on a program that would make us even with Russia . . . and probably leapfrog them . . .? I want to be firstest with the mostest in space, and I just don't want to wait for years. How much money do we need to do it?" [23] The second-ranking Republican member of the committee, Mr. Fulton, asked the question, and the outlook it reflected was obviously dominant on the committee. "The willingness of Congress to appropriate as much funds as were necessary was repeatedly stressed by the committee." [24] Those trying to get dollars out of Congress for foreign aid must have been green with envy.

[22] U.S. Congress, Senate, Committee on Armed Services, Preparedness Investigating Subcommittee, *Inquiry into Satellite and Missile Programs*, Hearings, 85th Cong., 1st Sess., 1957, Part 1, pp. 301-2.

[23] U.S. Congress, House, Committee on Science and Astronautics, *Missile Development and Space Sciences*, Hearings, 86th Cong., 1st Sess., 1959, p. 20.

[24] U.S. Congress, House, Committee on Science and Astronautics, *Space, Missiles, and the Nation*, H. Rpt. No. 2092, 86th Cong., 2d Sess., 1960, p. 16.

Expansion and Acceleration Under Kennedy

If to Quarles and Eisenhower the crucial test of the justifiability of space activities was their scientific or military significance, to John F. Kennedy, running for the presidency in 1960, it was their bearing on national prestige and national pride. He made much of the claim that the country's prestige had declined, principally because of its record in space.

The people of the world respect achievement. For most of the 20th century they admired American science and American education, which was second to none. But now they are not at all certain about which way the future lies. The first vehicle in outer space was called sputnik, not Vanguard. The first country to place its national emblem on the moon was the Soviet Union, not the United States. The first canine passengers to outer space who safely returned were named Strelka and Belka, not Rover or Fido.

If the Soviet Union was first in outer space, that is the most serious defeat the United States has suffered in many, many years. . . . Because we failed to recognize the impact that being first in outer space would have, the impression began to move around the world that the Soviet Union was on the march, that it had definite goals, that it knew how to accomplish them, that it was moving and that we were standing still. That is what we have to overcome, that psychological feeling in the world that the United States has reached maturity, that maybe our high noon has passed . . . and that now we are going into the long, slow afternoon.[25]

Kennedy saw "no reason why we should be second to anyone in outer space."

As was to be expected, a struggle over the future of the space program accompanied the transition from Eisenhower to Kennedy. The scientists on whom Eisenhower had relied (e.g., Killian and Kistiakowski) naturally favored a continuation of the same sort of program as the one Eisenhower had approved, putting the stress on scientific purposes and on the pursuit of them through instrumented satellites; they were very reserved about manned space flight, if not opposed. Others, including a number of scientists on the Space Science Board of the National Academy of Sciences as well as scientists in NASA, wanted a much bolder program and in-

[25] U.S. Congress, Senate, Committee on Commerce, Subcommittee of the Subcommittee on Communications, Final Report, Freedom of Communications, Part I: *The Speeches, Remarks, Press Conferences, and Statements of Senator John F. Kennedy, August 1 through November 7, 1960*, S. Rpt. No. 994, 87th Cong., 1st Sess., 1961, Part 1, pp. 159, 377.

creased emphasis on manned flight. There were pressures, too, for an increased role for the military.[26]

Questions about the future of the program were answered in part simply by the announcement that James E. Webb was to be the new Administrator, for his expertise was that of a professional administrator in a political environment. In earlier years he had served as an administrative assistant to a congressman, as Director of the Bureau of the Budget, and as Under Secretary of State, and he had business experience as well—as an associate of Senator Kerr, the new Chairman of the Senate Committee on Aeronautical and Space Sciences. He did not have noteworthy standing in the scientific community. Both Kerr and Vice President Johnson recommended his appointment, no doubt in anticipation of an expansion of the space program.

Webb himself favored an expansion, and secured interim approval from Kennedy, followed by funds from Congress, for an acceleration of the large launch vehicle program. The question of making a much more ambitious effort in space led to an extensive round of discussions, in which Vice President Johnson and the revived Space Council played important roles. In the midst of these discussions—on April 12—came the Gagarin flight, and renewed pressure from the House committee. The Chairman of the committee spoke of "the desire of the American people that we move from second into first position in the exploration of space." Mr. Fulton, the Republican quoted above, renewed earlier pleas. "Tell us how much money you need and we on this committee will authorize all you need. I am tired of being second to the Soviet Union. I want to be first."[27] Mr. Fulton thought of the race as "good peaceful competition" with great significance for American prestige and for American effectiveness at the diplomatic bargaining table. On April 20 President Kennedy is said to have directed a memorandum to Vice President Johnson raising various questions about the national standing and prospects in the space race,[28] and those with whom Johnson consulted—both in and outside the government—seemed generally to favor a much more extensive effort in space than had been made theretofore. A later memoran-

[26] Holmes, *op. cit.*, pp. 189-93.

[27] U.S. Congress, House, Committee on Science and Astronautics, *Discussion of Soviet Man-in-Space Shot*, Hearings, 87th Cong., 1st Sess., 1961, pp. 3, 7.

[28] Holmes, *op. cit.*, p. 199.

dum by one of the consultants from the business world included the following:

The goal that we must set is the achievement of leadership in space, leadership which is both clear-cut and acknowledged. Our objective must be, therefore, not merely to overtake, but substantially to out-distance Russia. Any program with a lesser basic objective would be a second-rate program, worthy only of a second-class power. And, most important, a lesser program would raise serious questions among other countries as to whether, as a nation, we had the will and the discipline necessary for leadership in the struggle to preserve a free society.[29]

The new NASA Administrator, Webb, and the Deputy Secretary of Defense, Roswell L. Gilpatric, are said to have worked out the final version of the plan that went to President Kennedy. The underlying motivations, some of them mentioned above, will be more fully discussed in subsequent chapters.

President Kennedy appeared before Congress in person on May 25, 1961, to make his recommendations concerning space. Referring by implication to the Gagarin flight, he spoke of "the impact of this adventure on the minds of men everywhere, who are attempting to make a determination of which road they should take." He thought that the time had come "for this nation to take a clearly leading role in space achievement." He asked Congress to endorse a very marked expansion and acceleration of the space program. "I believe that this nation should commit itself to achieving the goal, before this decade is out, of landing a man on the moon and returning him safely to earth. No single space project in this period will be more impressive to mankind, or more important for the long-range exploration of space; and none will be so difficult or expensive to accomplish. . . ." He did not say that the object was to beat the Russians to the moon, but he clearly hoped that we could. He also asked for increased funds for several additional purposes. He wanted to "accelerate development of the Rover nuclear rocket [which] gives promise of someday providing a means for even more exciting and ambitious exploration of space, perhaps beyond the moon, perhaps to the very end of the solar system itself." He wanted to "make the most of our present leadership by accelerating the use of space satellites for world-wide communications," and he wanted to accelerate the development of a satellite system for world-wide weather observation.

---

[29] Donald C. Cook, Executive Vice President for the American Electric Power Service Corporation of New York, as quoted by Holmes, *op. cit.*, p. 200.

Let it be clear—and this is a judgment which the members of Congress must finally make—let it be clear that I am asking the Congress and the country to accept a firm commitment to a new course of action— a course which will last for many years and carry very heavy costs of $531 million in fiscal 1962, an estimated $7 billion to $9 billion additional over the next five years. If we are to go only halfway, or reduce our sights in the face of difficulty, in my judgment it would be better not to go at all.

Kennedy did not explain in what sense the $7 to $9 billion would be "additional." NASA had previously worked out a space program —never officially endorsed by Eisenhower or Congress—calling for a lunar landing sometime after 1970. In effect, Kennedy took this program for granted, and asked that it be completed more quickly, which meant that money had to be spent earlier and thus required increased annual budgets. Whether it also meant an increase in total costs of a lunar landing is less certain.[30] Guesses about the probable total costs have varied widely. Eisenhower's Science Advisory Committee, in its "Introduction to Outer Space," had cited a "rough estimate" of "about a couple of billion dollars." At the time Kennedy spoke, $40 billion was frequently named. Edwin Diamond says $30 billion.[31] Hugh Odishaw of the Space Science Board of the National Academy of Sciences says $50 billion.[32] Webb and others in NASA for long said $20 billion and then, on at least one occasion, shifted to less than $3 billion. They arrived at the lower figure by assuming that most of the component parts of the lunar program would be carried out even if the lunar landing itself were abandoned; so the "extra" cost of getting a man to the moon would be relatively small. Leeway in deciding which costs to attribute to the lunar program and genuine uncertainty about future costs go far to explain the discrepancies in the estimates.

After Kennedy's message, Representative Pelly expressed the conviction that "this crash moon trip is a spectacular piece of nonsense. . . . The President, quite naturally, is concerned with national prestige. And well he might be when it is recalled what has happened

---

[30] U.S. Congress, Senate, Committee on Appropriations, *Independent Offices Appropriations, 1962*, Hearings . . . on H. Res. 7445, 87th Cong., 1st Sess., 1961, p. 650; U.S. Congress, House, Committee on Appropriations, *Independent Offices Appropriations for 1963*, Hearings Before a Subcommittee . . ., 87th Cong., 2d Sess., 1962, Part 3, p. 443.

[31] Edwin Diamond, "The Rites of Spring," *Bulletin of the Atomic Scientists*, 19 (May, 1963), 26.

[32] Hugh Odishaw, ed., *The Challenges of Space* (Chicago: University of Chicago Press, 1962), p. 157.

to our prestige [at the Bay of Pigs] since he took office." [33] There were a few other scattered comments of this sort, but it is nonetheless true that the message aroused little debate and little opposition. There is no doubt that Congress overwhelmingly approved, but for a talkative body it did so in virtual silence. It simply appropriated the money, perhaps with relief, and subsequently it has appropriated more and more. In May, 1962, Representative Gross hoped that "we will find a gold mine up there because we will certainly need it," and then joined the others in a unanimous vote.

Under Eisenhower and Glennan the space program grew rapidly. Under Kennedy and Webb there was leaping development. By June, 1964, NASA expects to employ some 32,500 persons, making it one of the largest of the independent agencies and larger than the Department of Labor. Budgets for NASA and other agencies participating in space activities are given in the accompanying table. In 1958 Dr. James A. Van Allen told a congressional committee that "something in the order of $500 million a year will be required for a vigorous national space program," but he was not even up to Eisenhower's definition of vigor. In 1959 the first NASA Administrator, T. Keith Glennan, told another congressional committee that he would not be surprised if the civilian space budget moved into the $1 billion range in the course of the next two or three years. In 1960 another NASA witness imagined the possibility of a future budget of $2.5 billion. In 1963 the second NASA Administrator, James E. Webb, indicated that under existing plans "the level-out of the program . . . should be between $5.5 billion and $6 billion" a year.[34] Whether his anticipations will fall as far short of reality as the others, time will tell. The President's budget for FY1964 called for $5.7 billion for NASA, putting it in fifth place among federal agencies—after Defense, Treasury, Agriculture, and Health, Education, and Welfare. From two-thirds to three-fourths of the $5.7 was to go into the manned space flight program.[35]

---

[33] *Congressional Record,* Vol. 107, No. 95 (June 7, 1961), 8990-91.

[34] U.S. Congress, Senate, Committee on Aeronautical and Space Sciences, *NASA Authorization for Fiscal Year 1964,* Hearings, 88th Cong., 1st Sess., 1963, Part 1, p. 90 (hereafter cited as Senate Hearings, *NASA Authorization for 1964*).

[35] Albert F. Siepert, "Organization and Funding of NASA," in NASA, Office of Scientific and Technical Information, *Proceedings of the NASA-University Conference on the Science and Technology of Space Exploration,* Chicago, Illinois, November 1-3, 1962 (Washington, 1962), I, 27; U.S. Congress, House, Committee on Science and Astronautics, *Space Posture,* Hearings, 88th Cong., 1st Sess., 1963, p. 38.

Congress had not finally acted on the appropriation at the time of writing, but each house had approved a figure of $5.1 billion.

Total costs for space are still higher. Counting the $5.1 billion for NASA and the budgetary recommendations for the Department of Defense and other agencies, the total for FY1964 comes to about $7 billion.

In February, 1962, John Glenn made the first American orbital flight, and since then other Soviet and American flights have occurred. Though some make dire predictions concerning the lunar venture,[36] Webb and others seem confident of its success. Whether or not the first effort succeeds, additional efforts will presumably be made. The Saturn V rocket is being developed for the purpose, with 7.5 million pounds of thrust—enough to put 100 tons into earth orbit (equivalent to 85 Mercury capsules) and 40 tons on the moon. To assemble it, a building is being constructed north of Cape Canaveral (now Cape Kennedy) with a volume half again that of the Pentagon. And human energies and other resources are being mobilized on a vast scale. The follow-on for the lunar project will apparently be manned orbital stations, and at some point the manned exploration of Mars will presumably occur.

Dreams for the future are almost endless. No one yet knows how many of them are realizable, and there is no need to recount them here. They are suggested by references to the possibility of gaseous fission rockets "which could turn solar system transportation into a convenient and economical operation." "It is clear that the missions which gaseous fission rockets can perform [if they are really developed] span the whole solar arena at a quite reasonable operating cost, with travel times at least to the inner planets no worse than typical 'wind-jammer' times of last century. . . . It should be possible to make spaceship operation as safe as any other form of transportation."[37]

From a technical point of view, possibilities of these sorts call for feasibility studies and then, perhaps, for development efforts. From a political point of view, they call for desirability studies, relating findings or assumptions concerning the feasible with an analysis of relevant values or interests or goals.

---

[36] Carl Dreher, "Martyrs on the Moon?" *Harper's*, 226 (March, 1963), 33-38. The article, and NASA's comments on it, appear in Senate Hearings, *NASA Authorization for 1964*, Part 1, pp. 323-29, 730-33.

[37] Maxwell W. Hunter, Jr., in U.S. Congress, Joint Committee on Atomic Energy, Subcommittee on Research, Development, and Radiation, *Space Nuclear Power Applications*, Hearings, 87th Cong., 2d Sess., 1962, pp. 271, 278.

SPACE ACTIVITIES OF THE UNITED STATES GOVERNMENT [a]
(New obligational authority. In millions of dollars.)

	NASA	Dept. of Defense	AEC	Weather Bureau	NSF	Space Total
1955	56.9	3.0				59.3
1956	72.7	30.3	7.0		7.3	117.3
1957	78.2	71.0	21.3		8.4	178.9
1958	117.3	205.6	21.3		3.3	347.5
1959	338.9	489.5	34.3			862.7
1960	523.6	560.9	43.3		.1	1127.9
1961	926.2	793.8	67.7		.6	1788.3
1962	1796.0	1284.3	147.8	50.7	1.3	3280.1
1963 Estimate	3622.6	1617.6	228.9	43.2	1.5	5513.8
1964 Recommendations	5663.6	1667.6	254.3	26.2	2.3	7614.0

[a] Source: U.S. President, Report to the Congress, *United States Aeronautics and Space Activities, 1962* (Washington: National Aeronautics and Space Council, 1963), p. 137.
NASA amounts for 1961 and subsequent years exclude amounts for aircraft and missile technology; amounts for 1960 and prior years are totals for all activities of NASA and include totals for NACA. Department of Defense amounts do not include the cost of developing missiles and related equipment or certain other costs that cannot be separated from other military expenditures. For other explanatory notes see Appendix D of the President's 1961 report to Congress on space activities.

PART ⊓ ⊓ MOTIVATIONS

Part II includes a series of chapters examining the reasons that are given to support and justify the space program—the motives, goals, purposes, values, interests that the program is supposed to serve. We have a space program, it is said, to promote our military security, to safeguard the peace, to stimulate progress in science and technology, to bring about economic and social progress, to enhance national prestige, and to provide an additional basis for national pride. Clearly, we also have a space program in part because of ulterior motives and special interests. And all of these factors differ in their importance to different groups and at different times.

The chapters rest on the assumption that the motives named are good—or at least are among the facts of life that we must accept. My purpose is not to argue for or against the desirability of military security or of the other goals, but rather to do the following: (1) to give a clear conception of the motive or goal, where clarification is needed; (2) to identify the persons or groups for whom the goal is significant, and to indicate how significant they deem it to be; (3) to show how they think the space program does or will serve the goal; and (4) to assess this claim or expectation. Note that though I am using the label "motivations," I will be discussing "method" to some extent too. For example, the chapters on military security as a goal consist largely of an examination of the possible methods of employing satellites in such a way as to contribute to security.

In sum, the chapters should provide both a conception of the reasons or motives or goals that figure prominently in discussions of the space program and a basis for judging their relative merit and cumulative force.

MILITARY SECURITY: "IMMEDIATE MISSIONS" IN SPACE

3

Several years ago a German scientist, Dr. Eugen Sänger, expressed the view that a trend toward peaceful ends was "ultimately dictated by the laws of nature," and he was pleased to see the trend appear in connection with space flight. Speeds were going beyond 17,500 miles per hour, producing trajectories that do not return to earth. Objects traveling at such speeds go into orbit and thus "become useless as instruments of war." "Looking over the list of new types of flying devices expected to come into existence between 1960 and 2000, it will be seen that there is not one machine of war amongst them." And when it comes to the speeds necessary for flight to other stellar systems, "it goes without saying that there is not the remotest possibility of exploiting this phase of the development for military purposes." [1]

In contrast to this is the view that military security is the principal justification for a space program. "The compelling motive for the development of space technology," General Bernard A. Schriever has said, "is the requirement for national defense." [2] "The establishment of a national space program [according to the report of the House Select Committee on Astronautics and Space Exploration in 1958] is a matter of the highest urgency both for reasons of immediate national defense and to insure that in the

---

[1] U.S. Congress, House, Select Committee on Astronautics and Space Exploration, *The Next Ten Years in Space, 1959-1969*, Staff Report, H. Doc. No. 115, 86th Cong., 1st Sess., 1959, p. 161.

[2] Eugene M. Emme, ed., *The Impact of Air Power* (Princeton: Van Nostrand, 1959), p. 844.

long run outer space is effectively utilized for peaceful purposes." [3]
The same committee reported some months later that "outer space
is fast becoming the heart and soul[!] of advanced military science.
It constitutes at once the threat and the defense of man's existence
on earth." [4] Senator John Stennis says, "Space technology will
eventually become the dominant factor in determining our national
military strength. Whoever controls space controls the world." [5]
And Senator Howard W. Cannon thinks that "the taxpayers would
not be inclined to continue and consistently maintain a large budget
for purely scientific space efforts if it were clear that there was no
military benefit or if the military requirements could be satisfied
in other ways. . . ." [6]

Where does the truth lie? Excluding missiles from consideration
(for they are not ordinarily considered a part of the space program
even though they travel through space), what are the implications
of space for national security and military power? What military
uses of space have been established, and what possibilities are
anticipated? What differences are there in the military potentialities of different reaches of space? To what extent do different
aspects of the space program seem to be motivated—and actually
justified—by security considerations?

We will see in this chapter that there are some definable immediate missions for the military in space, though the list is short.
In the following chapter we will discuss other missions that are
more problematic in terms of either their desirability or their
feasibility.

Communication, Navigation, Meteorology, and Geodesy

The most obvious and least controversial military applications of
space technology are in the fields of communication, navigation,
meteorology, and geodesy, where there is considerable overlapping
with nonmilitary applications.

[3] U.S. Congress, House, Select Committee on Astronautics and Space Exploration, *The National Space Program*, H. Rpt. No. 1758, 85th Cong., 2d
Sess., 1958, p. 37.

[4] U.S. Congress, House, Select Committee on Astronautics and Space Exploration, *The United States and Outer Space*, H. Rpt. No. 2710, 85th Cong.,
2d Sess., 1959, p. 6.

[5] *Congressional Record*, Vol. 107, No. 96 (June 8, 1961), 9174.

[6] "Space and National Security," *Air Force/Space Digest*, 45 (November,
1962), 72.

Early in the space age the Department of Defense (DOD) initiated projects looking toward the incorporation of satellites in its global communication network. The problem is much greater than was at first anticipated, and the effort has been beset with various kinds of difficulties.[7] In the fall of 1962 (during the development of the federal budget for the fiscal year ending in mid-1964), DOD and NASA agreed on a division of labor. DOD is focusing on medium altitude satellites (like the Relay satellite that NASA had earlier placed in orbit), and NASA on synchronous satellites (Syncom).[8] (A satellite is "synchronous" when it is in a 24-hour orbit, traveling in the same direction as the earth rotates, 22,300 miles from the surface; given an equatorial orbit, it would appear to hover over one spot.) Each agency gives certain types of assistance to the other, and it remains to be seen which satellite communications system DOD will, in the end, adopt. Though DOD will undoubtedly use the commercial facilities that the Communication Satellite Corporation expects to put into operation, it makes a good case for a separate system to serve its distinctive needs.[9]

Experiments are under way with satellites that will hopefully make possible an all-weather navigation system of high accuracy, useful to the Navy (including the Polaris submarines) and perhaps to the Air Force; the system may also have civilian applications.[10] Responsibility for exploring the potentialities of space for meteorology has been assigned primarily to NASA and the Weather Bureau, though of course the military will share the benefit of the results achieved. In addition to its efforts to improve weather forecasting through such devices as the Tiros satellites, the Weather

[7] U.S. Congress, House, Committee on Science and Astronautics, Subcommittee on Space Sciences, *Project Advent—Military Communications Satellite Program,* Hearings, 87th Cong., 2d Sess., 1962, esp. pp. 90-100 (hereafter cited as House Hearings, *Project Advent,* 1962).

[8] U.S. Congress, House, Committee on Science and Astronautics, Subcommittee on Applications and Tracking and Data Acquisition, *1964 NASA Authorization,* Hearings, 88th Cong., 1st Sess., 1963, Part 4, pp. 3212, 3274; Major General Ben I. Funk, USAF, "A Practical Approach to Military Space Programs," Space Systems Division (AFSC) News Release, January 23, 1963, p. 10.

[9] House Hearings, *Project Advent,* 1962, pp. 46-47.

[10] U.S. Congress, Senate, Committee on Aeronautical and Space Sciences, *NASA Authorization for Fiscal Year 1963,* Hearings, 87th Cong., 2d Sess., 1962, pp. 336, 723 (hereafter cited as Senate Hearings, *NASA Authorization for 1963*). For a description of Transit as an aid to navigation see U.S. Congress, House, Committee on Science and Astronautics, *Science, Astronautics, and Defense,* Staff Report, 87th Cong., 1st Sess., 1961, pp. 44-47.

Bureau is also exploring possibilities of modifying the weather, partly to avoid another situation of breathtaking potential import in which the United States would be second to the Soviet Union. If either country should develop a capacity to modify weather— above all, if it should actually attempt to do this abroad—the effect on the international political struggle might be profound. Satellites are being used for geodetic purposes, e.g., to refine earlier conceptions of the shape of the earth, to map portions of the earth, and to determine distances between points on the earth's surface more accurately than ever before. Both military and non-military implications are fairly obvious.

The possibility of using satellites in the ways suggested above depends on some basic facts that are well known but that perhaps had better be stated explicitly here. In successive orbits a satellite can give line-of-sight access to most or all of the surface of the earth, depending on its altitude and on the angle between the plane of the orbit and the plane of the equator. When the angle is zero (meaning that the satellite is in equatorial orbit) and when its altitude is low, it gives minimum coverage; and when the angle is 90° (meaning that the satellite is in polar orbit), its coverage is complete; its movement and the rotation of the earth make it pass sooner or later over every point on earth. This opens the way for the use of satellites not only for such purposes as navigation and weather forecasting but also for reconnaissance, which will be discussed below.

If a satellite is in anything other than a synchronous equatorial orbit, it is transient, giving line-of-sight access to any given area only a portion of the time. The frequency of passage over the area varies with circumstances, e.g., the period of the orbit. Once the Russian cosmonaut, Titov, went beyond his second orbit, he had to go on to the seventeenth orbit before it was again possible for him to land in the preselected target area. It is expected that a projected weather satellite, the Nimbus, in a 500-mile polar orbit, would go through 14 orbits before passing over the same area for a second time in daylight. Among other things, this means that if constant surveillance over any area is sought from satellites in low orbits, a number of them must be employed.

Reconnaissance and Early Warning

One of the major military efforts in space is the development of an effective reconnaissance system—a project that was known as Samos until the spring of 1962, when DOD banned the use of such names and sharply curtailed the release of relevant information. The Samos program employs "eye-in-the-sky" satellites, equipped with cameras and other devices designed to provide the kind of intelligence that was once obtained through the use of the U-2 airplanes, e.g., intelligence concerning the precise location of Soviet missile launching sites. Pictures obtained can be got back to earth via TV or by recovering film-carrying capsules ejected from the satellite. During World War II, photographs taken from an altitude of 30,000 feet provided "ground resolution"—the minimum distance between discernible points—of 15 to 20 feet. Developments since World War II apparently make it possible to do better than this from a satellite. "The accomplishment of 2-foot ground resolution from satellite-borne cameras would be a distinctly impressive achievement, and values of 8 to 10 feet or more are perhaps more realistic, at least for the next few years." [11] *Newsweek* reports that DOD launched at least 35 reconnaissance satellites in 1962, and that it is developing a "detailed master map of the Communist world." [12] The program is said to include what is unofficially called the Ferret, employing satellites that intercept radio, radar, and microwave telephone transmissions in the Soviet Union and that are thus useful in pinpointing the location of various strategic Soviet centers and in providing other types of intelligence. Electronic devices for this kind of purpose have been used before —e.g., in planes skirting the borders of the Soviet Union and perhaps in U-2 planes. Given the availability of satellites as carriers, the problem is not so much to intercept the transmissions as to select those that are worth intercepting and then to make good use of the data obtained.

Important enough to peacetime intelligence, the use of satellites for such purposes in case of unrestricted war might be vital. In such a war nuclear missiles would be directed against both airborne planes and the fields on which they depend, making it highly improbable that they could be relied upon for reconnaissance or for any other activity over enemy territory. Thus reconnaissance satellites might be the only available way of obtaining truly

[11] Donald G. Brennan, "Arms and Arms Control in Outer Space," in Lincoln P. Bloomfield, ed., *Outer Space. Prospects for Man and Society*, The American Assembly (Englewood Cliffs: Prentice-Hall, 1962), p. 136.

[12] *Newsweek*, 60 (December 31, 1962), 36.

crucial information. General Gavin takes the view that "to employ profitably an ICBM will require accurate and timely intelligence and this can only be secured through the use of a reconnaissance satellite." [13] Hopefully such satellites would already be in orbit at the outbreak of war, for massive nuclear strikes might quickly make further launchings impossible. Present reconnaissance satellites employ instruments only. There would be obvious potential advantages (e.g., in terms of the speed with which what is seen can be interpreted and an appropriate course of action selected) if men could be employed.

Though priceless data may be obtained through the use of reconnaissance satellites, considerations of both a legal and a practical sort raise questions. Senator Keating once declared that if the Soviet Union put a satellite in orbit "for the purpose of viewing what was going on in this country, we would try to shoot it down, and any other country would." [14] General Gavin, though urging the need for reconnaissance satellites, finds it "inconceivable . . . that we would indefinitely tolerate Soviet reconnaissance of the United States without protest, for clearly such reconnaissance has an association with an ICBM program." [15] But neither Keating nor Gavin anticipated the actual attitude of the U.S. government. The U.S. representative on the UN Committee on the Peaceful Uses of Outer Space has noted that "at least one of [the Soviet Union's] astronauts has taken photographs over the United States (without the slightest objection on our part). Such observation and photography from outer space are fully compatible with international law and the Charter." [16] According to the official view, it is irrelevant if the observations from space are made by the military.

Various considerations support this position. National advantage is probably the main one, for we can no doubt gain relatively more than the Soviet Union from space reconnaissance. Further, for some time at least, objection to reconnaissance would be tantamount to objection to space flight. An international system for

---

[13] James M. Gavin, *War and Peace in the Space Age* (New York: Harpers, 1958), p. 222.

[14] U.S. Congress, House, Committee on Science and Astronautics, *International Control of Outer Space*, Hearings, 86th Cong., 1st Sess., 1959, pp. 8, 15.

[15] Gavin, *op. cit.*, p. 224.

[16] U.S. Congress, Senate, Committee on Aeronautical and Space Sciences, *Documents on International Aspects of the Exploration and Use of Outer Space, 1954-1962*, Staff Report, S. Doc. No. 18, 88th Cong., 1st Sess., 1963, p. 326, and see pp. 271-72, 362.

the inspection of launches to make sure that reconnaissance is not attempted is scarcely to be expected in the visible future; and once a satellite is in orbit it cannot be steered around countries that object to flight over their territory. The ability to inspect satellites in orbit has not yet been developed. Thus, if space flight is to occur, the opportunity to engage in reconnaissance necessarily follows. Even after it becomes possible to inspect orbiting satellites and destroy those that are objectionable, it may not be worth the effort—at least as a routine matter—either for the Soviet Union or for the United States, for it may well be cheaper for one to keep launching reconnaissance satellites than for the other to take countermeasures. Moreover, in some circumstances it would be advantageous to a state to submit to reconnaissance from space. An international agreement on arms control, if one could be achieved, might well provide for inspection and surveillance from space. And whenever it is desirable to allow another state to obtain accurate and reliable information—whether to deter aggression on its part or to allay its fears—reconnaissance from space might be welcomed.

The Soviet press has denounced American reconnaissance from space, and the Soviet government has proposed in the United Nations that it be prohibited. But the Soviet government itself engages in the practice, and has not formally protested American activities.

The Midas program was originally coupled with Samos. Midas satellites were to put a different kind of eye in the sky—an infrared sensing device designed to detect the launching of missiles while in the hot-boost phase, and so provide early warning. In the fall of 1962, John H. Rubel, Assistant Secretary of Defense, spoke of "great technical difficulties and disappointments" relating to this effort. He indicated that efforts would persist, but there is no sign of any optimism about them.[17] Even if such an early warning system were developed, it is doubtful how much operational significance it might have. Surely it would take a very rare and extreme circumstance to justify the United States in launching a retaliatory strike with nuclear missiles simply on the basis of warning signals from a Midas satellite; the system could scarcely be absolutely reliable.

---

[17] Department of Defense, Office of Public Affairs, News Release No. 1642-62, October 9, 1962; *Aviation Week*, 79 (March 11, 1963), 121.

The Development of Basic Capabilities

The above brief list includes all of the specific military missions in space that deserve to be called immediate. Others that might be named, as we will see in the next chapter, must be ruled out, at least for the time being, either because they promise to be of little military value or because they are so far from being feasible.

This does not necessarily mean, however, that the military aspects of the space program should be equally limited. General capabilities might be developed, going beyond the requirements of the specific missions that can now be defined. And there is widespread agreement that this should be done. Air Force spokesmen, though granting that definable missions are few, like to say that we are still not far beyond the Kitty Hawk stage of the space age, and that just as Kitty Hawk opened the way to developments that no one could foresee at the time so do the first satellites. And they warn against a repetition of the American neglect that followed Kitty Hawk, a neglect that left the country without military planes of its own for use in World War I. They contend that it is imperative to develop various technologies and capabilities in the expectation (or against the possibility) that need for them will develop.

This is the conclusion that Major Richard C. Henry, USAF, comes to in a very perceptive article on the military potentialities of space. He says that the "immediate military mission . . . is to achieve a proficiency . . . in the fundamental capabilities for operation in space, to determine how these capabilities may be exercised in military applications, and to integrate these capabilities into definable hardware." [18] General Whisenand takes the same view in identifying three phases of a military space development program:

First, we should continue with the present military programs of unmanned satellites. . . .

Second . . . we should concentrate vigorously on obtaining certain basic capabilities for space operations. . . . The kind of capabilities I am talking about are the following:

The capability to put larger useful payloads in space on a repetitive, reasonably economical basis.

The capability to maneuver in space, to rendezvous in space, to dock with other space vehicles, to transfer personnel, fuel, and supplies from one space vehicle to another.

The capability to reenter the earth's atmosphere from both high and

---

[18] Major Richard C. Henry, USAF, "The Immediate Mission in Space," *Air University Quarterly Review*, 13 (Fall, 1961), 44.

low orbit, and to effect controlled horizontal landings back on the surface of the earth.

The capability to sustain life in space, and for man to perform useful work in space.

General Whisenand points out that there is already a "limited, specific mission which requires these capabilities," i.e., the inspection of suspect satellites, and he thinks that time (perhaps bringing new weapons) and experience may permit the identification of more. If so, "phase 3—a military space force—will become more definable in terms of mission and hardware." [19]

The general principle that the Air Force champions is accepted in DOD and elsewhere, even if controversy over its implementation sometimes gives the opposite impression. The Deputy Secretary of Defense, Roswell L. Gilpatric, affirmed the fact in saying, "We are very conscious of the need for taking out . . . certain technological insurance. . . . We don't want to be caught by surprise if any hostile use of space should occur." [20] John H. Rubel elaborated on the view in an address of October, 1962. [21] Mr. Rubel classified space projects under two principal headings: those "directed at clear, identifiable military needs and requirements" and those "aimed at evolving new opportunities, at creating a vigorous and broad base of new technology and even of devices and systems for possible future application, even though the requirements for these are incomplete or altogether absent." Undertakings in the second category "represent insurance against an uncertain future, a resolve to be prepared even though we often must be uncertain about how to prepare, or what to prepare for." Mr. Rubel said that efforts of DOD divide about half and half between the two categories; he thought that "our expenditures on space developments have been remarkably high in relation to viable concepts for military applications in space" and that perhaps we erred in allowing too generous a margin for safety.

Spokesmen for DOD like the term "building blocks." In its space activities, the Department is developing "building blocks." Not knowing just what kind of a "building" it may have to construct, it wants "blocks" available that can be put together in different

---

[19] Major General James F. Whisenand, USAF, "Military Space Efforts, the Evolutionary Approach," *Air Force/Space Digest*, 45 (May, 1962), 55.

[20] Senate Hearings, *NASA Authorization for 1963*, p. 25.

[21] Department of Defense, Office of Public Affairs, News Release No. 1642-62, October 9, 1962.

ways to meet whatever needs arise. "Building blocks" fit into Mr. Rubel's second category. Titan III is one of them—expected to be a "workhorse booster" costing a billion dollars to develop. Other developments in the second category "include a great variety of efforts in bioastronautics, the development of advanced sensors, the evolution of advanced propulsion systems and power supplies, developments in materials, and a multitude of exploration and research efforts aimed at learning more about space flight and the space environment." The reference to "advanced sensors" presumably relates to such problems as detecting the launching of missiles in order to get early warning, and inspecting satellites in orbit.

Agreement on the principle that technologies and capabilities should be developed that go beyond specific needs does not mean agreement on the projects that are actually to be undertaken. In fact, controversies—intense and bitter controversies—have occurred in DOD since the beginning of the space age. One of the first issues was whether the military should develop boosters larger than those required for missiles. General Medaris, onetime Commander of the Army Ballistic Missile Agency, reports that he wanted to do so, but could not get approval from DOD because he could not cite a specific military need that would be served. His argument was that we should develop engines, guidance systems, and so on, even if we didn't know what we would do with them, "because just as sure as they come through, by that time there will be plenty of use for them." [22] Wernher von Braun, speaking of establishing "control" of outer space, took a similar view.[23] In 1958 DOD authorized the development of the booster that is now known as Saturn, but obviously put it toward the bottom of the priority list as far as funding was concerned.[24] Finally, in 1959 DOD joined with NASA in endorsing a memorandum for President Eisenhower declaring that "there is, at present, no clear military requirement for super boosters, although there is a real possibility that the future will bring military weapons systems requirements." The memorandum went on to recommend that Eisenhower transfer to NASA the part of the Army Ballistic Missile

[22] U.S. Congress, Senate, Committee on Armed Services, Preparedness Investigating Subcommittee, *Inquiry into Satellite and Missile Programs,* Hearings, 85th Cong., 1st Sess., 1957, Part 1, p. 554.

[23] *Ibid.,* p. 597.

[24] Major General John B. Medaris, USA (Ret.), *Countdown for Decision* (New York: Putnam, 1960), p. 263.

Agency that was working on Saturn, which Eisenhower proceeded to do.[25] The action—and the principle that it reflected—obviously caused dismay to space enthusiasts in both the Army and the Air Force. Perhaps the most significant point is, however, that the super boosters are in fact being developed, even though in the name of nonmilitary requirements; and when and if military needs develop they will be available.

One of the persistent issues concerning the military aspects of the space program relates to manned space flight. During most of the period since Sputnik DOD has been probing into the question; it has carried out wide-ranging studies and experiments of a scientific and technical sort, has sponsored the development of some relevant technologies, and has given various forms of assistance to NASA in connection with the Mercury, Gemini, and Apollo programs, including the assignment of military personnel to NASA. But the Air Force has persistently pressed for more, claiming that there are enough special features of manned space flight for distinctively military purposes to justify either a fuller share in NASA's program or, preferably, a separate program.[26] Spokesmen for DOD have been resistant, stressing the absence of a definable military requirement for man-in-space. This is indicated by the testimony of Dr. Harold Brown, Director of Defense Research and Engineering, to the Senate Committee on Aeronautical and Space Sciences in June, 1962.

When it comes to manned orbital systems for rendezvous it is not at all clear that there is a military need. Neither is there a military program for manned orbital rendezvous. . . .

We cannot at this time identify . . . a manned military space flight mission. . . .

In the past, and again now, I have expressed my doubts that manned military space vehicles will be a requirement.[27]

Similarly, Assistant Secretary Rubel, in the address cited above, said that "most manned military missions in space still, after years of study, seem little or no more viable than they ever did." Earlier, Mr. Rubel had said, "We do not have an acknowledged mission for

[25] U.S. Congress, House, Committee on Science and Astronautics, *Transfer of the Development Operations Division of the Army Ballistic Missile Agency to the NASA,* Hearing . . . on H. J. Res. 567, 86th Cong., 2d Sess., 1960, p. 29; U.S. President, *Public Papers of the Presidents of the United States,* Dwight D. Eisenhower, 1960-61 (Washington, 1961), p. 33.

[26] *Missiles and Rockets,* 11 (November 26, 1962), 46-48; *New York Times,* October 21, 1962, 68:1.

[27] Senate Hearings, *NASA Authorization for 1963,* pp. 346-47.

a man in space. There is no man-bomber requirement. There is no man-on-the-Moon requirement." [28] Secretary McNamara and others testified to the same effect in 1963.[29]

Air Force spokesmen disagree more with the spirit than with the letter of these statements, and with the inferences drawn from them. They do not literally claim that there is an existing definable military mission for man-in-space. But they choose to emphasize the point expressed by Major Henry and General Whisenand in the quotations given above, that the military ought to develop manned flight capabilities just in case. They stress the undoubted fact that man has capacities that cannot be built into any instrument or combination of instruments, however sophisticated they may be. An intelligent being, man can exercise judgment, choosing the ends to pursue and the appropriate means for pursuing them—perhaps changing his mind on occasion and otherwise adjusting himself to unanticipated circumstances. "Man has certain qualitative capabilities which machines cannot duplicate. He is unique in his ability to make on-the-spot judgments. He can discriminate and select from alternatives which have not been anticipated. He is adaptable to rapidly changing situations. Thus, by including man in military space systems, we significantly increase the flexibility of the systems, as well as increase the probability of mission success." [30] More specifically, the argument is that man will be highly useful in tending to instruments in space vehicles, in reconnaissance and reporting, in maneuvering a space vehicle (whether to achieve or to avoid rendezvous), and in deciding upon and taking any hostile action that might be staged in or from space (whether against targets in space or on the ground). General Medaris once expressed a different version of the thought.

It was perfectly clear to me . . . that the first nation to establish a permanent, manned space station would have taken a giant step toward domination of the whole planet. . . .

[28] U.S. Congress, House, Committee on Science and Astronautics, *1963 NASA Authorization,* Hearings . . . on H. R. 10100, 87th Cong., 2d Sess., 1962, Part 2, p. 746.

[29] U.S. Congress, Senate, Committee on Armed Services, *Military Procurement Authorization for Fiscal Year 1964,* Hearings, 88th Cong., 1st Sess., 1963, p. 152 (hereafter cited as Senate Hearings, *Military Procurement Authorization for 1964*); U.S. Congress, House, Committee on Science and Astronautics, *Space Posture,* Hearings, 88th Cong., 1st Sess., 1963, p. 180 (hereafter cited as House Hearings, *Space Posture, 1963*).

[30] Lieutenant General James G. Ferguson, USAF, in U.S. Congress, House, Committee on Armed Services, *Hearings on Military Posture and H.R. 9751* . . ., 87th Cong., 2d Sess., 1962, p. 3771.

As for possible combat in space, we knew that wherever man has gone, on land or in the air or under the sea, sooner or later he's managed to get into a fight. We saw no reason to suppose that space would be any different.[31]

Pressures from the Air Force finally led to an agreement between DOD and NASA designed "to assure that the scientific and operational experiments undertaken as part of the Gemini Program are directed at objectives and requirements both of the Department of Defense and the NASA manned space flight program." The agreement calls for the establishment of a joint Gemini Program Planning Board "to insure maximum attainment of objectives of value to both the NASA and the Department of Defense." NASA continues to exercise managerial control. The agreement provides that if there are significant changes in the Gemini program to meet military requirements, DOD will contribute funds to meet the additional costs.[32] In May, 1963, the Gemini Program Planning Board decided that Air Force participation would be "limited to providing experiments on a 'space available' basis only," which suggests that changes will be minor.[33] The implication seems to be that within the limits of the possibilities afforded, NASA's plans for Gemini will substantially serve military needs; and advocates of the Dyna-Soar program may be happy to safeguard it by restricting Air Force participation in Gemini.

The Dyna-Soar or X-20 program is, in a sense, the sequel of the program based on the X-15 which Dr. Hugh L. Dryden suggests "may be a lot more significant in the long run than the Mercury capsule." [34] The object of the X-20 program is to develop a one-man space glider that can be launched into orbit (Titan III is scheduled to be used for the purpose) and that, within limits, will be maneuverable on re-entry into the atmosphere, permitting the pilot to "extend or shorten the flight path and . . . turn to either side over distances of several thousand miles." The Department of the Air Force has sought an expansion of this program, against resistance in the Office of the Secretary of Defense. As Dr. Harold Brown puts it, "It is not possible to lay down military needs which

---

[31] Medaris, op. cit., p. 135.

[32] "NASA-DOD Gemini Agreement," NASA News Release No. 63-12, January 22, 1963; U.S. Congress, House, Committee on Science and Astronautics, 1964 NASA Authorization, Hearings, 88th Cong., 1st Sess., 1963, Part 2(a), p. 423 (hereafter cited as House Hearings, 1964 NASA Authorization).

[33] House Hearings, 1964 NASA Authorization, Part 2(b), p. 869.

[34] National Aeronautics, 41 (November, 1962), 18.

would be fulfilled in an obviously useful way by such a vehicle."[35] From his point of view the X-20 is in the "building block" category, and there is an obvious question whether it is different enough from Gemini to be worth the cost. At the time of writing, the issue is not resolved.[36]

For the Air Force and DOD a major additional issue in the field of manned space flight concerns a prospective orbital space station. The Air Force has recommended the inclusion of such a station in its space program, but has failed to win approval in the Office of the Secretary of Defense.[37] NASA is also intensely interested. Both DOD and NASA have sponsored studies of the potential project, and both would undoubtedly want to manage it. In the fall of 1963 they made a relevant agreement.[38] They view the "possible new manned earth orbital research and development project" as "a major technical and financial undertaking . . . involving spacecraft larger and more sophisticated than Gemini and Apollo." They agree to coordinate their studies pertaining to it with a view to the development of a single project that will meet "all foreseeable future requirements of both agencies in this area." They will "attempt to arrive at a joint recommendation as to whether to proceed" with the new project, and will also make a recommendation concerning the location of managerial control "based on predominant interest and consideration of other pertinent factors, such as management competence, relation to other programs in progress, and international political implications." If the Administration endorses the recommendation, the two agencies will establish a joint board to formulate the specific objectives to be pursued and to approve the experiments to be conducted, and the managerial agency will prepare the plan for submission to the Administration and to Congress.

Additional issues are associated with the principle that basic capabilities in space ought to be developed, either as a way of looking for military applications or as a way of obtaining a kind of contingency insurance. But such serious doubts and uncertainties attend them that it seems best to consign them to a separate chapter.

---

[35] Senate Hearings, *NASA Authorization for 1963*, p. 346. Cf. James Trainor, "AF Fights for Bigger Space Role," *Missiles and Rockets*, 10 (March 5, 1962), 12.

[36] Senate Hearings, *Military Procurement Authorization for 1964*, pp. 154-55.

[37] House Hearings, *Space Posture*, 1963, p. 230; *Aviation Week*, 79 (March 11, 1963), 116.

[38] NASA News Release No. 63-231, October 17, 1963.

MILITARY SECURITY: POTENTIALITIES

In addition to the immediate missions in space described in the preceding chapter, there are other possibilities. The United States might put H-bombs in orbit, or weapons designed to give protection against missiles. It might try to develop the technology and skills required to permit the interception and inspection of objects in space. It might attempt to establish a military base on the moon, or otherwise use the moon for military purposes. It might finance research aimed at producing exotic weapons useful in space warfare. And, in more general terms, it might stimulate scientific and technological progress for many reasons, including the long-run implications of such progress for military power.

Orbital Weapon Systems?

The UN General Assembly has called upon states "to refrain from placing in orbit around the earth any objects carrying nuclear weapons or any other weapons of mass destruction. . . ." [1] Both the United States and the Soviet Union supported the resolution, and this suggests that currently both intend to observe it. But it is of some interest and potential significance to examine possibilities.

One of the projects that has been discussed, called Bambi, is designed to provide a defense against ballistic missiles. To understand it we need to recall a fact alluded to in the preceding chapter: that a satellite is transient. In any one orbit it is over a given

[1] *New York Times,* October 17, 1963, p. 14:2.

area for only a brief period, and a number of orbits occur before it covers the same area again. How, then, could one make sure that a satellite is at the right place for the interception of any ballistic missiles that might be launched? The answer is to put such great numbers in orbit that at least one of them will always be where it is needed. "Hundreds" of them might be required.[2] According to one proposal, they would be unmanned, and each would carry "many" small anti-missile missiles. Each anti-missile missile would be equipped with an infrared homing device that would hopefully guide it to its target. If this were feasible, and if the system could be made reliable, the gain for national power and security would obviously be immense.

Reference was made in the preceding chapter to the efforts of DOD to develop satellites that would give early warning of missile launchings, and to the "great technical difficulties and disappointments" associated with the effort. Obviously, the great technical difficulties would also attend the Bambi satellites, and others would be added. The Bambi satellites would have to distinguish between heat emanating from missiles being launched and heat emanating from other sources. They would have to do their discriminating and make their "decisions" while still some hundreds of miles away from the potential target to make it possible to get their anti-missile missiles deorbited in time. Some way would have to be found to make sure that the missiles strike only against enemy targets and not against rockets launched by the United States itself —or, for that matter, by any other country. These problems are formidable in a technical sense, and it is doubtful whether they can be solved. And even if the Air Force were to convince itself that they were solved, widespread fears of accidents would undoubtedly exist both in this country and abroad, poisoning the climate of international politics. Moreover, the costs of a Bambi operational system would be enormous. Studies of the proposal have been under way in DOD, with rather negative results. "Detailed technical assessments . . . indicate that considerable additional research is required in a variety of areas before the technical,

[2] Dr. Walter R. Dornberger, "Dornberger Sees Space as Military Area," *Aviation Week/Space Technology*, 75 (September 18, 1961), 57-59. Cf. Philip J. Klass, "Bambi ICBM Defense Concept Analyzed," *Aviation Week/Space Technology*, 75 (October 23, 1961), 82-83; Michael Golovine, *Conflict in Space* (London: Temple Press, 1962), pp. 98-99.

operational, and economic feasibility of the Bambi concept can be verified." [3]

Another kind of possibility is a space bombardment system. Both the United States and the Soviet Union undoubtedly have, or could shortly have, the capacity to put nuclear and thermonuclear bombs in orbit. Bombs of several hundred megatons, detonated in low orbit, could reportedly set fire to vast areas—to the whole area within sight of the point of detonation, except for portions protected at the time by cloud cover.[4] Smaller bombs could be deorbited and brought close to the target for detonation.

The proposal that such a space bombardment system be created raises a number of questions, most of which have not been thoroughly explored—at least not in publicly available materials. What would be the relative cost of a weapon system depending on orbiting bombs rather than on earth-based bombs? How would the accuracy of a strike from different orbits compare with the accuracy of missile strikes? Would a counterforce strategy still be feasible, or would reliance on bombardment satellites require the adoption of a countervalue strategy—that is, could the strikes be confined to the more strictly military targets, or would they have to be aimed at urban centers? If we relied on bombardment satellites rather than on missiles, what would the effect be on our ability to strike a number of targets at approximately the same moment, and how important would this be? Would bombs brought down out of orbit penetrate defenses more reliably, or less, than the warheads of missiles? Do we need bombs in orbit—perhaps in deep space—to be sure of preserving a second-strike capacity? How vulnerable would bombardment satellites in different orbits be to enemy action, or to natural forces that would produce malfunctions, and how vulnerable would the communication and control system be? How would we keep sure that bombs in orbit are in working order? If we used bombardment satellites at all, would we keep them in orbit on a routine basis, or would we put them up irregularly, e.g., in times of special crisis? How would each kind of strategy be likely to affect our own attitudes and those of other

---

[3] U.S. President, *United States Aeronautics and Space Activities, 1961 . . .*, H. Doc. No. 324, 87th Cong., 2d Sess., 1962, p. 35.

[4] Donald G. Brennan, "Arms and Arms Control in Outer Space," in Lincoln P. Bloomfield, ed., *Outer Space. Prospects for Man and Society*, The American Assembly (Englewood Cliffs: Prentice-Hall, 1962), p. 130.

governments and peoples? If we simply added bombardment satellites to other weapon systems, rather than adopting them as alternatives, to what extent would we complicate the preparations and calculations of a potential enemy? If we added significantly to the uncertainties that he faces, to what extent would we enhance or reduce our safety? To what extent may our decision on the question of putting nuclear bombs in orbit influence comparable decisions in the Soviet Union and in other countries that develop space capabilities? To what extent would the possibility of catastrophic accident be increased if nuclear bombs go into orbit? If a number of countries eventually put nuclear bombs in orbit, as opposed to keeping missiles with nuclear warheads based on earth, what kinds of consequences may ensue? If the United States led the way in placing nuclear bombs in orbit, would it be promoting or impeding the development of a desirable world order? If another country led the way, would it be necessary to follow suit?

Thomas C. Schelling raises most of the above questions without attempting to answer them.[5] Given the possibility of doing with missiles almost everything that could be done with bombardment satellites, and doing some things better or more surely, the case for using satellites is, to say the least, not at all obvious.

The United States and the Soviet Union have apparently both followed the policy of refraining from placing weapons in orbit. After leaving active service, General Gavin spoke of the possibility, suggesting that in the future a manned orbital vehicle might be able to launch a warhead from space and guide it into a selected target area. He granted that the earth is a better launching platform now, but suggested that once an anti-missile missile is developed it may be well to have alternative launching platforms in space.[6] Lieutenant General James Ferguson has spoken of the potential advantages of "space bombers in low orbit."[7] General Bernard A. Schriever speaks of potential space weapons, such as large bombs in orbit, but holds that "their value as stabilizing or retaliatory

---

[5] Thomas C. Schelling, "The Military Use of Outer Space: Bombardment Satellites," in Joseph M. Goldsen, ed., *Outer Space in World Politics* (New York: Praeger, 1963), pp. 97-113.

[6] James M. Gavin, *War and Peace in the Space Age* (New York: Harpers, 1958), p. 224.

[7] U.S. Congress, House, Committee on Armed Services, *Hearings on Military Posture and H.R. 9751 . . .*, 87th Cong., 2d Sess., 1962, p. 3769 (hereafter cited as House, *Hearings on Military Posture, 1962*).

factors is still questionable." [8] Major Richard C. Henry concludes at least tentatively that "the tactical disadvantages of orbiting systems outweigh the advantages." [9] Loftus Becker, former Legal Adviser in the Department of State, once predicted that "if anybody attempted to put up a military satellite which had any offensive capabilities with respect to the United States . . . this government would take the position that that was not legally permitted." [10] And in the fall of 1962 Deputy Secretary of Defense Roswell L. Gilpatric said:

We have no program to place any weapons of mass destruction into orbit. . . . The United States believes that it is highly desirable for its own security and for the security of the world that the arms race should not be extended into outer space, and we are seeking in every feasible way to achieve that purpose. Today there is no doubt that either the United States or the Soviet Union could place thermonuclear weapons in orbit, but such action is just not a rational military strategy for either side for the foreseeable future.[11]

In the light of these considerations and attitudes, it is not surprising that the United States would support the UN resolution against putting weapons of mass destruction into space.

A Capacity to Intercept and Inspect

Air Force spokesmen and others place considerable emphasis on the potential importance of an ability to intercept and inspect objects in space, coupled with an ability to eliminate whatever threat they may be found to involve. The most likely threats have already been indicated. Despite Soviet denunciations of American "eye-in-the-sky" (or "spy") satellites, it is to be assumed that the Soviet government has launched or might launch such satellites itself. Further, it could undoubtedly place thermonuclear bombs in orbit. Other possibilities exist, e.g., in the use of communications

---

[8] U.S. Congress, House, Committee on Science and Astronautics, *1963 NASA Authorization*, Hearings . . . on H. Res. 10100, 87th Cong., 2d Sess., 1962, Part 2, p. 657 (hereafter cited as House Hearings, *1963 NASA Authorization*).

[9] Major Richard C. Henry, USAF, "The Immediate Mission in Space," *Air University Quarterly Review*, 13 (Fall, 1961), 39.

[10] U.S. Congress, House, Select Committee on Astronautics and Space Exploration, *Astronautics and Space Exploration*, Hearings . . . on H. Res. 11881, 85th Cong., 2d Sess., 1958, p. 1283 (hereafter cited as House Hearings, *Astronautics and Space Exploration*, 1958).

[11] Department of Defense, Office of Public Affairs, News Release No. 1426-62, September 5, 1962, p. 3.

satellites. And, of course, there is always the chance of revolutionary developments that will bring new weapons into play.

Given these possible threats from space, there is no doubt that it would be desirable to be able to meet them. The issues concern feasibility and relative urgency.

Rendezvous must first be accomplished if inspection in space is to occur. Ideally the inspecting satellite should go in the same direction in the same orbital plane as the satellite to be inspected, and its speed should be adjusted so as to bring it within range and keep it there for a considerable period. I have seen nothing in print to indicate the maximum useful range, but have heard it said that much can be learned from a distance as great as 50 miles. Clockwork precision might permit the launching of an American inspecting satellite into the same orbital plane as that of a Soviet satellite. If this is not achieved, some maneuvering would be necessary, and maneuvering cannot be accomplished in space simply by turning a wheel or a rudder. Fuel must be used—fuel equal to half of the weight of the spacecraft if it is to be deflected to the right or left by 15°; and fuel is also required to speed a satellite up or slow it down.[12] Obviously, then, the amount of maneuvering that any one satellite can engage in is strictly limited. As Major Richard C. Henry says, "the basic cost in energy that must be expended to extensively maneuver an orbiting system is simply so high that it must be applied with great care and deliberation." [13] The problem becomes all the greater, of course, if the satellite to be intercepted is maneuvered evasively. The outcome may then be determined by the amount of fuel available to each satellite and therefore the number of maneuvers that can be executed. The development of nuclear methods of propulsion may affect the problem profoundly.

Once rendezvous is achieved, inspection also involves problems. Cameras, or a man's eyes, can provide information concerning the size and shape of the object, the length of the antennas, the presence or absence of apertures for cameras, etc. Other sensors can determine the temperature of the object and the speed with which its temperature changes when it passes from sunlight into shadow. I do not know to what extent firm conclusions can be drawn from these types of evidence. Further, it should not be very

---

[12] Major General Osmond J. Ritland, USAF, "The Need for Man in Space," mimeo. (issuing agency not identified; apparent date Spring, 1963).

[13] Henry, loc. cit., p. 37.

difficult for the Soviet Union to send decoys into orbit that would seriously complicate the problem of inspection.

The Air Force has a program under way that was originally designed to demonstrate the practicality of unmanned interception and inspection. But toward the end of 1962 it announced that it was "reorienting" the program, terminating some of the relevant contracts. The reorientation was "towards the development of sensor components which would yield an inspector capability of military value." [14] This suggests serious problems. Possibly experience with Gemini will shift the emphasis toward manned inspection systems.

Little has been said publicly about the course of action to pursue if inspection revealed something objectionable. Should the Soviet Union begin to interfere with our reconnaissance or other satellites, we would want to retaliate in kind. And should the Soviet Union place thermonuclear bombs in orbit, we would no doubt want to remove them somehow, or render them harmless. Otherwise, as already suggested, forbearance might be the best rule, for, within limits, the principle of the freedom of space may be as desirable as the principle of the freedom of the seas.

It is uncertain how we would go about removing or destroying an objectionable satellite, or rendering it harmless, if the decision should be for this course of action. Philip Siekman says that the problem "should be relatively simple." "A squirt of paint would blind an observation satellite. Its infrared sensing devices could be destroyed by focusing the sun on them with a small mirror. And some ingenious space engineers have suggested that it would be possible to destroy a satellite in such a fashion that its owner would charge off the damage to natural phenomena rather than an enemy attack [e.g., through the use of sand or chemicals]." [15] One wonders a bit about the behavior of paint in the vacuum of space (to say nothing of the thought that spacemen may go into the wild black yonder armed with paint can and brush). One wonders too about the possibility of booby traps on vehicles being inspected, and about the problem of safely disposing of an orbiting thermonuclear bomb.

The possibility of defense against a hostile satellite is not necessarily limited to such actions as might be taken by or from a

[14] Department of Defense release, December 3, 1962. Cf. New York Times, December 4, 1962, 5:3.
[15] Philip Siekman, "The Fantastic Weaponry," Fortune, 65 (June, 1962), 218.

satellite in the same orbit. In principle, a crossing orbit might be employed, or an anti-satellite missile might be launched from the ground. Dr. Harold Brown, Director of Defense Research and Engineering, says "you can probably do it better from the ground, and we have a program that will allow us to do it from the ground." [16] Presumably the reference is to the Nike-Zeus and perhaps to a further development of the Nike-Zeus. The problem of intercepting a satellite from the ground is comparable to the problem of intercepting an incoming missile. Launching sites within the United States might or might not be adequate. If the hostile satellite is not itself a weapon but is instead a vehicle from which weapons are launched, and if it can launch the weapons so as to strike targets well outside the plane of its own orbit, it might never fly over the target area. In this event, launching sites for anti-satellite missiles would have to be located in the general region of the equator to maximize the possibilities of interception. The satellite to be intercepted would fly faster and at a higher altitude than a missile; but whereas the anti-missile missile has only one chance to do its job and must get it done in a matter of minutes, an anti-satellite missile might have repeated opportunities over a number of days. Especially if the satellite is not maneuvered, singularly skillful performance might bring about an interception. Sand or shrapnel placed in the path of spacecraft traveling at such a tremendous speed would probably render it useless. Blast effects in the vacuum of space would be nonexistent, whether the warhead is nuclear or conventional; but nuclear radiation would apparently be highly effective as a weapon in space. "The range of significant dosages will be many times greater than is the case at sea level." Lethal radii from thermonuclear explosions in space "may be of the order of hundreds of miles." [17] Further, heat effects might be damaging. Thus, unless adequate shielding can be provided, it may be that in wartime neither men nor instruments would have a good prospect of remaining useful for long in space. Nuclear radiation may also provide a method of defense in case the Soviet

---

[16] U.S. Congress, Senate, Committee on Armed Services, *Military Procurement Authorization for Fiscal Year 1964,* Hearings, 88th Cong., 1st Sess., 1963, p. 476 (hereafter cited as Senate Hearings, *Military Procurement Authorization for 1964*). Cf. *New York Times,* October 20, 1963, 1:7.

[17] U.S. Congress, House, Select Committee on Astronautics and Space Exploration, *Space Handbook: Astronautics and Its Applications,* 85th Cong., 2d Sess., 1959, pp. 132-34.

Union should place H-bombs in a parking orbit, and the possibility raises another question about the wisdom of such a policy. "An American physicist estimates that the neutrons released by a very small one-kiloton atomic blast would neutralize a bomb at distances up to one-quarter of a mile." [18]

One obvious difficulty with the use of an anti-satellite missile is that it cannot be equipped to do any inspecting before exploding. If it were used at all in peacetime, it would presumably be only after a satellite inspector had done its work. Citing a need for such prior inspection, the Air Force (which has been skeptical of the Army's Nike-Zeus program for defense against missiles) has indicated that it was not seeking an "anti-satellite Nike-Zeus" development program. [19]

Some conjure up the possibility that either the United States or the Soviet Union might develop reliable methods of intercepting the missiles and satellites of the other, and they then suggest striking possibilities. Consider, for example, a proposal made by Dr. Alton Frye and published in *Air Force/Space Digest* in July, 1962. It is that the lunar program should be subordinated to "another, more proximate goal . . . the development of an efficient interception system." The system would encompass both anti-missile missiles and satellite interception, which, as we have already seen, would involve very considerable problems. But if we can somehow manage to solve these problems, Dr. Frye suggests, "a new vista of political opportunities is open to us." In brief, what he proposes is that we should lay down the conditions that the Soviet Union (and, presumably, any other power) will thereafter have to meet if it is to have access to space. The principal condition Dr. Frye names includes various measures designed to give assurance that Soviet space projects are nonmilitary. If our conditions are rejected, "the United States will be compelled to destroy every vehicle which the Soviets fire into orbit or in a trajectory toward our territory." Should the Soviet Union develop similar capabilities for interception at about the same time, Dr. Frye expects that it would seek an accommodation with the United States rather than

[18] Siekman, *loc. cit.*, p. 218.

[19] U.S. Congress, House, Committee on Science and Astronautics, *Defense Space Interests*, Hearings, 87th Cong., 1st Sess., 1961, p. 111 (hereafter cited as House Hearings, *Defense Space Interests*, 1961). Cf. Ralph E. Lapp, *Man and Space, The Next Decade* (New York: Harpers, 1961), pp. 118-19; Golovine, *op. cit.*, pp. 98-100.

accept a mutually frustrating situation in which each power substantially excludes the other from space activities.

The proposal is farfetched on several counts. First of all, if there were any doubt at all about our ability to intercept a Soviet missile or satellite, it would be foolish to attempt to impose the suggested conditions. Moreover, the interception and presumed destruction of Soviet vehicles would have to occur without inflicting destruction anywhere outside the United States, even within the Soviet Union, unless we are willing to precipitate war. Barring a very revolutionary development, an interception system that will meet these requirements is not to be expected.

In the second place, quite apart from the question of technological feasibility, it is highly doubtful whether the proposal would be politically acceptable within the United States. It calls for a policy of imperialist arrogance and truculence and for establishing the United States as the overlord of space. But this would be alien to the dominant national style. It would subvert the kind of world order that the country has in the past been supporting and in the long run it would probably not be compatible either with the kind of domestic order we have and want. The principles of freedom, tolerance, equality, and reciprocity can scarcely be maintained in one area of activity and denied in another.

In the third place, the policy would almost certainly alienate both friendly and neutral powers. They would surely resent the new form of imperialism even if to some extent they benefited from it, and even if they themselves lacked space capabilities. And they would resent it all the more if they had such capabilities. Suppose that France sometime should choose to defy American rules concerning access to space. Would we enforce the rules? What would be the effect on our alliance system?

I mention the Frye proposal not because it has merit or because of any prospect that it will be adopted, but rather because it provides a basis for discussing a fear that a number of Americans have expressed: that the Soviet Union might actually attempt something like what Frye proposes. Thus General Gavin in 1960 spoke of the possibility that the Soviet Union might develop a surveillance system that would be "so effective as to deny us use of space." [20]

[20] U.S. Congress, House, Committee on Science and Astronautics, *To Amend the National Aeronautics and Space Act of 1958*, Hearings . . . on H. Res. 9675, 86th Cong., 2d Sess., 1960, p. 364.

And General Whisenand says, "If a hostile power develops the basic capabilities which I have outlined—the capability to maneuver, to rendezvous, dock, reenter, and so forth—it would seem evident that these capabilities might be exploited to deny our use of space for any purpose whatever." [21] Similarly Major Henry, though building up a case for skepticism of the value of orbital weapon systems, adds a warning:

Note, however, that the advantage of access and the control of access has been a key factor in the power struggles of the past and in fact has often been the key to victory. This is probably the one aspect of orbital operations that gnaws at every military officer who seriously considers the military applications of the space environment. . . . If access control should be gained to the extent that the space environment is denied to all but the favored few, those few can control the earth.[22]

If the Frye proposal is farfetched, is the corresponding fear of the Soviet Union in the same category? Probably so, at least for the visible future, though the answer is not quite so sure. The technological problem would be the same for the Soviet Union as for the United States. Even if the Soviet Union is closer than the United States to mastering a technique for rendezvous, this does not necessarily mean that it is close to solving the problems of intercepting missiles and uncooperative satellites. And it would be just as foolish for the Soviet Union as for us to seek to deny others access to space without the ability to enforce the denial with complete effectiveness. The other considerations that would prevent the United States from implementing the Frye proposal would probably operate on the Soviet Union less decisively, if at all. From an ideological and political point of view, the Soviet Union might be pleased to take on the role of overlord of space. I do not know how much it might be deterred by the prospect of adverse reactions abroad—for example, in China and in the neutralist countries.

Without going nearly so far as Dr. Frye, a number of others speak of obtaining mastery or control or supremacy in space. Thus General Curtis E. LeMay, Chief of Staff of the Air Force, says that we "will need in-being forces that can control each stratum of aerospace." [23] General Thomas S. Power, Commander of the Strategic Air Corps, says: "Absolute superiority in space is essential

[21] Major General James F. Whisenand, USAF, "Military Space Efforts, the Evolutionary Approach," *Air Force/Space Digest*, 45 (May, 1962), 54.

[22] Henry, *loc. cit.*, p. 39.

[23] *Congressional Record*, Vol. 108, No. 51 (April 3, 1962), 5338.

to the future welfare and security of the Free World. In order to reserve space for peaceful purposes we must achieve the capability to defend ourselves against the wartime use of space, and we must achieve a strategic space capability of our own which will help us preserve if not improve our deterrent posture throughout the future." [24] The Office of the Secretary of the Air Force has declared that "military supremacy in space is as essential to our security as military supremacy at altitudes near earth," [25] and Secretary of the Air Force Zuckert indicates that "the obligation is . . . to assure that space remains free for man's constructive exploitation." [26] President Kennedy played on a similar theme in saying that "only if the United States occupies a position of preeminence can we help decide whether this new ocean will be a sea of peace, or a new terrifying theater of war." [27]

Precisely what these various statements mean, and how the indicated objective is to be pursued, is left in some doubt, especially where "control" or "supremacy" is concerned. The words are reminiscent of the classic conception of "command" of the sea or of the air—a concept that is also somewhat vague. According to Bernard Brodie, "Sea command, at least in the days of battleship supremacy, was won by the ability of a superior fleet to intercept and destroy an inferior fleet when the latter sortied for an attack within the area in dispute." [28] Brodie goes on to describe Douhet's conception of "command" of the air. "Douhet made clear that by 'command' he did not mean such totality of control that 'even the enemy flies are prevented from flying.' But it is essential to the idea of command that the enemy be put in a position where he finds it impossible 'to execute aerial actions of any significance.' " [29] "Command" of the air was to be achieved not simply by interception of enemy planes in flight but even more by the destruction of the bases from which they operated. Perhaps General LeMay means something comparable when he speaks of establishing "control" of each stratum of aerospace. If so, the concept applies

[24] Speech of April 10, 1962, New York City.

[25] House Hearings, *Defense Space Interests*, 1961, p. 93.

[26] House, *Hearings on Military Posture*, 1962, p. 3700.

[27] U.S. President, *Public Papers of the Presidents of the United States*, John F. Kennedy . . . January 1 to December 31, 1962 (Washington, 1963), p. 669 (hereafter cited as *Public Papers of the Presidents*).

[28] Bernard Brodie, *Strategy in the Missile Age* (Princeton: Princeton University Press, 1959), p. 83.

[29] *Ibid.*, p. 85.

more to wartime than to peacetime and calls not simply for the interception of enemy missiles and satellites but also—and perhaps primarily—for the destruction of the launching sites from which they spring. The problem has gained a different order of magnitude since Douhet's day, however; it is one thing to speak of having "command" of the air even if a few hostile planes of the prenuclear age get through, and another thing to speak of "control" of each stratum of aerospace when the few vehicles that get through carry thermonuclear bombs.

Even in wartime, with attacks against launching sites, it may not be possible to "control" space. This is suggested, among other things, by an exchange that occurred during hearings by the Senate Armed Services Committee in February, 1963. Senator Thurmond asked, "Do you feel . . . that the nation that controls space will control the world . . . ?" To this, Dr. Harold Brown responded as follows:

I would not subscribe to that statement partly because I am not quite sure what control of space means. I do not see that it is really feasible to control space because a country will always have an advantage in space over its own territory because it can easily operate from the ground up into space.

I do not see a way, for example, in which space can be controlled to the extent that one can prevent ballistic missiles from firing here going through space and coming down there. If a country could do that it would indeed be in a fair way to control the world, and we continue to work on ideas that might have that effect. But I think in the end it is not going to be feasible.[30]

It would obviously be desirable to have a capacity to intercept, inspect, and, if need be, destroy space vehicles, and efforts to solve the various problems should certainly continue. But an effective system is apparently some years away.

Military Use for the Moon?

Scarcely anyone contends that a base on the moon would be useful for defense on earth.

Several years ago there were some claims that the moon constituted "high ground" in relation to the earth, and that it is vital for military purposes to occupy "high ground." Those who took the view did not say how many light years away from the earth they were willing to go in the pursuit of high ground. Presumably the advantage they saw in a base on the moon relates not to the normal

---

[30] Senate Hearings, *Military Procurement Authorization for 1964*, p. 477.

meaning of high and low but to the fact that, due to gravitational differences, it would take less energy to move a given object from the moon to the earth than from the earth to the moon. But the advocates of using the moon for military purposes clearly underestimated an appalling set of difficulties. They might gain safety from enemy attack by going to the moon, but they would not improve their ability to strike at the enemy.

Those who think about the relationship between national security and space generally decide to confine their thoughts to near space. "For today," says Major Henry, "it is quite reasonable to restrict discussion to near space—that is, out to the synchronous altitude." Dr. Harold Brown takes the same view. He says that the definable military uses of space all involve low orbits. "As one gets to larger distances [than the synchronous altitude], the military applications become more and more difficult to describe. In fact, they do not now exist." [31] General Bernard A. Schriever, Commander of the Air Force Systems Command, thinks that "in a decade from now we would perhaps be interested in escape velocities and orbits that are quite a bit outside of the earth orbits which we are considering now." [32] But he thinks that today "our interest lies in the area from here to the moon, and probably even in lower orbits than that." [33] General Curtis E. LeMay says that "the present area of military interest is within the sphere bounded by the synchronous orbit." [34] Dr. Edward C. Welsh describes the moon as "not a particularly useful military base for operations against earth targets." [35] And Dr. Dornberger says, "Let NASA go to the moon, let them go to Mars, let them go to Venus. It seems to me that presently there is no military interest in far outer space." [36] Dr. Simon Ramo even suggests that if the Soviet Union should "take" the moon, it might only be adding a much more remote Siberia to its domain, and that the effort to make it useful might lead to weakness rather than strength.[37] Obviously, the thought is potentially applicable to the United States as well.

[31] House Hearings, *1963 NASA Authorization*, Part 2, p. 609.

[32] "Space and National Security," *Air Force/Space Digest*, 45 (November, 1962), 78.

[33] House Hearings, *1963 NASA Authorization*, Part 2, p. 672.

[34] Senate Hearings, *Military Procurement Authorization for 1964*, p. 897.

[35] Edward C. Welsh, "Space Dollars, Sense, and Defense," *Air Force/Space Digest*, 45 (November, 1962), 68.

[36] Dornberger, *loc. cit.*, pp. 57-58. Cf. House Hearings, *Astronautics and Space Exploration*, 1958, p. 1082.

[37] House Hearings, *Astronautics and Space Exploration*, 1958, p. 479.

Though NASA and DOD are cooperating in the Gemini program, involving manned flight in near-earth orbit, nothing similar is contemplated for Apollo, "because it is a mission that does not appear to have possible military ramifications." [38]

This does not deny, of course, that what is learned in getting to the moon (e.g., about the problems of manned space flight) may later be useful for military purposes in near space.

The above discussion rests on the assumption that what we are concerned about is military security on earth—the defense of the United States and the free world. The nature of the problem will be transformed if the time comes when we want to defend specific areas on the surface of the moon or the planets. A nonmilitary writer, Dandridge M. Cole, addresses himself to the latter possibility in discussing what he calls the "Panama Hypothesis," consisting of a number of propositions that he admits cannot now be proved. "The moon, because of its low gravity and lack of atmosphere, is a 'Panama Canal' to the riches of the deep space 'Pacific' beyond." Cole's summary of his propositions runs about as follows: that man can learn to live and work beyond the Van Allen belts, that space transportation costs can be very drastically reduced, that there will be need for extra-terrestrial colonies, that access to the moon will be of critical importance (he envisages the manufacture of propellants on the moon and the in-flight refueling, from the moon, of interplanetary rockets), that some areas on the moon will be of much greater strategic importance than others (e.g., because water-bearing rocks are available in some areas and not in others), and that there will be international competition for control over the strategic areas. "There are strategic areas in space— vital to future scientific, military, and commercial space programs —which must be occupied by the United States, lest their use be forever denied us through prior occupation by unfriendly powers." [39] In an age of technological miracles, it would perhaps be rash to dismiss such imaginings as preposterous, but consideration of them can safely be postponed.

---

[38] U.S. Congress, House, Committee on Science and Astronautics, Subcommittee on Manned Space Flight, *1964 NASA Authorization*, Hearings, 88th Cong., 1st Sess., 1963, Part 2(a), p. 424 (hereafter cited as House Hearings, *1964 NASA Authorization*).

[39] Dandridge M. Cole, "Response to the 'Panama Hypothesis,'" *Astronautics*, 6 (June, 1961), 36-39+. Cf. I. M. Levitt, "Now the Space Age Opens," in Richard Witkin, ed., *The Challenge of the Sputniks* (Garden City: Doubleday, 1958), pp. 79-86.

New Weapons?

There is a rather natural tendency, which everyone agrees we should guard against, to judge the military potentialities of space on the basis of existing weapons. The point was made in 1958 by Roy W. Johnson, then Director of the Advanced Research Projects Agency in DOD: "Let's not look at the problem of tomorrow in terms of weapons of today and just automatically say that there will be no military uses of space way out, including the moon. If we think in terms of present weapons, that is probably right." But Johnson expected that nuclear bombs would be obsolete within 20 years, intimating the possibility of developing a death ray that a man in space could use and control.[40]

In 1962 General Curtis E. LeMay took up the same theme. He did not believe that the nuclear weapon was ultimate, or that the weapon replacing it would be. There was technological change in weapons as in other fields. Tomorrow's weapons might employ entirely new principles. "If a new generation of armaments operating in space could neutralize an aggressor's ICBMs, then the world would enter a new era in warfare, or in the prevention of warfare."

Beam-directed energy weapons may be used in space. And the energy directed by these weapons could travel across space essentially with the speed of light. This would be an invaluable characteristic for the interception of ICBM warheads and their decoys.

Suppose the Soviets were first to develop advanced weapons of this sort and to employ them aboard maneuvering spacecraft? . . . If they could neutralize satellites and spacecraft with such a weapon, they could prevent us from developing an equal defense against their ICBMs. And they could even prevent us from going into space for peaceful purposes.[41]

The search for exotic weapons, or at least for military applications of exotic scientific developments, is known to be going on in several areas.[42] Prospects are apparently most exciting in connection with the optical maser, or laser, a discovery that, according to General Bernard A. Schriever, "may prove to be even more important to the world than the development of the ballistic missile, the discovery of the transistor, or the reality of Telstar."[43] It is

---

[40] House Hearings, *Astronautics and Space Exploration*, 1958, p. 1180.

[41] Department of Defense, Office of Public Affairs, News Release No. 451-62, March 28, 1962.

[42] Philip J. Klass, "U.S. Increases Radiation Weapons Studies," *Aviation Week/Space Technology*, 75 (December 4, 1961), p. 55.

[43] General Bernard A. Schriever, USAF, "A New Spectrum in Technology," Hq. Air Force Systems Command, Office of Information, Release No. 50-62, August 6, 1962.

a device that renders light coherent. Ordinary light diffuses as it travels, and differs in frequency. A laser converts such light to the same frequency and keeps the rays parallel. "If focused by a telescope, a master beam would shine a one-foot spot on a screen 100 miles away. . . ."[44] Under laboratory conditions, according to General Schriever, lasers can create temperatures "millions of times hotter than the surface of the sun." He expects lasers to "open up a completely new area of microtechnology, by giving us the ability to drill or cut to tolerances measured in hundreds of molecules. All materials—including diamonds—can now be drilled or cut with extreme precision." This indicates an ability to shear holes in metal. "With an increase in the energy level of a Laser beam, or with more precise aiming techniques, it might have increasingly destructive and lethal effects and perhaps could be used to degrade or destroy the sensors and structure of the space vehicle at which it was directed." Others have been less restrained in their speculations about lasers as weapons. Thus *U.S. News and World Report* speaks of "weapons now being talked about":

Antimissile weapons. Light rays, vast in power and range, and aimed like searchlights, would be swept across the heavens at almost the speed of light. Enemy warheads would be knocked off course or, ideally, destroyed in flight. [The Pentagon is said to be pushing topsecret studies of the possibility of placing such anti-missile weapons in satellites.]

Antisatellite weapons. A beam concentrated on a satellite would exert enough power to send it flying off its course. Its electronic gear could be heated beyond critical limits. For other purposes, the orbit of an enemy satellite might be controlled by gentle pulses, nudging it first one way and then another—taking control from the enemy.[45]

There are also references to the possibility of using lasers as antiaircraft guns, igniting the fuel in enemy planes, or as weapons that could be employed from satellites to produce destruction and terror below. It is said to be "almost within the capability of present lasers [to start] backfires as a means of fighting forest fires"—and to do this from aircraft.[46] The possibility is mentioned that lasers might be employed instead of A-bombs to detonate thermonuclear bombs, which might make the diffusion of thermonuclear capabilities occur more rapidly. Along less violent lines, General Schriever expects that lasers will be useful "as a part of various sensing devices. Sur-

[44] George A. W. Boehm, "What We Know About Solids Is Getting Solid," *Fortune*, 64 (November, 1961), 154.

[45] *U.S. News and World Report*, 52 (April 2, 1962), 48.

[46] *New York Times*, May 22, 1963, 37:1.

veillance, data readout, mapping, surveying, and navigation and control may be revolutionized by the full application of the laser principle." He also says that the laser offers a method for energy transfer in space. "If a high-energy laser beam were directed at a satellite, most of its energy could be transferred to an apppropriate receiver." Above all, lasers are expected to revolutionize communications—at least in space. "In the next few years lasers will open more than a million times the present communications spectrum." [47]

Let it not be thought that there is general confidence in all of the above anticipations. The laser suffers a humbling limitation of a very elementary sort: anything that diffuses light—e.g., fog, clouds, rain, snow—destroys its usefulness.[48] The London *Economist* reports that "there are no immediate commercial prospects for the laser." [49] Skepticism seems to be especially strong about the potentiality of the laser as an instrument of violence, the report being that "current models produce a beam only about 1% as powerful as the energy pumped into it." On this basis it is said that it would take "practically the nation's entire power supply" to produce a destructive ray that would be effective at a substantial distance.[50] Though General Schriever speaks of using a laser to transfer energy to a satellite, he does not say whether a laser on board a satellite could be fed enough power to make it effective as a weapon. And if the laser does become effective as a weapon, it is not yet clear whether the potential military role of satellites, such as it is, will be enhanced or jeopardized.

The principal point here is not that lasers will or will not be made into weapons that are useful in space, but rather that the possibility exists; and this strengthens the thought expressed by Roy Johnson and General LeMay: that new weapons of some sort may well appear, affecting military potentialities. This consideration reinforces others in suggesting that military capabilities should be developed in space going beyond those for which there is an

---

[47] In addition to the above citations concerning lasers, see *New York Times*, November 13, 1962, 20:4; *Wall Street Journal*, March 9, 1961, p. 4; Siekman, *loc. cit.*, p. 218.

[48] House Hearings, *1964 NASA Authorization*, Part 2(a), p. 637.

[49] *Economist*, 206 (February 9, 1963), 507. Cf. Anon., "The 'Secrecy of Space,'" *Vectors*, 2 (Fourth Quarter, 1960), 5-10.

[50] Howard Simons, in *Washington Post*, November 18, 1962, E5; *Aviation Daily*, August 7, 1962.

immediate definable need. The question is what capabilities should be developed on this basis, how, and how urgently.

New Technology?

In Chapter 6 I will cite the view that the space effort is at least in part justifiable as a stimulus to technological progress. Let it be noted here, however, that the subject has implications for national defense, for though an advanced technology does not guarantee security, it is one of its necessary conditions. The importance of the point is suggested by imagining what might have happened if Hitler had developed nuclear weapons ahead of the United States and Britain or if, after the war, the East rather than the West had had a nuclear monopoly. And it might have been. If the Nazi or the Soviet government had decided at the end of the 1930's to make a major effort to develop nuclear weapons, it is quite possible that either could have succeeded. The importance of the point is also suggested if one contemplates the fate that retarded or static societies (e.g., those of the American Indians) have suffered at the hands of the dynamic. The possibilities and facts of the past give warning for the future. Security and survival depend on many factors, not least among them the extent to which a country develops latent scientific and engineering talent and the way in which it chooses to employ that talent.

General Gavin has stressed this point. "As war becomes increasingly complex, technology becomes more and more important. In fact, if the strategy of the Soviets or of the West were to be decisively successful without tactical battle, it would be in the field of technology, for technology contains all of the elements short of war itself."[51]

James E. Webb, Administrator of NASA, takes a somewhat similar view. He lists "five principal reasons for the national commitment to sustained and resolute action in space on a large scale, a crucial element of which is the augmented drive to land Americans on the moon during this decade," and he states the first as follows:

1. The United States cannot risk continuing (and discounting) the lag of past years in the space competition with the Soviet Union. We must master spaceflight in both its unmanned and manned aspects. This is insurance against finding ourselves at some stage with an over-all tech-

[51] Gavin, op. cit., p. 236.

nology inferior to that of the Russians. . . . If we permitted the Russians to surpass us, eventually we would almost certainly find ourselves on the receiving end of their advanced space technology, employed for military and economic aggression.[52]

There is here no mention of specific danger or of a specific method by which the Soviet Union might use space capabilities in military aggression. There is, rather, a general assumption that significant technological developments are likely to lead to new methods of economic and military struggle.

General Gavin's conception of technology is very broad. To him it includes "economics, natural resources, decision-making and lead time, and superior weapons systems." He says that each of these elements, "if not properly understood and carefully planned, could directly contribute to strategic defeat." This constitutes a reminder that the natural scientists and the engineers are not the only ones involved. Perhaps it will not be out of place for a social scientist to suggest that the security and survival of a state depend at least as much on the wisdom of its policies, especially its foreign policies, as on technological strategy. The strength of the dinosaur, when guided by the brain of the dinosaur, leads to extinction.

Conclusion

At the beginning of the preceding chapter two views of the potentialities of space for military security were cited. Under the one view, expressed by Dr. Sänger, orbital velocities preclude military uses. Under the other view, security and even survival depend upon space power.

No one goes quite as far as Dr. Sänger in denying that orbiting vehicles may somehow be instruments of war, but some approach that position. Eisenhower himself was asked a few days after Sputnik I went into orbit whether the event made him more concerned about our nation's security, and he responded as follows: "Now, so far as the satellite itself is concerned, that does not raise my apprehensions, not one iota. I see nothing at this moment, at this stage of development, that is significant in that development as far as security is concerned, except, as I pointed out, it does very definitely prove the possession by the Russian scientists of a very powerful thrust in their rocketry, and that is important." [53] This

[52] *New York Times*, October 8, 1961, 1:2.
[53] *Public Papers of the Presidents*, Eisenhower, 1957, p. 730.

attitude—or, more usually, the few words that can be taken out of context to indicate that nothing about Sputnik raised Eisenhower's apprehensions one iota—has been cited rather frequently, and always scornfully; and it is true that if Eisenhower had been dedicated more to complete frankness than to his responsibilities for the defense of the United States and its allies, he might have put much more stress than he did on the revolutionary potentialities of Soviet rocket power. But he is scarcely to be blamed for not emphasizing to the world, including the potential enemy, that the strategic power position of the country had deteriorated badly. And he may well have been right in his estimate of the military potentialities of satellites.

Many others have expressed views more or less similar to those of Eisenhower. Dr. Simon Ramo, former adviser to the Air Force and manager of space projects for the Air Force, put a very reserved interpretation on "The Potentialities of Space Weapons Systems" in testimony to a House committee in 1958.[54] Dr. Jerome B. Wiesner mixes skepticism with caution. The Wiesner report submitted to President-elect Kennedy in January, 1961, seemed to deny (though rather unclearly) what it described as the general assumption that the space program was designed primarily to meet security needs. A later comment by Dr. Wiesner is that "although most people say that they see no military use for space, not to have a space capability is a risk that I don't want to take." [55] Roswell L. Gilpatric, Deputy Secretary of Defense, said in March, 1961, "Whether we will ever have space systems for operational use as weapons systems is something we cannot predict today." [56] Two years later his statement was: "While acknowledging that space is not inevitably or predictably the key to future military power, we must remain, and we are, alert to the possibility that it could grow in importance as technology evolves." [57] A study prepared for a House Subcommittee on Manned Space Flight in 1962 concluded that "to date [military applications] are quite restricted in nature

---

[54] House Hearings, *Astronautics and Space Exploration*, 1958, pp. 482-87.

[55] "Thinking Ahead with Jerome Wiesner," *International Science and Technology*, February, 1962, p. 32.

[56] House Hearings, *Defense Space Interests*, 1961, p. 14.

[57] U.S. Congress, Senate, Committee on Aeronautical and Space Sciences, *NASA Authorization for Fiscal Year 1964*, Hearings, 88th Cong., 1st Sess., 1963, Part 1, p. 605.

and it is difficult to see offensive military missions which absolutely require the development of space systems." [58] Keith A. Brueckner, Vice President for Research of the Institute for Defense Analysis, cites a 1959 statement by Herbert York, Director of Defense Research and Engineering, that the Soviet lead in space propulsion was "'more a question of acute embarrassment than national survival,'" and says that this estimate "appears now to have been correct." [59] Senator Proxmire, though acknowledging the "magnificent potentialities of space," thinks that "there is no great urgency involved." "It is not a matter of defending freedom; it is not a matter of defending the world; it is not a matter of protecting the United States against possible aggression from a Communist opponent. It is a matter of developing, in time, an exciting future for mankind, particularly for Americans." [60] President Kennedy placed little public stress on military reasons for a space program, whether because he thought that they are not very substantial or because of a decision to play them down.[61] In May, 1963, the Special Assistant for Space in the Office of the Director of Defense Research and Engineering commented that "most task groups" that have studied the military space program "have arrived only at very general conclusions and recommendations, most of which involved expanding on a broad front to do more of everything without any real definition of what the over-all objectives or goals should be. . . . There is little common agreement . . . on the ultimate military significance of space technology." [62] When General Ferguson, USAF, was testifying before the House space committee in March, 1963, a member distinguished between "passive" space systems such as communications and reconnaissance and "offensive" systems; and he asked the General what we were doing "offensively." The answer was, "We are studying it and we are analyzing it. But I think the underlying statement that needs to be made when we discuss the military opportunities in space is

[58] House Hearings, *1963 NASA Authorization*, Part 2, Appendix IV, p. 1041.
[59] Review of Donald W. Cox, *The Space Race*, in *Washington Post*, November 25, 1962.
[60] *Congressional Record*, Vol. 108, No. 116 (July 10, 1962), 12,199.
[61] Richard Witkin, "Pros and Cons," in Walter Sullivan, ed., *America's Race for the Moon. The New York Times Story of Project Apollo* (New York: Random House, 1962), p. 150.
[62] Dr. Lawrence L. Kavanau, "The Military Space Program in Perspective," Department of Defense, Office of Public Affairs, News Release No. 718-63, May 21, 1963, pp. 9, 14.

that we don't know what they are and we have to get up there and find out what they are." [63]

In April, 1963, reportedly after Secretary McNamara "turned down some proposals for manned spacecraft that seemed outlandish to him," the Air Force initiated "Project Forecast"—including studies of the potentialities of space power. The mood of the Air Force in sponsoring the studies—and getting some 200 persons to help with them—is said to be that of a service approaching a fight for existence. [64]

As to the view that space power is potentially vital to security, there is no doubt that it has been and is widely held. Especially in the months following Sputnik I, congressional deliberations relating to the event were dominated by dire fears and warnings and vague forebodings. The attitude was justified more by Soviet missiles than by Soviet satellites. And the same is still true. In the light of this, it is strange to see how much stress some observers put on the notion that military space power is somehow tremendously important but is being neglected. Senator Dodd says, "We must accept the harsh fact that our very survival as a nation may very well depend on our ability to control our space environment." [65] Precisely what he means and what leads him to the conclusion he does not say. Senator Cannon complains that the major emphasis is being placed on civilian pursuits "to the detriment of development of vitally needed military capabilities in space. If continued, this could prove to be a fatal mistake." [66] He does not say precisely why the military capabilities are vitally needed, or precisely what military capabilities he has in mind. Senator Goldwater has spoken to the same general effect. In the House, both Mr. Teague and Mr. Fulton seem to regard DOD as remiss for not pressing for a military man-in-space program. Mr. Fulton believes that "we must be the first nation having vehicles orbiting in space, both manned and unmanned, with nuclear and nonnuclear weapons." [67] Representative Waggoner says, "I personally would not support a program of this magnitude if I was not convinced it was part of our national security." But implicitly he indicated that his conviction was based on intuition or faith rather than on evidence. "When will

---

[63] U.S. Congress, House, Committee on Science and Astronautics, Space Posture, Hearings, 88th Cong., 1st Sess., 1963, p. 235.

[64] New York Times, May 27, 1963, 1:4.

[65] Congressional Record, Vol. 108, No. 151 (August 24, 1962), 16,445.

[66] Ibid., Vol. 108, No. 147 (August 20, 1962), p. 16,052.

[67] House Hearings, 1964 NASA Authorization, Part 2, p. 633.

we be able to define a military value of this space program? There is a good question for anybody." [68]

There is always room for argument on whether a defense program is adequate, particularly when it is a question of preparing against vague and uncertain future dangers. The problem is made all the greater by the fact that lead times are so long. "The time required for development, once it appears that a new system is practical, is in the order of five or six years. If you have made the wrong bet on the technology, the consequences could be grave." [69] Some seize upon this to argue for the urgent development of virtually everything that might conceivably turn out to be useful, fearing that any omission might be fatal. And attitudes toward the problem are affected by assumptions concerning the intentions and capabilities of the Soviet Union. Strident advocates of the development of space power tend to make the very simple assumption that the Soviet Union is out to dominate the world, and that an all-out defense effort is therefore urgently imperative. They do not ask whether the Soviet government has any other interests and values that may qualify the desire for domination and thus modify the threat.

The Air Force, and the whole Department of Defense, are automatically in an invidious position in estimating defense needs, for relevant considerations are contradictory and every significant decision is almost bound to involve controversy.

On the one hand, a series of considerations suggest extreme askings. No commanding officer can relish the prospect of finding himself caught short in the future—finding himself without vital capabilities when and if crisis and war overtake him. To safeguard himself against such an eventuality, he naturally wants capabilities fully adequate for every need he can imagine, with a comfortable margin for safety. In a sense it is his duty to view with alarm— to give insistent warning of every military danger he can conceive. If he expects to get less than he asks for, he is under great temptation to exaggerate his needs, and the knowledge that others will review his requests and assume formal responsibility for decisions may temper his own sense of responsibility. His desire to retain

---

[68] U.S. Congress, House, Committee on Science and Astronautics, *Panel on Science and Technology. Fifth Meeting*, 88th Cong., 1st Sess., 1963, pp. 42-43, 46-47.

[69] Department of Defense, Office of Public Affairs, News Release No. 1684-62, October 16, 1962.

the loyal support of those in his own service and to buttress their belief in the importance of their role and the significance of their future may inflate his claims and expectations. He is commonly goaded toward extremes by militarist or profit-minded elements, e.g., lobbyists, trade journals, and some congressmen.

On the other hand, there is every reason to assume the general honesty, integrity, and competence of those in responsible positions in DOD. Each service can look with a jealous eye on the askings of the others, and the Office of the Secretary of Defense has the opportunity to subject all service recommendations to rigid scrutiny. Though those in military command may aim to provide for every need they can imagine, their imaginations do not always keep up with the possibilities, especially in periods of rapid and extreme technological change. They are under some practical compulsion to keep askings within "reasonable" bounds, and they may have to operate under more or less severe restrictions imposed by the President and the Bureau of the Budget.

Conflicting forces such as those listed above produce varying outcomes. Perhaps the only generalization that can safely be made is the obvious one that interpretations of needs should not necessarily be taken at face value, especially those of the individual services and even those of DOD. To seek maximum guarantees against every imaginable danger is scarcely a sensible policy when every dollar spent for the purpose comes at the expense of other values that are also precious. Further, an exaggerated defense effort may incite comparable exaggerations abroad, accentuating the dangers that are supposed to be countered. Though it is always possible that more should be done, the fact is that the military space program is already very extensive. Arguments that it is inadequate do not seem strong.[70]

No over-all conclusion will be attempted here on the extent to which security considerations explain and justify the various aspects of the space program. A number of motives are operating, and it will be best to identify all of the major ones before attempting an assessment of the influence that they have or ought to have. Even then the conclusions will reflect judgment more than objectively verified fact. Tentatively, however, the question may be raised whether there has not been a rather general tendency to

---

[70] Cf. address of George P. Miller, Chairman of the House Committee on Science and Astronautics, in *Congressional Record*, Vol. 108, No. 160 (September 6, 1962), 17,584.

overemphasize the security motive, both in relationship to the weight it should have in relationship to the role that it has really played. If so, this suggests either that some parts of the space program are not as fully justified as they have been thought to be, or that other motives have been operating without being recognized or adequately emphasized.

PEACE

5

"If any ask, why do we do what we are doing in space—what do we expect to attain—the first answer of America is a one-word answer: peace. . . . The avenues of space offer man's best hope for bringing nearer the day of peace on earth." So speaks Lyndon B. Johnson, and a number of others express similar thoughts. Moreover, the National Aeronautics and Space Act of 1958 declares it to be "the policy of the United States that activities in space should be devoted to peaceful purposes for the benefit of all mankind." The question is how the space program might bring peace and what the limitation to "peaceful purposes" means. And another kind of question necessarily intrudes itself: whether the references to peace are to be classified simply as propaganda ploys and pious hopes that lack operational significance.

Theories About Space and Peace

The thought that space activities might contribute somehow to peace has been prominent from the first, expressed particularly in political and scientific circles. The most common theory is that space activities provide a basis for international cooperation and that cooperation will build a sense of unity; in other words, the assumption is that cooperative space efforts may eliminate the kinds of thoughts and purposes that bring on war. At the opposite extreme is another theory: that the military potentialities of space can be exploited in such a way as to render states incapable of attacking successfully, whatever the thoughts and purposes of the governmental leaders may be.

In 1958 the majority leaders of both houses of Congress endorsed the first of the theories named above. The House majority leader, Mr. McCormack, declared: "Not least among the possibilities of this great adventure is the potentiality of a reemphasis in men's hearts of the common links that bind the members of the human race together and the development of a strengthened sense of community of interest which quite transcends national boundaries. It is my belief that in such a development lies our strongest hope of world peace and security." [1] And the Senate majority leader, Mr. Johnson, said: "If we proceed along the orderly course of full cooperation, we shall by the very fact of cooperation make the most substantial contribution yet made toward perfecting peace. Men who have worked together to reach the stars are not likely to descend together into the depths of war and desolation." [2] The first NASA Administrator, T. Keith Glennan, thought that out of cooperation might come "that common understanding and mutual trust that will break the lock step of suspicion and distrust that divides the world into separate camps today." [3] Ambassador Lodge expressed similar sentiments at the United Nations. A statement of the Federation of the American Scientists, submitted to the Senate special committee in 1958, urged that international cooperation be fostered: "We can best improve our national security by initiating cooperative programs which will draw together the peoples of the world in the joint conquest of outer space." [4] Five years later the Editor of the *Bulletin of the Atomic Scientists*, confronting the question being debated especially among scientists, whether the lunar program was justifiable, took up the same general line of thought.[5] "In facing cosmic space, the quarrels and struggles between different factions of humanity appear petty and irrelevant." The dimensions and costs of space exploration impress nations and their leaders with the need for cooperation, despite their bitter rivalry and conflict.

[1] *Congressional Record*, Vol. 104, Pt. 8 (June 2, 1958), 9913.

[2] *Department of State Bulletin*, 39 (December 15, 1958), 979.

[3] T. Keith Glennan, "Opportunities for International Cooperation in Space Exploration," *Department of State Bulletin*, 42 (January 11, 1960), 63.

[4] U.S. Congress, Senate, Special Committee on Space and Astronautics, *National Aeronautics and Space Act*, Hearings . . . on S. 3609, 85th Cong., 2d Sess., 1958, Part 2, p. 381.

[5] Eugene Rabinowitch, "Previews of Space," *Bulletin of the Atomic Scientists*, 19 (May, 1963), 7.

Common effort could help to create bonds and foster the trust which comes from participating in a common enterprise.

If space exploration could help bring together the two alienated parts of humanity and reduce, even slightly, the danger of all-destroying nuclear war, that alone would make worthwhile investing in it many billions of dollars.

And President Kennedy endorsed the theme in calling for joint Soviet-American space projects. He suggested that the gains for world peace might be more significant than the gains for science. "For a cooperative Soviet-American effort in space science and exploration would emphasize the interests that must unite us, rather than those that always divide us. It offers us an area in which the stale and sterile dogmas of the Cold War could be literally left a quarter of a million miles behind." [6]

There is no way of knowing how well founded such thoughts and hopes may prove to be. They are suggestive of the idea of seeking a "functional integration" of the world, i.e., getting peoples so interrelated and interdependent through a network of activities serving common interests that war becomes almost unthinkable, and getting problems transferred from the political category to the technical or administrative category. The idea undoubtedly has merit. Functional integration within countries is plainly one of the factors contributing to domestic peace. At the same time, where peace is stable it depends upon much more than this. As long as men have varied desires, issues over which they struggle are bound to arise. Moreover, functional integration is bound to be extremely slow and uncertain, even if pursued simultaneously in connection with many different kinds of activities and not alone in connection with space. Further, as experience with space activities has demonstrated, it is likely to be least applicable where it is most needed, i.e., in the relationships of states that are more or less hostile to each other. It is one thing to cooperate with friends and allies, with whom trusting relationships have been established, and another thing to cooperate with an unfriendly government given to distrust and suspicion. Despite some degree of cooperation between the United States and the Soviet Union, each country has so far treated its space program much more as an instrument of struggle than as a means of ameliorating relationships. In view of the close

---

[6] U.S. Congress, Senate, Committee on Aeronautical and Space Sciences, *Documents on International Aspects of the Exploration and Use of Outer Space, 1954-1962*, Staff Report, S. Doc. No. 18, 88th Cong., 1st Sess., 1963, p. 253 (hereafter cited as Senate, *Documents on International Aspects*, 1963).

association between space activities and missile power, it is to be expected that those primarily concerned with security in both Washington and Moscow will be extremely cautious about coopera- tive arrangements. Even so, such cooperation as is possible may help a little to relax tensions, and given the horrible prospective costs of war, even slight contributions to peace may be precious.

A study by the staff of the House space committee in 1961 ex- pressed a variation on the above theme: ". . . that the absorption of energies, resources, imagination, and aggressiveness in pursuit of the space adventure may become an effective way of maintain- ing peace." The thought was that the "urge to overcome the un- known" might dwarf the other kinds of desires that have led to wars in the past.[7] The thought seems very fanciful. Preoccupied as many are with the moon, there is no sign that Berlin or Cuba or Vietnam are being forgotten either in Washington or in Moscow —or in Peking.

In addition to the contribution that scientific and exploratory cooperation may make to peace, there is another possibility: that satellites will contribute by facilitating "people-to-people" com- munication. Already the Telstar and Relay satellites have provided a trans-Atlantic link giving TV audiences on each side a more immediate and intimate conception of life and events on the other side. Further, as has been demonstrated, satellites permit the hold- ing of "Town Meetings of the World," with speakers in different countries seeing each other and being seen by untold millions of viewers. Frank Stanton, President of CBS, points out that people have already been captivated by trans-Atlantic TV. "The pressing need of mankind is to advance . . . unity of purpose. . . . A com- munications satellite system can make a most valuable contribution. It can do this, I think, primarily on two great fronts, reporting and discussing. . . . We cannot achieve a common purpose or a unity of values unless people know what is going on and are able to conduct a dialog on its meaning and its implications."[8]

Again predictions of the effect of transoceanic TV on peace must be cautious. It is perhaps symbolic that France refused to cooperate in the first "Town Meeting of the World" because of the political

[7] U.S. Congress, House, Committee on Science and Astronautics, *The Prac- tical Values of Space Exploration* (revised August, 1961), H. Rpt. No. 1276, 87th Cong., 1st Sess., 1961, p. 22.

[8] Speech of October 25, 1962, reprinted in *Congressional Record*, Vol. 109, No. 92 (June 19, 1963), A3894.

nature of the program. If people-to-people communication is limited to programs whose content is pleasing to each government, or if it occurs only among countries that have already established a friendly, common understanding, the contribution to peace will necessarily be slight. Moreover, it sometimes happens that fuller knowledge of the purposes and practices of other people produces antipathy more than friendship and respect.

General Curtis E. LeMay, Chief of Staff, USAF, is an exponent of the second theory: "maintaining peace in space, as elsewhere, will be accomplished through deterrence." [9] Lyndon B. Johnson also seems to endorse this second theory of peace, as well as the first one, though less clearly. "If peace is to be maintained on earth, free men must acquire the competence to preserve space as a field of peace before it can be made into a new battlefield of tyranny. . . . If we abandon the field, space can be preempted by others as an instrument for aggression." [10] And President Kennedy said that "only if the United States occupies a position of pre-eminence can we help decide whether this new ocean of space will be a sea of peace, or a new terrifying theater of war." [11]

By general consent, a capacity for effective retaliation is a vital factor in deterrence, and it is quite plausible that reconnaissance and communications satellites—and perhaps other space developments that are militarily useful—might significantly enhance the prospect of effective retaliation. At the same time, the extension of the arms race into space would no doubt add to international tensions. And, quite apart from this, there is as yet no reason to believe—in fact it is absurd to believe—that the actual or foreseeable contributions of space to military capabilities are such as to give real assurance that war can be prevented. Nuclear weapons and long-range missiles come much closer to providing the assurance, but no one can be sure that even they will be effective.

The Limitation to "Peaceful Purposes" in Space

In a letter to Chairman Bulganin in January, 1958, President Eisenhower proposed an agreement "that outer space should be

[9] U.S. Congress, Senate, Committee on Armed Services, *Military Procurement Authorization for Fiscal Year 1964*, Hearings, 88th Cong., 1st Sess., 1963, pp. 896-97.

[10] *Congressional Record*, Vol. 109, No. 91 (June 18, 1963), A3867.

[11] U.S. President, *Public Papers of the Presidents of the United States*, John F. Kennedy . . . January 1 to December 31, 1962 (Washington, 1963), p. 669.

used only for peaceful purposes. . . . Both the Soviet Union and the United States are now using outer space for the testing of missiles designed for military purposes. The time to stop is now."

Agreement was not reached, and the reasons are fairly easy to identify. Khrushchev recognized the strategy, for it was one that the Soviet Union has very commonly employed. He said that the United States was attempting to ban weapons it did not possess and to protect itself from those weapons that would harm its own territory.[12] The Chairman of the House Committee on Science and Astronautics, the late Overton Brooks, spelled the idea out at a later time. He saw the possibility of both propaganda and practical benefits from championing the principle that activities in space should be devoted to peaceful purposes only.

About the only way our land can be hurt by Russia, in the event of anger, is through outer space. You take away the ballistic missiles; you take away the satellites and the rockets, and we can keep our own nation impervious, more or less, to attack.

So we have not only the propaganda value but we also have a very strong nationalistic reason for wishing to make outer space peaceful.[13]

Despite the failure to obtain an agreement with the Soviet Union, the United States endorsed the principle unilaterally. In enacting the National Aeronautics and Space Act of 1958 Congress, on Eisenhower's recommendation, used the words quoted above, declaring it to be "the policy of the United States that activities in space should be devoted to peaceful purposes for the benefit of all mankind." It seems likely that the principle was endorsed primarily for its propaganda effect, without being clearly thought out. Moreover, it expresses an aspiration rather than a rule that limits the government in what it can do. Even if the principle did involve a limitation, it could be abrogated just as it was adopted—by unilateral action. But regardless of all this, it is interesting and it may be significant to see what the words mean, or whether they have any clear meaning at all. For present purposes, the crucial word is *peaceful,* though there is also room for disagreement about the meaning of *space.* (Where does it begin?)

[12] U.S. Congress, House, Select Committee on Astronautics and Space Exploration, *The National Space Program,* H. Rpt. No. 1758, 85th Cong., 2d Sess., 1958, p. 221.

[13] U.S. Congress, House, Committee on Science and Astronautics, *International Control of Outer Space,* Hearings, 86th Cong., 1st Sess., 1959, p. 66 (hereafter cited as House Hearings, *International Control of Outer Space,* 1959).

SOME ANTONYMS OF "PEACEFUL"

When a country declares that activities should be devoted to peaceful purposes, what kinds of purposes, if any, does it propose to forgo? The usual antonym for *peace* is *war*. Does the notion that space is to be devoted to peaceful purposes mean that no hostile act is to be committed in it or through it in time of war? This is a possible construction, but it is unlikely that a belligerent which might secure a significant advantage via space would forgo the opportunity; and Eisenhower and Congress clearly thought of themselves as formulating a rule pertaining not to wartime but to peacetime. The apparent assumption, despite later disclaimers, was that peacetime activities can be divided into two categories: peaceful and nonpeaceful.

The problem of ascertaining the meaning of *nonpeaceful* might be simplified if the English language included the word *warful*. But it does not; and, in any case, what government would admit in peacetime that it was conducting *warful* activities? *Bellicose, war-like, hostile, aggressive, violent,* and *military* are all possible antonyms for *peaceful,* and perhaps the intention was that activities that could be characterized by one of them were to be excluded. But there are difficulties about all of them in the present context. Given the fact that the declared, general purpose of the United States is to deter war and keep the peace, what activities in which it might wish to engage would it describe by one of these adjectives? Are war games necessarily bellicose? If warlike, are they necessarily to be described as nonpeaceful? No doubt an *aggressive* act would be nonpeaceful, and is therefore forsworn. But Eisenhower's reference to the testing of weapons in space indicates that he was thinking of acts in addition to, or other than, those that might be classed as aggressive. And we might note incidentally that the term *aggressive* is horribly difficult to define in a satisfactory, general way. If one country orbits nuclear bombs and another destroys them or somehow removes them from orbit, is either guilty of an aggressive act? Which one? If the object orbited and destroyed is a reconnaissance satellite, has aggression occurred? If so, who is guilty? Acts of violence are clearly nonpeaceful when associated with a state of war, but otherwise some kinds of them are commonly described (though perhaps with some strain) as peaceful. Did not the UN pursue peaceful purposes in applying violence in the Congo?

ARE MILITARY PURPOSES NONPEACEFUL?

It is common to speak of *peaceful* purposes as if the contrast is with *military* purposes. In fact, before enacting the National Aeronautics and Space Act of 1958 both houses of Congress had already passed a resolution containing this meeting. The resolution asserted that it was the wish of peoples everywhere "that the exploration of outer space shall be by peaceful means and shall be dedicated to peaceful purposes." It went on to declare that "the nations of the world . . . should ban the use of outer space for military aggrandizement." It was the sense of Congress "that the United States should strive, through the United Nations or such other means as may be most appropriate, for an international agreement banning the use of outer space for military purposes." [14]

Now the usual antonym for *military* is *civilian*. To contrast peaceful purposes with military purposes, then, is to suggest the thought that peaceful and civilian somehow go hand in hand. The force of the suggestion is indicated by the actual tendency to discuss "military and peaceful uses" as if "military and civilian uses" is what is actually meant. But generals do not always seek war, nor do diplomats always try to maintain peace. Military forces may have a pacifying and stabilizing influence, and military personnel may put as much (or as little) value on peace as civilians do. The assumption that civilian purposes are peaceful and military purposes nonpeaceful is quite untenable.

Testifying on the above resolution, the General Counsel of DOD urged that we must condition our acceptance of any international agreement on the subject "upon the need for adequate safeguards, including inspections" and also "upon the need to continue to develop military weapon systems for outer space until such time as adequate safeguards can be established." He did not interpret our unilateral endorsement of the principle of peaceful purposes to preclude the development of "defensive weapons and vehicles." [15] Later, in another context, Admiral Ward, the Navy's Judge Advocate General, spoke of "the stubborn, unpleasant, inescapable fact

---

[14] U.S. Congress, Senate, Special Committee on Space and Astronautics, *Final Report* . . . Pursuant to S. Res. 256 of the 85th Congress, S. Rpt. No. 100, 86th Cong., 1st Sess., 1959, p. 17.

[15] U.S. Congress, House, Committee on Foreign Affairs, *Relative to the Establishment of Plans for the Peaceful Exploration of Outer Space,* Hearing Before the Subcommittee on National Security and Scientific Developments Affecting Foreign Policy . . . on H. Con. Res. 326, 85th Cong., 2d Sess., 1958, p. 33.

. . . that scientific and commercial uses of space are so inextricably intermixed with security and defense interests that they simply cannot be severed therefrom." Evidently not realizing that the congressional resolution had spoken of forgoing the pursuit of *military* purposes in space, he identified this wording with a Soviet proposal.

Limiting the use of outer space to "peaceful purposes" certainly does not necessarily exclude harmless scientific testing of weapons. On the other hand, an international agreement banning use for "military" purposes would most likely be construed to ban the testing of weapons even though the tests were completely harmless. Also, the latter type of agreement would furnish a basis for fierce contention that any type of reconnaissance satellite, regardless of whether its primary purpose was scientific, was a "military" use.

Agreements of the latter type, therefore, might very well preclude the United States from developing types of nuclear weapons necessary to deter war and to insure our survival.[16]

Senator Keating, who championed the principle that space should not be used for military purposes, was once asked whether he would forbid the military use of space communication facilities, but he indicated that he did not intend this. However, as we have seen in an earlier chapter, his attitude supported Admiral Ward's fears with regard to reconnaissance satellites. He thought that such a satellite should be classified as serving a military and nonpeaceful purpose, and he said that if we knew that such a satellite was in space "for the purpose of viewing what was going on in this country, we would try to shoot it down, and any other country would." To Jessup and Taubenfeld, it would be a nonpeaceful use of outer space if satellites with nuclear warheads were placed in orbit, if one state used space vehicles in jamming the attack-warning system of another state, or if space vehicles were used to provide "weather and other observations in advance of military movements on earth." They say that "the definition of 'peaceful' remains, of necessity, inadequately specific and subject to change with time. In outer space the most peaceful uses may be suffused with military potentials. . . . If weather can be controlled, droughts or storms may become a *casus belli* some day."[17]

A comparable problem arose in connection with the treaty of

---

[16] House Hearings, *International Control of Outer Space*, 1959, pp. 100, 103.

[17] Philip C. Jessup and Howard J. Taubenfeld, *Controls for Outer Space and the Antarctic Analogy* (New York: Columbia University Press, 1959), p. 222.

1959 pertaining to Antarctica, to which both the United States and the Soviet Union are parties. A number of spokesmen, including representatives of the Department of State, have cited this treaty as providing a precedent that may be helpful in delimiting the realm of the permissible in space. Article 1 of the treaty contains two paragraphs:

1. Antarctica shall be used for peaceful purposes only. There shall be prohibited, *inter alia*, any measures of a military nature, such as the establishment of military bases and fortifications, the carrying out of military maneuvers, as well as the testing of any type of weapons.

2. The present treaty shall not prevent the use of military personnel or equipment for scientific research or for any other peaceful purpose.

Again the contrast is between *peaceful* and *military* purposes, but it is incomplete. Some activities of the military are accepted as peaceful. The fact is that the U.S. armed forces, especially the Navy, have played a substantial role in the exploratory and scientific work that has been done in Antarctica, and under the treaty they continue in this role.

The very term *peaceful purposes* suggests that intent may be a crucial factor in the classification of activity, whether in Antarctica or in space. The exploratory and scientific work that goes on in Antarctica is obviously undertaken, predominantly at least, for reasons that have nothing to do with war. Given peaceful intent, then, the treaty makes certain activities permissible even if carried on by military personnel with military equipment. But the treaty also suggests that some activities (e.g., the testing of any type of weapon), are of such a nature that their intent must be presumed to be nonpeaceful.

Even the criterion of intent leads into difficulties. It is one of the rules of international politics that governments profess a love of peace. In everything that they do, their intentions are peaceful. Certainly the United States takes this position, which raises the question whether it was consistent in accepting the view in the Antarctica treaty that military bases and the testing of weapons are nonpeaceful.

ALL PEACETIME ACTIVITIES ARE PEACEFUL

Obviously, our unilateral policy that activities in space should be devoted to peaceful purposes has not been interpreted to exclude military purposes. As the Assistant Secretary of the Air Force, Brockway McMillan, has said, ". . . our policy of peaceful use of outer space has never been intended or interpreted to deny the military the use of space for peaceful or for stabilizing purposes." [18] Stressing the same point, Dr. Edward C. Welsh, Executive Secretary of the National Aeronautics and Space Council, points to the fact that the Space Act itself denies any general incompatibility between our peaceful and our military purposes. While endorsing peaceful purposes, the Act specifies that "activities peculiar to or primarily associated with the development of weapons systems, military operations, or the defense of the United States (including the research and development necessary to make effective provision for the defense of the United States) shall be the responsibility of, and shall be directed by, the Department of Defense." Moreover, it obliges NASA to make available to DOD any "discoveries that have military value or significance." Dr. Welsh goes on to say that "the Defense Department's space vehicles such as ICBMs, Midas, Samos, and others, in the hands of the United States, are designed for peaceful purposes. Nothing is more essential for peace than the capability to discourage or deter attack." [19] He holds that "the true mission of our military strength is to protect the peace. That mission is to deter war." [20] And he believes that the attempt to make a distinction between peaceful and nonpeaceful activities has "hampered clear thinking on our national space programs." [21] Lyndon B. Johnson, as Chairman of the National Aeronautics and Space Council, expressed the same general view: "The United States does not have a division between peaceful and non-peaceful objectives for space, but rather has space missions to help keep the peace and space missions to improve our ability to live well in peace." [22] In other words, in saying that activities in space should be devoted to peaceful purposes only, we do not limit ourselves at all; for all of our peacetime purposes are peaceful.

This is no doubt true, yet at the same time it is a rather unsatisfactory conclusion. Not only does it make the profession of peaceful intent seem disingenuous (which it may have been in part), but

---

[18] Department of Defense, Office of Public Affairs, News Release No. 1206-62, July 18, 1962.

[19] Address of September 22, 1961, Air Force Association Symposium on Space and National Security, mimeo., p. 2.

[20] "Economic Aspects of Space Program," address of June 12, 1962, mimeo.

[21] Hal Bamford, "Dr. Edward C. Welsh, Executive Secretary, NASC: 'I'm Never Satisfied with Our Space Efforts,'" *Armed Forces Management,* 9 (December, 1962), 20.

[22] U.S. President, *United States Aeronautics and Space Activities, 1961* . . ., H. Doc. No. 324, 87th Cong., 2d Sess., 1962, p. 6.

it suggests that one of the major considerations supporting the principle of civilian control rests on intellectual confusion.

"PEACEFUL PURPOSES" VS. "MILITARISM"

A U.S. delegate to the United Nations, Senator Gore, pointed toward a way out of the confusion in 1962. He rejected the contrast between peaceful and military uses and indicated that "the question of military activities in space cannot be divorced from the question of military activities on earth." Until such activities could be banished in both environments, "the test of any space activity must *not* be whether it is military or non-military, but whether or not it is consistent with the United Nations Charter and other obligations of international law." Senator Gore saw no workable dividing line between military and nonmilitary uses of space, and suggested that purposes are peaceful so long as they are "nonaggressive and beneficial." [23] And Richard N. Gardner, Deputy Assistant Secretary of State for International Organization Affairs, holds: "The test of the legitimacy of a particular use of outer space is not whether it is military or non-military, but whether it is peaceful or aggressive. . . . The United States has military space programs, but all of our space activities will continue to be for peaceful, i.e., defensive and beneficial, purposes." [24]

Even these statements, though reflecting the fact that a problem has been identified, are not entirely satisfactory in solving it; and the ambiguities of the English language are such that some semantic difficulties may be inevitable. But it seems to me that the sense of the emphasis on "peaceful purposes" is indicated by the following. We want to give assurances—to ourselves and to others—that the thought of war does not dominate our behavior. We want to avoid militarism, to avoid accentuating the arms race, to avoid contributing to an atmosphere of war. We do not want to appear to be acting on the assumption that war will come, still less to be planning to bring it on. Though giving attention to our military power in due proportion to the danger we face, we do not want to appear to be completely preoccupied or obsessed by military concerns. We hope for peace—for the good life rather than for the garrison state. We want to put the stress on goals selected predominantly for reasons that do not relate to war.

---

[23] Senate, *Documents on International Aspects*, 1963, p. 362.
[24] Richard N. Gardner, "Cooperation in Outer Space," *Foreign Affairs*, 41 (January, 1963), 359.

The Operational Significance of the Stress on Peace

Though the stress on peace has obvious propaganda purposes, this does not mean that it can be dismissed, for it does have operational significance. Most obviously, it very strongly reinforced other considerations in bringing about the decision to place the space program largely under the management of a civilian agency, NASA. And, though there is cooperation between NASA and DOD, NASA has gone to considerable lengths at times to avoid identification with strictly military endeavors—withdrawing from the geodetic satellite project, for example, when DOD insisted that it be classified "secret." [25] The man-in-space program remains under NASA's management, despite Air Force ambitions in this field. And the general aura of publicity surrounding the space program obviously emphasizes its civilian, scientific, and exploratory aspects. Further, the determination to stress peace and our peaceful purposes in space has a great deal to do with the program of international space cooperation, to be described below in Chapter 14.

Obviously the goal of peace and the policy of pursuing only peaceful purposes are secondary rather than primary. The proper statement is not that we have a space program in order to promote peace and to pursue peaceful purposes, but rather that since we have a space program it is desirable to give reassurances concerning it and to utilize it to promote goals that we would want to be pursuing in any case. Moreover, goals pertaining to peace do little to indicate the appropriate extent of space activities. The expansion and acceleration of the program in May, 1961, obviously did not mean a proportionate expansion and acceleration of a contribution to peace. Concern for peace could be manifested in relation to an Eisenhower-size program as readily as in relation to a Kennedy-size program; it has little to do with the question whether or not the lunar trip is really desirable or necessary.

[25] D. S. Greenberg, "Space Accord: NASA's Enthusiasm for East-West Cooperation Is Not Shared by Pentagon," *Science*, 136 (April 13, 1962), 138.

PROGRESS IN SCIENCE AND TECHNOLOGY

The promotion of progress in science and technology is cited as a motive of the space program almost as frequently as the enhancement of military security. And, as in the case of the security motive, there are many doubts and questions. Early in the space age Dr. Lee A. DuBridge, President of the California Institute of Technology, declared: "In my view the predominating and overpowering reason for developing a substantial program of space exploration is the vast new extension in our knowledge which this will yield and the great value which this knowledge is certain to have as it is applied, as time goes on, to the practical problems of human welfare." [1] And the first objective named in the National Aeronautics and Space Act of 1958 was "the expansion of human knowledge of phenomena in the atmosphere and space." But no one who goes through the *Congressional Record* and the committee hearings and reports since Sputnik is likely to believe that this consideration has ever been uppermost in Congress. The first NASA Administrator, T. Keith Glennan, once commented that though the expansion of knowledge "in the long run must certainly be the most important motivating force," the desire for it "seemed to play a very minor role in the generation of the pressures for speed and progress we were feeling in those early days." [2]

[1] U.S. Congress, House, Select Committee on Astronautics and Space Exploration, *Astronautics and Space Exploration, Hearings . . .* on H. Res. 11881, 85th Cong., 2d Sess., 1958, p. 776.

[2] Speech at Yale Convocation, October 7, 1960.

The question of the importance of the desire to promote scientific and technological progress as a motive is all the greater since the development of the very costly man-in-space program. Dr. DuBridge should be cited again. Asking "why are we going into space?" he asserts that he does not mean why Congress voted the money. He knows that "Congress voted the money to put a man on the Moon ahead of the Russians," but this is a motive that he chooses not to count. It apparently does not seem entirely worthy to him, and therefore should be ignored. "The purpose of the space program, as far as the civilian space program is concerned, operated under NASA, is to conduct scientific research. It is a quest for more knowledge." [3] But Dr. Eberhardt Rechtin of Caltech's Jet Propulsion Laboratory, which devotes itself to work for NASA, holds that "science is not, and cannot be, the driving force for space exploration." [4] And Dr. DuBridge himself later described "valid" objectives in addition to the enhancement of knowledge.[5] We will note further exchanges on this subject below.

There is less give and take on the question of using the space program as a means of stimulating technological progress, but Dr. Hugh L. Dryden and others give it considerable emphasis, as we will see.

I discussed military security as a motive of the space program mainly by asking what immediate and potential military missions there might be in space. The counterpart of this question is not of much moment in connection with the role of scientific and technological progress as a motive. I will note some of the possibilities, of course, but the question of the kinds of experiments that might be conducted and the kinds of knowledge gained does not have much to do with the reasons for the program. Everyone assumes that scientific knowledge is there to be gained, and that the space program will in fact promote technological development.

[3] "Impact of Space Programs on Society," in NASA, Office of Scientific and Technical Information, *Proceedings of the Second National Conference on the Peaceful Uses of Space*, Seattle, Washington, May 8-10, 1962 (Washington, 1962), p. 235; U.S. Congress, House, Committee on Science and Astronautics, *Panel on Science and Technology. Fifth Meeting*, 88th Cong., 1st Sess., 1963, pp. 50-51.

[4] Dr. Eberhardt Rechtin, "Why the Space Race?" *Vectors*, 2 (Fourth Quarter, 1960), 15-16.

[5] U.S. Congress, Senate, Committee on Aeronautical and Space Sciences, *Scientists' Testimony on Space Goals*, Hearings, 88th Cong., 1st Sess., 1963, pp. 138-40 (hereafter cited as Senate Hearings, *Scientists' Testimony on Space Goals*).

The issues concern costs—costs in terms of either money or talent or both. And costs have to be judged in terms of prospective results, which means that it is important to keep in mind the kinds of results or goals that are being contemplated.

The Desire for Knowledge

The first reason that President Eisenhower's Science Advisory Committee gave for a space program was "the compelling urge of man to explore and discover, the thrust of curiosity that leads men to try to go where no one has gone before." Secretary of the Air Force Zuckert makes a similar statement: "The first compulsion to conquer space is, I believe, from within us. . . . Man continuously seeks new knowledge about himself and his surroundings. . . . There is some quality in man's growth pattern which impels us to seek knowledge, to embrace it philosophically, and apply it. . . . Man cannot contemplate the means of exploring space and leave it alone." [6]

These statements suggest related but distinguishable motives: on the one hand, exploration as a matter of adventure, as a matter of climbing the mountain because it is there, as an activity that is a self-justifying manifestation of a need for achievement; and, on the other hand, exploration as a more disciplined and directed search for knowledge. We will discuss the first of these motives in Chapter 9. Here the focus is on the second, with which natural scientists are especially concerned.

The development of the rocket has made it possible to acquire new knowledge in several categories: knowledge of the earth itself, knowledge of space, and knowledge of celestial bodies; and at the same time the exploitation of these possibilities requires the development of other sorts of knowledge, e.g., knowledge of the medical and other problems that men will confront when they leave the earth's atmosphere. The questions are endless. And the pursuit of scientific knowledge through the use of rocket technology calls also for further technological developments in many areas.

Supporters of the space program are not content to point simply to the new knowledge that can be gained in the categories named above. They anticipate much broader intellectual and cultural benefits. Dr. Dryden sometimes recalls the question of a Russian

---

[6] Speech of February 13, 1962, p. 4.

workman, who asked, "What do Sputniks give to a person like me?"

To this question frequently asked by men in many countries, including our own, we can of course reply with discussions of practical benefits from weather and communication satellites and from technological developments. . . . But perhaps a better reply would be: "The exploration of space can give you new interests and new motivations arising from an expansion of your intellectual and spiritual horizons as you take a longer view of man's role in time and space at this point in the history of the human race." [7]

James E. Webb, the NASA Administrator, claims that the Apollo program "will add zest and stimulation to almost every level of education, industry, government, and to life in general." An interesting bit of supporting testimony comes from an analysis of the General Electric Company's relationship to the space program. "Space exploration has had a benign effect on the whole atmosphere at G.E. Without that refreshing atmosphere, G.E. probably could not recruit or keep top-drawer scientists of the new kind. These men come to the company principally because there they find the excellent facilities, and the government dollars, that give them the freedom to follow where their scientific noses may lead." [8] And the London *Economist* concludes that "one must envy American manufacturers the intellectual stimulus that they get from a space program, pushing them against the frontiers of knowledge." [9] Moreover, some scientists emphasize the same general theme. For example, Dr. Martin Schwarzschild, Professor of Astronomy at Princeton, thinks that the "basic justification" of the lunar program is "the sparking of the Nation as a whole to a new level of vitality." He thinks that it has a "wonderfully energizing effect . . . particularly on the younger generation who will determine the spirit of this country a decade hence." [10] In the summer of 1962 at the University of Iowa the National Academy of Sciences sponsored an intensive review of space research. Participants in the review cited the fact that in the past certain historical events and technical innovations had "created major 'discontinuities' in thought, with

---

[7] Hugh L. Dryden, "The National and International Significance of the Lunar Exploration Program," NASA News Release No. 61-286, December 29, 1961, pp. 10-11.

[8] Walter Guzzardi, Jr., "G.E. Astride Two Worlds," *Fortune*, 65 (June, 1962), 260.

[9] "Skybolt's American Shadow," *Economist*, 206 (January 12, 1963), 128.

[10] Senate Hearings, *Scientists' Testimony on Space Goals*, p. 167.

consequent profound changes in outlook, customs, political and economic institutions, and in art, literature, and religion." They cited the discovery and settlement of the New World as a major example, and suggested that "the opening of outer space to human exploration may prove to be another." [11] The staff of the House Select Committee on Astronautics and Space Exploration has made a bolder assertion. "The creative forces of modern science and technology, through which man is beginning to realize some of his finest powers of reason and constructive ability, are now moving like the breakup of an Arctic river in the spring. . . . The changes have accelerated, so that today we seem about to witness a major loosening of the ice jam of our intellectual past." [12] And, still bolder, Krafft A. Ehricke lays it down as a "historical fact" that "man's mind and spirit grow with the space in which he is allowed to operate." [13]

Though the enthusiasms associated with space lead to some extreme claims, there is no doubt that the program is in fact having effects going in the direction indicated. Knowledge is being acquired as a result of the space program, both directly and indirectly, and the stimulation toward further research is undoubtedly there. Clearly this is one of the main reasons why some persons —especially some scientists—support the program. At the same time, appropriations for scientific research relating to space have gone up far more than appropriations for research not so related, which automatically raises a question about the importance of a desire for knowledge as the motive. The man-in-space program makes the question especially sharp.

Man-in-Space for Science?

There is really no argument on the question whether the man-in-space program is justifiable in the name of science. No one

[11] National Academy of Sciences, Space Science Board, *A Review of Space Research,* report of a summer study conducted at the State University of Iowa, Iowa City, June 17–August 10, 1962, Publication 1079 (Washington: National Academy of Sciences—National Research Council, 1962), Ch. 16, p. 9 (hereafter cited as NAS, *A Review of Space Research*).

[12] U.S. Congress, House, Select Committee on Astronautics and Space Exploration, *The United States and Outer Space,* H. Rpt. No. 2710, 85th Cong., 2d Sess., 1959, p. 7.

[13] Krafft A. Ehricke, "The Anthropology of Astronautics," in Richard Witkin, ed., *The Challenge of the Sputniks* (Garden City: Doubleday, 1958), p. 91.

contends that it is. The real issue (debated in an indirect and implicit way) concerns the goals or values that are to be considered, the standard of judgment that is to be employed. The scientists who oppose the lunar program (or, at least, its timing) see the enhancement of scientific knowledge as its only significant purpose, whereas the scientists who support the program cite non-scientific goals as well.

Confusion concerning the nature of the issue precedes the man-in-space program. Perhaps the most interesting illustration of it appears in the "Introduction to Outer Space," prepared by President Eisenhower's Science Advisory Committee, of which Dr. James R. Killian, Jr., was Chairman. Formally, as indicated in the quotation given in Chapter 1, the "Introduction" at the outset acknowledges a number of different reasons for a space program. But when, at a later point, it takes up the question whether the results will justify the costs, the scientific results are the only ones considered. This outlook—that, though there are various reasons for a space program, the only one that really counts is science—has seemed to prevail in Dr. Killian's thought ever since. He wants a space program that is "in balance with our other vital endeavors in science and technology," and he thinks that we should "plan our national program for space science and technology as part of a balanced national effort in all science and technology." [14] Given this context, he takes a very reserved view of man-in-space. "From reading the record of Congress one can be led to conclude that a strange and hazardous inversion of values plagues our nation today. Funds to send a man to the moon seem easier to come by than funds to send a young American to a better classroom. Advances in space seem to take priority over advances in education; investment in things seems to take priority over investment in people." [15]

Dr. Philip H. Abelson, Editor of *Science*, who came forward in the spring of 1963 as a principal critic of the man-in-space program, takes a similar position. He speaks of "making a judgment as to the scientific potential inherent in space studies," and he finds that "manned space exploration has limited scientific value and has been accorded an importance which is quite unrealistic." [16] He

[14] James R. Killian, Jr., "Shaping a Public Policy for the Space Age," in Lincoln P. Bloomfield, ed., *Outer Space. Prospects for Man and Society,* The American Assembly (Englewood Cliffs: Prentice-Hall, 1962), pp. 184, 191.

[15] *Ibid.,* p. 186.

[16] Senate Hearings, *Scientists' Testimony on Space Goals,* p. 4.

does not want to discontinue the lunar program, but he objects to the priority assigned to it; "eventually" the manned exploration of space is desirable, but it is undesirable to try to get to the moon in this decade.[17] He attaches very little importance to purposes other than the enhancement of scientific knowledge. Dr. Warren Weaver, Vice President of the Sloan Foundation, is more explicit in acknowledging that military and political reasons for man-in-space may be important, but he leaves it to others to say how much expense they may justify. These reasons apart, he holds that scientific considerations do not justify the magnitude of the program or, still less, what he considers "its frantic, costly, and disastrous pace." [18]

It is not surprising that some scientists regard the space program as a scientific program. Among the basic reasons for the confusion is probably the early association between the space effort and the IGY, which suggested that the enhancement of scientific knowledge was the main or only purpose. Moreover, the decision of the Eisenhower Administration to stress peaceful purposes in space and to avoid the appearance of militarism made a stress on science convenient, and the criticism that the space effort was aimed more at the glamorous and spectacular than at "substantive" results could be countered by emphasizing science. In a small way these tendencies are illustrated by a statement of Senator Cooper after the first American satellite, Explorer I, went into orbit some months after Sputnik. The event brought great relief and exhilaration, including many self-congratulatory speeches in Congress. Quite obviously the reaction reflected a concern for values other than the enhancement of scientific knowledge, but Senator Cooper did not perceive the fact. He said, "In our exultation we should not forget that the primary purpose of launching a satellite is to extend man's knowledge for peaceful purposes." [19] The same kind of outlook shows up in the treatment accorded the Mercury program. The public position of the Eisenhower Administration was that this program aimed at scientific accomplishment; Eisenhower's budget message of January, 1961, included the statement that "further testing and experimentation will be necessary to establish whether there are any valid scientific reasons for extending manned space flight beyond the Mercury program." There was no reference to

[17] *Ibid.*, pp. 12, 16.

[18] Warren Weaver, "Dreams and Responsibilities," *Bulletin of the Atomic Scientists,* 19 (May, 1963), 11.

[19] *Congressional Record,* Vol. 104, Pt. 2 (February 3, 1958), 1548.

possible nonscientific reasons. The Glenn flight in February, 1962, brought a veritable congressional orgy of expressions of pride, as we will see in Chapter 9, but again the same singular note was struck, this time by Representative George P. Miller, Chairman of the House Committee on Science and Astronautics: "This was in no way a stunt or an exhibition. It was . . . a great contribution to science. What we have seen today was a scientific experiment whose end object was not the entertainment of the people of this country and the world, although it means a lot to us in international prestige. That was not the end object either. Its end object is to wrest from space her secrets that can be used for the betterment of mankind." [20] Others joined in endorsing this theme.

In contrast, Dr. Eberhardt Rechtin, of Caltech's Jet Propulsion Laboratory, reports:

It is evident to most people, including most of the people in the Mercury program, that the "pure science" in that program is zero. (The few people who believe that the program is scientific in nature use a definition of science which is so broad as to include all of advanced technology.)

The scientist will invariably say that [Mercury] is a terrible program.[21]

A rather extreme view of the place of science in the space program is given in a statement by Representative Fulton immediately after the Gagarin flight—the first orbiting of man-in-space.

I feel that we in the United States should publicly say we are in a competitive race with Russia and accept the challenge in science.

I am tired of coming in second best all the time by 30 days. . . .

I would . . . work the scientists around the clock, and stop some of this WPA scientific business. . . .[22]

To Mr. Fulton, science was a tool to use in pursuing a political objective; and where an immediate application of scientific research was not envisaged, support for it was a form of work relief.

No doubt the scientists who support the space program resent Mr. Fulton's views on this point. But they very definitely acknowledge and insist upon goals in space in addition to the promotion of scientific knowledge. The point is stressed in the *Review of Space Research*, cited above. Participants in the review were obviously

---

[20] *Ibid.*, Vol. 108, No. 24 (February 20, 1962), 2391.

[21] Eberhardt Rechtin, "What's the Use of Racing for Space?" *Air Force/ Space Digest*, 44 (October, 1961), 51.

[22] U.S. Congress, House, Committee on Science and Astronautics, *H.R. 6169 —A Bill to Amend the National Aeronautics and Space Act of 1958*, Hearing, 87th Cong., 1st Sess., 1961, pp. 5-6.

troubled about the question of the justifiability of manned space flight, and more specifically about Apollo. "There was concern that the Apollo mission was being mislabeled as primarily a scientific effort in its own right and that such misrepresentation could react unfavorably on the more basic scientific parts of the program." Speaking of the "proper justifications" of Apollo, the report of the summer study puts the stress in the first instance on nonscientific motives. "The Apollo program is related to man's innate drive to explore unknown regions, to national prestige, and to national security." The report goes on to describe the program as "primarily a technological and engineering effort." "Scientists should recognize that Apollo is the first phase in a continuing engineering enterprise that will ultimately enable man to move about in space and provide him with the capacity for conducting his scientific investigations. . . . Appreciation of these concepts is of critical importance to the acceptance of the current Apollo program by scientists throughout the country." The argument is that, though the immediate purpose of Apollo is not primarily scientific, the capabilities developed will be very useful to science, and that therefore "scientific validity" is acquired. Further, given the national commitment to the program, duty calls. "The lack of an adequate scientific endeavor could invite serious criticism of the program, while the impact of a successful scientific mission by means of a lunar landing will enormously enhance the importance of the Apollo program in the eyes of the world." [23]

Along the same line, a group of scientists who issued a statement in the spring of 1963—presumably in answer to editorials in Science by Dr. Abelson—indicated through a rhetorical question that congressional support for the expanded space program was not "tendered for scientific reasons primarily," but was "motivated by a broader concern with national interests and national goals." [24] Moreover, the scientists who testified before the Senate space committee in June, 1963, divide fairly clearly between those who evaluate the space program in terms of its potential scientific contributions and those whose conception of its purpose is much broader. Some of the nonscientific purposes that they cited are discussed in other chapters, especially Chapter 9.

Dr. H. H. Hess, Chairman of the Space Science Board of the National Academy of Sciences, notes that the lunar program "does

[23] NAS, *A Review of Space Research*, Ch. 1, pp. 21-22; Ch. 11, p. 3.
[24] *Science*, 140 (June 7, 1963), 1078.

not have the enthusiastic support of many scientists," and explains the fact by describing it as "primarily an engineering, technological, and biomedical project, not a basic scientific effort." [25] So far as it goes, the explanation is no doubt good. It is understandable if scientists are disappointed at the fact that what started as a scientific enterprise has become something else. But the change goes much beyond the one that Dr. Hess identifies; because of Sputnik—or rather because of a complex set of factors that Sputnik brought into play—the enterprise has become primarily political and psychological. Many scientists either fail to perceive this change or refuse to accept it.

Criticisms of the Space Program by Scientists

The chief criticisms of the space program offered by scientists —as well as by some others—are that it costs too much in terms of money and trained manpower. Whether the costs are too high depends, of course, on the value attached to the various goals that are pursued—a subject discussed through most of this book.

Dr. Warren Weaver, cited above, refers to a forecast that it will cost $30 billion to put a man on the moon and then names alternative projects that could be financed with that much money.

We could give a 10% raise in salary, over a 10 year period, to every teacher in the United States, from kindergarten through universities, in both public and private institutions (about $9.8 billion); give $10 million each to 200 of the best smaller colleges ($2 billion); finance 7-year fellowships (freshman through Ph.D.) at $4,000 per person per year for 50,000 new scientists and engineers ($1.4 billion); contribute $200 million each toward the creation of 10 new medical schools ($2 billion); build and largely endow complete universities with medical, engineering, and agricultural faculties for all 53 of the nations which have been added to the United Nations since its original founding ($13.2 billion); create 3 more permanent Rockefeller Foundations ($1.5 billion); and still have $100 million left over to popularize science.[26]

Some of these possibilities are beguiling and tantalizing, and it is quite arguable that the American political system should be reformed so as to permit clear-cut choices between alternatives. But in a realistic sense we do not now have the choice. There is no assurance at all that an abandonment of the lunar program would

---

[25] H. H. Hess, "Manned Lunar Landing Defended," *Science*, 140 (June 14, 1963), 1173.
[26] Warren Weaver, "What a Moon Ticket Will Buy," *Saturday Review*, 45 (August 4, 1962), 38.

be followed by appropriations for such purposes as those listed by Dr. Weaver; it very probably would not. Furthermore, the idea of a choice between alternatives is somewhat illusory in another sense. Some of the money has already been spent or committed. More important is the fact that few really seek the complete abandonment of the lunar program. The question is not so much whether to have the program as whether to slow down or postpone its implementation. A slowdown might produce either marginal reductions or marginal increases in the total cost, but would not, in the long run, release anything like the $30 billion that Dr. Weaver mentions for alternative purposes. Further, it should not be assumed that the money spent for the lunar program—whether it be $30 billion or some other figure—will be a total loss. There will be some material returns, however small, as we will see in the next chapter.

On the question of timing, I might note that while Dr. Abelson and others object to the commitment to reach the moon in this decade, other scientists, e.g., Dr. Frederick Seitz, President of the National Academy of Sciences, takes the view that the program of space exploration is "pretty well paced." [27]

Some scientists are troubled not simply by the thought that man-in-space may cost more than the scientific returns will justify; it is not simply a question of diverting resources from pursuits having nothing to do with science. There is also a more specific fear: that the emphasis on research relating to space will lead to a slighting of scientific work of other sorts—that the funding of space projects may preclude the funding of others. Dr. Killian obviously had this in mind when he spoke of planning a program for space science and technology as part of a balanced national effort in all science and technology. I have not attempted to determine to what extent, if at all, this fear may be justified. Dr. Jerome B. Wiesner, Chairman of President Kennedy's Science Advisory Committee, held that it was groundless. "The space program will augment the whole science program, because there is a great deal of related science that will be supported by the space program. . . . Furthermore, the climate will be such that it will be generally easier to get support for science." [28] A similar kind of debate has

---

[27] Senate Hearings, *Scientists' Testimony on Space Goals*, p. 98. Cf. the statement of Dr. Martin Schwarzschild in *ibid.*, pp. 156-57, 167.

[28] "Thinking Ahead with Jerome Wiesner," *International Science and Technology*, February, 1962, p. 32.

occurred in Britain. For a variety of reasons, among which financial considerations were apparently not controlling, the official Advisory Council on Scientific Policy reported that it would be gross folly for Britain to launch an independent space program. The astronomer, Fred Hoyle, later argued to the same effect, citing financial reasons primarily. There followed a series of "for and against" letters, which struck several familiar and unfamiliar notes. One was that "space research is certainly one of the great and exciting things of our age," and that it would be a "national misfortune" if Britain could not afford it. Another is the same point that Dr. Wiesner made: "Nor let us delude ourselves by supposing that by not spending money on space research there will be more to spend on other scientific projects. There will probably be less. One really first class project having been refused, lesser ones will stand little chance." [29] To the argument that a space program leads to a disproportionate emphasis on some areas of science, one answer was, in effect, so what? The writer held that another distortion could "surely be faced with equanimity by a nation which already and very reasonably spends annually some £980 million on tobacco . . . and £4 million on medical research." [30] This is reminiscent of the fact that the American people are spending more on cigarettes each year than on NASA's share of the space program.

Another kind of cost is also a source of concern: cost in terms of trained manpower. Dr. Killian speaks of cost in terms of "talent," saying that we "face an acute shortage of exceptional talent possessing that level of education in science and engineering which enables it to master and use effectively the new and advanced technologies." [31] Given a strict enough interpretation of "exceptional talent," he is no doubt correct. Dr. Abelson holds that "the crucial bottleneck is brains not money." And he too is in a sense no doubt correct. But the terms "exceptional talent" and "brains" are vague. It is more common to speak of the utilization of scientists and engineers, though to count them without differentiating in terms of their quality involves problems too. NASA's statement

---

[29] Sir George Thomson, "For and Against a British Space Programme," *New Scientist*, 8 (August 18, 1960), 446.

[30] Alexander Haddow, "For and Against a British Space Programme," *New Scientist*, 8 (August 25, 1960), 508.

[31] James R. Killian, Jr., "The Crisis in Research," reprinted from the *Atlantic Monthly* in *Congressional Record*, Vol. 109, No. 46 (March 28, 1963), 4768.

is that on its own staff for the fiscal year ending in June, 1964, it will require a total of approximately 11,300 scientists and engineers and that its contractors will require about 62,000. The sum represents approximately 5 per cent of the total supply.[32] The declared expectation is that under present plans no more than 7 per cent of the country's scientists and engineers will be employed on the space effort by NASA itself or by NASA's contractors.[33] The percentage goes up some, of course, if the portion of the space program managed by DOD is considered.

Dr. Simon Ramo, who has been for some years a ranking officer in a leading missile and space business concern, testified in June, 1963, on the question of a shortage of scientific and technical personnel. His statement was: "We are not limited by engineers and scientists in performing the typical engineering project which characterizes so much of the space program and almost all of the defense program. In fact, on the contrary, we have today an over-expanded capability with a surplus of organizations, large and small, equipped with experienced technical teams geared to handle more projects than the Nation has in the offing. True, we have no oversupply of the great, creative genius."[34]

We do not yet know what effect the space program will have, if any, on the tendency of young people to choose careers in engineering, mathematics, and the natural sciences. Conceivably, even if NASA does strain resources in these fields in the short run, it may provide compensation in the long run. Its fellowship program, to be described in Chapter 13, is designed to bring this about. There have been complaints abroad, too, about the loss of scientists and engineers through emigration to the United States, but the space program is so new that its effect in this respect is uncertain.[35]

[32] U.S. Congress, House, Committee on Science and Astronautics, Subcommittee on Applications and Tracking and Data Acquisition, *1964 NASA Authorization,* Hearings, 88th Cong., 1st Sess., 1963, Part 4, p. 2916; J. Herbert Holloman, "The Brain Mines of Tomorrow," *Saturday Review,* 46 (May 4, 1963), 47.

[33] U.S. Congress, Senate, Committee on Aeronautical and Space Sciences, *NASA Authorization for Fiscal Year 1964,* Hearings, 88th Cong., 1st Sess., 1963, Part 1, p. 37.

[34] Senate Hearings, *Scientists' Testimony on Space Goals,* p. 27.

[35] National Science Foundation, *Scientific Manpower from Abroad. U.S. Scientists and Engineers of Foreign Birth and Training* (NSF 62-24); D. S. Greenberg, "The Manhunters: British Minister Blames American Recruiters for Emigration of Scientists," *Science,* 139 (March 8, 1963), 893.

Technological Progress

In Chapter 4 I noted the importance of technology to military security, and the possibility that the fate of nations may be determined by the technological strategy that they pursue. It is time now to consider this matter in a broader framework. Several of the objectives named for NASA in the National Aeronautics and Space Act of 1958 concern the promotion of technological development, and both of the top officials of NASA, Dr. Hugh L. Dryden and James E. Webb, have stressed its importance again and again. The purpose is a very familiar one to Dr. Dryden, for in his earlier role as Director of the National Advisory Committee for Aeronautics his main job was to promote scientific and technological progress in the field of aeronautics. In June, 1961, soon after President Kennedy asked for an expansion and acceleration of the space program, Dr. Dryden declared that the President "has become convinced that we should accelerate the pace of manned exploration in order to accumulate knowledge and experience in space science and technology more rapidly." "In my opinion, the lunar landing and return of man, dramatic and impressive as it may be, is but the symbol of a more important result—exploration of the new frontiers of science, engineering, and technology. . . ." [36] Later, when Senator Allott asked whether the propaganda value of the new lunar program would be worth the $20 billion that Dr. Dryden thought it would cost, the answer was that the propaganda effect was not the main consideration. "Setting this goal will force you to do a scientific and technological development in this country that otherwise would not be done. . . . [It] requires you to stretch your legs in science and technology." [37]

The billions of dollars required in this effort . . . will insure the nation against technological obsolescence in a world of explosive advances in science and technology and against the hazard of military surprise in space. The specific goal set by the President has the highly important role of motivating the scientists and engineers who are engaged in this effort to move forward with urgency, and of integrating their efforts in a way that cannot be accomplished by a disconnected series of research investigations.[38]

---

[36] "Building for Tomorrow's World," June 2, 1961, mimeo.

[37] U.S. Congress, Senate, Committee on Appropriations, *Independent Offices Appropriations, 1962*, Hearings . . . on H. Res. 7445, 87th Cong., 1st Sess., 1961, p. 653.

[38] Hugh L. Dryden, *The National Significance of the Augmented Program of Space Exploration* (NASA pamphlet), (Washington, 1962), p. 6.

It isn't the lunar landing as such that matters so much, then; rather, it is the component elements of the effort that really count.

James E. Webb advances an identical argument. "The country needs the stimulus, the knowledge, and the products that will evolve from the program to land Americans on the moon. In marshalling and developing the scientific and technical resources required for manned lunar exploration, we shall be creating a technology that is certain to radiate great and diversified benefits to almost every area of material and intellectual activity." [39] He describes the lunar goal as not so much an end in itself as "a challenging focal point for the initial stages of an enormous national effort." Without recalling some of his own earlier pronouncements, he decries the tendency to think in terms of "winning, in a contest with the Soviet Union, 'A race to the moon.'" "This statement of purpose has one grave defect. It does absolutely nothing to enlighten anyone with respect to what our space program is really all about. It overlooks the significant, and seldom appreciated, fact that *learning how to get to the moon, developing the technology which will be required to get there, and employing this technology for many purposes in space, is more important than the lunar landing itself.*" [40]

It is difficult for a layman to judge the validity of this reason for the space program. On one aspect of the matter, I might cite statements by Dr. Lloyd V. Berkner, who speaks of the "new technological explosion." "At the core of our situation today lies the fact that the mid-century saw the beginning of a technological revolution of a new order of power. This is a revolution that is as profound in its social and economic implications as the industrial revolution of two centuries ago." The technological revolution, according to Dr. Berkner, is very different in character from the old industrial revolution—different because of the role played by scientific knowledge. The industrial revolution depended upon inventions hit upon through trial-and-error methods, but the technological revolution "is based on a complete new insight into nature, and the new ability to uncover natural phenomena, and to manipulate natural processes that were heretofore inconceivable. So we can confidently predict that the new technological revolution now rising from an infinitely more encompassing science will have, inevitably, a most

---

[39] *New York Times,* October 8, 1961, 1:1.

[40] James E. Webb, address of October 1, 1962, NASA News Release, p. 2.

profound effect on our industry, our daily living, and our future society." [41]

So far, the "technological explosion" has had its significance mainly in the military realm, and especially insofar as missiles and nuclear weapons are concerned its significance cannot be exaggerated. Whether it has anything like a similar significance in the civilian realm is a much more difficult question—one that will be taken up in the following chapter.

Conclusion

A brief recapitulation may be in order. Before Sputnik it was probably correct to think that the central purpose of the developing Vanguard program was scientific. But Sputnik ushered in a revolution, and Kennedy's recommendation of the lunar program brought a second revolution. The enhancement of scientific knowledge and the promotion of technological development remain significant purposes, but they are no longer central. They do much to justify research employing satellites that carry instruments. But they are subordinate purposes so far as manned space flight is concerned and especially so far as the lunar program is concerned.

It is relevant to note an exchange that occurred between American and Soviet delegates (Drs. Dryden and Sedov) discussing the possibilities of cooperation in space. Dr. Dryden is said to have commented that it was too bad that the two countries were competing in space rather than cooperating, to which Dr. Sedov is said to have responded that the scientists should be thankful for the competition, for otherwise neither country would have a manned space flight program.

---

[41] "Science and the World Tomorrow," lecture of January 19, 1962, Industrial College of the Armed Forces, mimeo., pp. 2, 7.

ECONOMIC AND SOCIAL PROGRESS

7

No one contends that the desire to promote economic progress was a major motive under Eisenhower for the initial development of a space program, and few cite the motive as decisive today. Other considerations are commonly accepted as more important, at least in the short run. Nevertheless, both the space enthusiast and the more skeptical are interested in prospective economic effects, even if only to reinforce views arrived at for other reasons. As usual, contradictory assertions are made. According to Lyndon B. Johnson,

The funds going into space research are investments which will yield dividends to our lives, our business, our professions, many times greater than the initial costs.

It is estimated conservatively that our space outlays will yield $2 return for every $1 invested. For every nickel we put into it, we get a dime back.[1]

Representative George P. Miller, Chairman of the House space committee, also takes an optimistic view.

The technological advances that have evolved from NASA research and development activities have implications to American industry and economy that are really beyond accurate evaluation. . . . The translation of NASA discoveries or innovations into useful economic tools is benefiting our people of almost every walk of life.

I can't think of any other aspect of our space program that could better justify our space expenditures to the average taxpayer than industrial

---

[1] Remarks of March 16, 1962, in *Congressional Record*, Vol. 108, No. 57 (April 12, 1962), A2857-58.

applications. Here is the tangible evidence that he is getting something in return for his investment. His return will be a wide variety of new or better products, at reasonable cost, which in turn will give rise to a greater consumer demand and economic stimulus.[2]

Mr. Webb is much more cautious. "We in the space agency do not seek to justify our program on the basis of the industrial applications which will flow from it. . . . Since we are committed to this great effort in space, however, a responsibility exists to glean from it the maximum public benefits which can be obtained." [3] William Meckling's view is that "unfortunately, research and development is a very uncertain business, and confident assertions emanate only from the uninitiated, the unbridled enthusiast, or the charlatan." [4] He thinks it "unlikely that the nonmilitary products of the space program will generate sufficient income to repay the investment, or even a very large portion of it." [5] Edwin Diamond, far from anticipating material returns, likens the space race to a practice of the Kwakiutl Indians called the potlatch. In the potlatch, persons who have become enemies fight each other by destroying their own possessions, and the one who has the most to destroy wins. Presumably he is gratified, but necessarily he is poorer.[6]

The variety of anticipations suggests that no one has yet proved his case to the satisfaction of others, and I cannot claim sufficient expertise to resolve the problem. What I hope to do is to call attention to some of the uncertainties and to some relevant considerations that are often ignored.

The claims and counterclaims that are made concerning the potential economic effects of the space program can conveniently be placed in four categories. In the first are those based simply on the fact of government spending, which commentators on the space program usually seem to regard, quite uncritically, as either good in itself or bad in itself. I will not attempt to analyze the prob-

---

[2] *Ibid.*, Vol. 109, No. 108 (July 17, 1963), A4508.

[3] James E. Webb, address at the Space, Science, and Urban Life Conference, Oakland, California, March 30, 1963, NASA News Release, p. 13.

[4] William H. Meckling, "The Economic Importance of Space Technology," in NASA, Office of Scientific and Technical Information, *Proceedings of the Second National Conference on the Peaceful Uses of Space*, Seattle, Washington, May 8-10, 1962 (Washington, 1962), p. 202 (hereafter cited as *Seattle Proceedings*).

[5] William H. Meckling, "Economics and Space Technology," *Bulletin of the Atomic Scientists*, 19 (May, 1963), 17.

[6] Edwin Diamond, "The Rites of Spring," *Bulletin of the Atomic Scientists*, 19 (May, 1963), 26-27.

lem, noting only that, as economists have demonstrated, it is considerably more complex than the unsophisticated usually assume it to be. In the second category are claims relating to the prospect of "spill-over" or "spin-off" or "fall-out." In the third are those concerning specific space enterprises, mainly communications and meteorological satellites. And in the fourth there is a miscellany.

Spill-over Benefits

Spill-over benefits are those that come incidentally. The concept applies to the fact that techniques, processes, materials, etc., developed for the space program are sometimes found to be useful elsewhere. There is a transfer of innovations from space to nonspace pursuits. The term itself may be misleading in that it suggests a natural or automatic process, whereas in fact the transfer of innovations often requires deliberate effort.

Supporters of the space program very commonly have great hopes for spill-over benefits. The statement by Representative Miller, quoted above, illustrates the point, and so does the following one by the Deputy Administrator of NASA, Dr. Hugh L. Dryden.

. . . the influence of the technical progress required [to implement the accelerated and expanded space program] will be felt throughout our economy. . . . Many of the instruments, equipment, power sources, and techniques which we must devise as we accelerate and push into space will be adaptable to a host of other uses. The result will be a great variety of new consumer goods and industrial processes that will raise our standard of living and return tremendous benefits to us in practically every profession and activity.[7]

Dr. Dryden speaks of the "vast, unforeseeable dividends" that have come to man in the past through "striving toward difficult technical goals," and he speaks of the impact on the United States of the development of the automobile and the airplane, and the release of nuclear energy. "The forward movement of space technology, with its many ramifications in our industrial life, will stimulate our economy just as these other great technological developments have done in the past."[8] As we have noted, not everyone is this optimistic.

[7] U.S. Congress, Senate, Committee on Appropriations, *Independent Offices Appropriations, 1962,* Hearings . . . on H. Res. 7445, 87th Cong., 1st Sess., 1961, p. 649.

[8] Hugh L. Dryden, "Industry's Toughest Assignment: Make It Work," *Missiles and Rockets,* 9 (November 27, 1961), iii.

Studies of the transfer of innovations from space to nonspace pursuits are handicapped by the inevitable time lag. The results are not in. But a somewhat longer period for study can be had if the focus is on transfer not only from the space effort but also from the missile program; and a still greater fund of data can be obtained if it is assumed that experience with military R&D (research and development) is applicable. At best, however, the exploration of the subject is still incomplete.

The Denver Research Institute, working on the basis of a grant from NASA, reports that R&D pertaining to missiles and space have made contributions to the commercial economy in six categories: [9] (1) the stimulation of basic and applied research; (2) the development of new or improved processes and techniques—"new ways of fabricating a material, forming a part, or scheduling a job"; (3) the improvement of already existing products, e.g., through stress on quality and reliability; (4) the increased availability of materials, testing equipment, and laboratory equipment; (5) the development of new products; (6) cost reduction, e.g., through the improvement of production techniques and through fuller utilization of laboratories and research equipment. "The total contribution of missile/space R&D to the commercial economy is broader, more complex, more indirect, and more difficult to identify than is generally realized. . . . Because of the scope and complexity of the total contribution, it is probably more significant than is frequently envisioned, although this significance does not appear to lend itself to quantitative measurement." This rather restrained conclusion is in marked contrast to those of several other organizations that have prepared reports describing numerous and sometimes wondrous devices, processes, and materials developed for the space program but also having applications in other fields.[10]

The skeptics present relevant but inconclusive data. Their questioning relates to topics like the following: the great increase in federal expenditures for R&D and the concomitant increase in the manpower devoted to R&D; the fact that the increases for military and space R&D are much greater than the increases for R&D

---

[9] John G. Welles et al., The Commercial Application of Missile/Space Technology (Denver: University of Denver, Denver Research Institute, 1963), Part 1, pp. 1-5.

[10] For a particularly enraptured treatment of the subject see "Civilian Dividends from Space Research," prepared by Edward Gottlieb and Associates, in Congressional Record, Vol. 108, No. 61 (April 19, 1962), 6475-80.

aimed directly at meeting everyday civilian needs; the lack of a correlation between increased expenditures for R&D, on the one hand, and the rate of economic growth and the development of patentable innovations, on the other; and the possibility that the stress on military and space R&D may be disproportionate.

The increases in federal expenditures for R&D have been leaping. As late as 1940 they were still under $100 million a year. Ten years later they had risen to about $1.1 billion. In FY1953 they were $3.1 billion, and in FY1963 about $12.4 billion.[11] The expenditures of government for R&D have been going up much faster than those of industry. "In 1953, 60% of the R&D performed in industry was financed by industry for commercial-industrial purposes; 40% was financed by the government for defense, space, atomic energy and other public purposes. In 1961 that proportion was exactly reversed—60% of the industry-performed R&D was being done for the government."[12]

Increased expenditures for R&D have called for increased manpower. According to J. Herbert Holloman, Assistant Secretary for Science and Technology in the Department of Commerce, the number of scientists and engineers in industry doing R&D doubled from 1954 to 1962, the figure jumping from 160,000 to 320,000. But the increase was very uneven. The number engaged in R&D for nongovernmental purposes went up by only 30 per cent, while the number engaged in it for governmental purposes (defense, space, atomic energy, etc.) jumped by 300 per cent.[13] It is significant to note, incidentally, that, according to these figures, government R&D is not draining scientists and engineers away from commercial-industrial R&D; the numbers engaged in both categories have gone up.

At the same time, those who are skeptical about the alleged economic benefits of the space program point out that the rate of economic growth has not responded to increased expenditures for R&D. "In the period from 1947 to 1954, the average annual rate of growth was 3.7%. From 1954 to 1960, the average rate dropped to

[11] U.S. Congress, Senate, Committee on Government Operations, *Report to the President on Government Contracting for Research and Development*, prepared by the Bureau of the Budget, S. Doc. No. 94, 87th Cong., 2d Sess., 1962, pp. 1, 34.

[12] J. Herbert Holloman, "Technology and Its Impact on the National Economy," no date (Spring, 1963?), mimeo., p. 5.

[13] *Ibid.*

3%. This occurred during the period when our expenditures for research and development . . . tripled and the percentage of our gross national product spent for R&D doubled (rising from 1.4 to 2.8%)." [14] And the skeptics also note that "in spite of the tremendous increase in R & D expenditures and, presumably, of the deployment of a larger proportion of the population for technologically creative activities, the number of patents applied for [since 1920] declined, both absolutely and per capita." [15] Defense R&D apparently produces relatively few patents. From 1954 to 1956 only about 4 per cent of the patents sought by private firms stemmed from work done for DOD, even though it was financing about 50 per cent of their R&D. Moreover, according to a forthcoming volume by Merton J. Peck, patents stemming from defense R&D are not nearly as likely to be exploited commercially as patents stemming from other kinds of R&D.

The Secretary of Commerce, Luther H. Hodges, has called attention to the above kinds of data. His view is that an R&D effort concentrated so much on defense and space "is not the incubator of demand and productivity that people think it is, or that the country needs for a growing, healthy economy." [16] He describes other industrial nations—our competitors in world markets, as "free from the burden of large military and space commitments [and thus] able to devote almost their entire scientific and technical effort to developing the civilian economy and their social welfare." Japan, West Germany, Sweden, and the Netherlands, he says, "spend about 50% more than we do for civilian research—for the civilian technological advances that promote economic growth." [17] "West Germany has more than twice as many scientists and engineers, per 1000 workers in their labor force, working on new consumer products and new industrial processes, as do we in the U.S." [18]

In response to considerations of these sorts, the Department of Commerce in 1962 inaugurated a Civilian Industrial Technology Program. The intent was both to sponsor research on the scientific and technological problems of various industries and to establish

[14] J. Herbert Holloman, "The Brain Mines of Tomorrow," *Saturday Review*, 46 (May 4, 1963), 46.

[15] Robert A. Solo, "Gearing Military R&D to Economic Growth," *Harvard Business Review*, 40 (November-December, 1962), 53.

[16] Address of January 22, 1963, mimeo., p. 2.

[17] *Ibid.*, pp. 2, 5.

[18] Luther H. Hodges, "The Age of Excellence," address of April 4, 1963, mimeo., p. 4.

an experimental industrial extension service patterned after the agricultural extension services and their county agents. Special attention was to be given to the industries that have been least inclined to engage in research on their own. The January, 1963, Economic Report of the President included a reference to the problem: "In the course of meeting specific challenges so brilliantly, we have paid a price by sharply limiting the scarce scientific and engineering resources available to the civilian sectors of the American economy. . . . I believe that the Federal Government must now begin to redress the balance in the use of scientific skills. . . ." And the President's budget for FY1964 included a $7.4 million item for the Civilian Industrial Technology Program.[19] A good many industries, however, were unhappy about the prospect of federal research and services that might assist their competitors, and the House of Representatives was willing to appropriate only $1 million of the $7.4 million requested by the President.[20] At the time of writing, the Senate had not yet acted.

As already suggested, the above arguments concerning the effects of space R&D on economic progress are not conclusive, even if data relating to military R&D are wholly applicable. A great many factors affect economic growth. If the rate of growth has declined while federal expenditures for R&D have been rising sharply, the fact does not really prove anything. Possibly the R&D has been counterbalancing other forces that might have slowed the rate of economic growth still more. Moreover, the number of patents obtained per dollar invested in R&D is not a very reliable indicator of economic effects either. The more realistic question—if more difficult to investigate reliably—concerns transfers in categories like those established by Mr. Welles of the Denver Research Institute, referred to above. Even so, the lack of a correlation between R&D, on the one hand, and economic growth and patentable innovations, on the other, underscores legitimate questions—questions with which NASA itself is much concerned.

One other caveat ought to be entered on the question of the unevenness of the increases in expenditures for R&D. The comments of Mr. Hodges and Mr. Holloman of the Department of Commerce are similar to the comments of various scientists who

[19] D. S. Greenberg, "News and Comment," *Science*, 139 (February 15, 1963), 576.

[20] D. S. Greenberg, "Civilian Technology: Program to Boost Industrial Research Heavily Slashed in House," *Science*, 140 (June 28, 1963), 1380.

think that the rewards would be greater per dollar if the money spent for the lunar program were only spent some other way. But no one has shown that expenditures for pure research, or for research aimed directly at commercial-industrial application, are less because of the space program than they otherwise would be. Mr. Holloman's own statistics, as noted above, indicate that the number of scientists and engineers engaged in R&D for nongovernmental purposes has been going up, increasing by 30 per cent from 1954 to 1962. It is possible that the sharp increases in military and space R&D bring about more rather than less R&D of a civilian-commercial-industrial sort. One of the main spill-over benefits may well be the dramatic demonstration of the potential values of large-scale, organized research. Moreover, even if space R&D were reducing nonspace R&D, no one has shown that it is politically possible to get expenditures for R&D allocated on a more "rational" basis. The fate of the Department of Commerce's Civilian Industrial Technology Program in the House of Representatives is a warning.

NASA's concern about the problem of spill-over is, in a sense, required by law. The Space Act obliges NASA to require that contractors supply it with full and complete information concerning any invention, discovery, improvement, or innovation conceived or made in the course of work under the contract. The obligation applies not only to inventions that are patentable, but to all innovations or improvements. As the skeptics about the economic benefits of the space program would expect, experience under the clause has been discouraging. A NASA spokesman reports that "the number of inventions, innovations, improvements and discoveries that were reported . . . appears to fall short of what might reasonably be expected." [21] NASA hopes that the problem is not so much the failure of space R&D to lead to innovations as the failure of industry to report them, and, as we will note in Chapter 13, it is taking steps to improve the situation. Further, it is making strenuous efforts, described in Chapter 15, to disseminate information concerning innovations to potential civilian-commercial-industrial users.

Perhaps the best concluding statement that can be made is the unsatisfactory one that it remains to be seen how great the spill-over effects of the space program are. That the facts call for some

---

[21] G. D. O'Brien, "NASA Patent Policy and Procedure," in NASA, Office of Scientific and Technical Information, *Proceedings of the Second NASA-Industry Conference,* Washington, D.C., February 11-12, 1963 (Washington, 1963), p. 203.

reserve on the question is indicated by the following statement of the Director of NASA's Technology Utilization Program: "The space exploration program stands on its own merits; our nation must occupy a position of preeminence. The benefits from industrial applications are not now—and never will be—the justification for the high costs of this major effort." [22]

Communications

Space activities are expected "to revolutionize communications— radio and television, telephone and teleprinter messages, wirephotos and radiophotos, and the like." [23] They are "about to multiply our long distance communications capacity by a hundred times, and to reduce costs." [24] Telstar and Relay have given dramatic evidence of the potentialities for world-wide TV, and less dramatic evidence is being collected concerning the potentialities of different sorts of satellite systems (passive and active-repeater; low, medium, and synchronous orbit) for the various communications needs. Lasers, discussed in Chapter 4, might conceivably bring about a vast extension of the revolution, though serious problems stand in the way (e.g., the fact that laser beams do not penetrate clouds and rain, and that it is difficult to aim them accurately from a satellite). Moreover, it is not simply a question of handling current communications more efficiently. Past growth suggests very striking increases in future demands for communications facilities, and improved facilities will presumably generate still greater demands. Frederick R. Kappel, Chairman of the Board of A.T.&T., says that "last year—1962—there were about 5 million oversea calls. By 1980 we expect something like 100 million. Right now, with our foreign partners we operate about 700 oversea circuits. We expect that by 1980 at least 10,000 will be needed." [25] New kinds of uses for communications satellites may sooner or later increase needs to a much greater extent. NASA is already considering a data-collection satellite system, which would retrieve data from buoys and

[22] Louis B. C. Fong, "The NASA Program of Industrial Applications," in NASA, Office of Scientific and Technical Information, *Proceedings of the Conference on Space-Age Planning*, Chicago, Illinois, May 6-9, 1963 (Washington, 1963), p. 190.

[23] Lloyd V. Berkner, "Are Space Probes Worth It?" *Air Force/Space Digest*, 43 (November, 1960), 90.

[24] Lloyd V. Berkner, "Science and the World Tomorrow," lecture of January 19, 1962, Industrial College of the Armed Forces, mimeo., p. 46.

[25] *Congressional Record*, Vol. 109, No. 45 (March 25, 1963), A1676.

perhaps from posts on land and which might include an iceberg patrol; and utilization in the processing of data and the transmission of mail are possibilities.

A Communication Satellite Corporation is developing a communications satellite system under an act of 1962. For international transmissions, the corporation must work out arrangements with foreign agencies. Utilization of the satellite system will depend on terminal stations on the ground at various points over the world, providing a hook-up with the conventional facilities of communications carriers. All transmissions will be through the terminal stations and the connected facilities. Direct broadcasting from satellites to radio or TV sets in homes is not anticipated in the visible future. The expectation is that satellites will be used mainly for transoceanic transmissions; they are not expected to be competitive with microwave relays for overland transmissions. In principle, and partly for political reasons, the communications satellite system is to be "global," and the "national interest" is to supplement the profit motive in determining at what points terminal stations on the ground are to be established. The system is to provide services "to the economically less developed countries and areas as well as to those more highly developed." [26] If the Secretary of State decides that the national interest calls for the establishment of a terminal station at a given point, he can take steps to require its establishment. It will not be enough for the communications system to consist of one synchronous satellite providing services only to the North Atlantic area, however profitable that might be. Much has been made of the possibility of world-wide TV, but various considerations dictate caution in estimating its commercial value. Differences of time and language, as well as differences in culture, create imposing obstacles to regular world-wide TV aimed at mass audiences, and so do differences in technical standards. Telephonic and other transmissions directed to specific persons seem more likely to be profitable.

It is obvious from the above that the commercial prospects of a communications satellite system are contingent on a number of kinds of developments, and the venture is therefore speculative. Moreover, prospects of a pay-off depend in part on the basis for calculations. If most of the costs of developing rockets and space vehicles and instrumentation are charged to other purposes, and if

---

[26] Sec. 102(a) of the Satellite Communication Act of 1962.

the only costs counted are those incurred specifically and exclusively to get a communications satellite system into operation—and apparently this is what is to be done—then the chance that the system will show profits is obviously much more favorable than it would otherwise be. NASA spokesmen seem confident of the prospects. Thus the Director of NASA's Office of Applications, Morton J. Stoller, says: "Economic studies . . . indicate that with the development of the communications satellite it will be possible to provide services closely comparable in performance to those of the underseas cables, at lower costs per channel than we now experience with the cables, and that we will be able to expand the system to a capacity well beyond that which would be economic with cables alone." [27] That A.T.&T. expects a communications satellite system to be profitable is indicated by the fact that it went ahead with Telstar at its own expense in 1962 after NASA had decided to support Relay, proposed by RCA.

Contemplation of the possibilities of communication via satellite sometimes leads to interesting suggestions, e.g., the following by Lyndon B. Johnson:

Advances in the realm of rapid data transmission will permit the transmission in 2 weeks' time of every page in every book in the Library of Congress anywhere in the world.

That means that scholars in the new nations of Africa and Asia no longer need yearn for libraries or source materials. They will have access to the world's greatest stores of knowledge within a matter of seconds.[28]

I wonder when such manna from heaven will be available to scholars in Iowa, and how it could be managed! The then Vice President also predicted that the satellite communications system "will permit face-to-face television communication at any hour between heads of state," and said that "major conferences can be held without the principal participants ever leaving their own country." [29]

Meteorology and Weather Forecasting

As in the case of communications satellites, extremely optimistic

---

[27] U.S. Congress, House, Committee on Science and Astronautics, Subcommittee on Applications and Tracking and Data Acquisition, *1963 NASA Authorization*, Hearings . . . on H. Res. 10100, 87th Cong., 2d Sess., Part 5, p. 2056 (hereafter cited as House Hearings, *1963 NASA Authorization*).

[28] Remarks of March 16, 1962, in *Congressional Record*, Vol. 108, No. 57 (April 12, 1962), A2858.

[29] *Ibid.*

statements are very common concerning the prospective economic benefits of the space meteorology program. The more conservative of the space enthusiasts claim only that the savings made possible by improved forecasts "will exceed by several orders of magnitude the total cost of the meteorological program." The less conservative claim that the savings will "easily" pay not only for the meteorological program but for all the rest of the space program as well.

The most publicized achievements made possible to date by meteorological satellites have been the identification and tracing of hurricanes at sea, permitting warning to coastal areas about to be struck. Important as this kind of achievement is, it is relatively simple. The more difficult problem is to utilize data from meteorological satellites and other sources to develop scientific law and theory on the basis of which weather forecasts can be improved in many different kinds of circumstances. The object is to increase the accuracy of the forecasts and to extend the period of time that they cover. Progress in these directions will undoubtedly occur, but nobody really knows yet how far or how fast the progress will go. The still greater problem is to learn how to modify or control the weather.

Soon after the inauguration of President Kennedy, an Ad Hoc Panel of the President's Science Advisory Committee was asked to appraise a proposed expansion of the meteorology space program. It endorsed the program, saying that it would "provide a real contribution to forecasting . . .," but it was restrained.

The immediate contribution to civilian forecasting in the United States will be confined to very special circumstances. . . .

The ultimate contribution to civilian forecasting in the United States may be expected to be substantial, though one cannot assess how, or in what way, this contribution will arise. Research in the basic processes of the atmosphere, and development of techniques of interpretation of satellite data, will be necessary before this ultimate contribution is available.[30]

There is question not only about the extent to which forecasting can be improved but also about resultant benefits. Reliable forecasts are potentially valuable to everyone: to those in the path of a severe storm, to farmers, to those concerned with the conservation of water resources, to those engaged in marketing, construction, transportation, to those who provide or seek recreation, to those

[30] U.S. Congress, Senate, Committee on Aeronautical and Space Sciences, *Meteorological Satellites*, Staff Report . . . Prepared by the Library of Congress, March 29, 1962, 87th Cong., 2d Sess., p. 174 (hereafter cited as *Meteorological Satellites*, Senate, 1962).

concerned with health, convenience, and comfort. The list plainly shows that the value of reliable forecasts can in many cases not be translated into dollars in a meaningful way. Moreover, there are obvious problems about estimating the amount saved by averting damage; how do you know how great the damage would have been? And you cannot assume that those who should benefit from a forecast will actually hear and heed it, doing everything needful to minimize losses and maximize gains.

There is another area of uncertainty, too: the potential military value of more accurate forecasts. Memories of D-Day in 1944 suggest the possible magnitude of the stakes, and the following does so even more pointedly:

There is one special group of new military problems that are now demanding the concentrated attention of meteorologists both in the Soviet Union and the United States. These relate to the use of nuclear weapons. In what kind of weather situation can a 10-megaton bomb be detonated 3 miles above Moscow without endangering Poland? How many megatons of H-bombs can be detonated over the United States before the atmosphere will become so saturated with radio-active dust that even the Soviet Union, 5,000 miles downwind, will suffer from the consequences? [31]

In connection with communications satellites, DOD has its own separate program, so the civilian program is relatively less vital for defense purposes. But in meteorology the armed forces are depending mainly on civilian research and civilian operations. Quite obviously, the military benefit of accurate weather forecasts might in some circumstances be literally priceless. Further, techniques of modifying the weather, if they can be developed, will be important not only to a considerable variety of commercial and personal pursuits but also to military pursuits. Reliable techniques for substantially modifying the weather would have a significance that would be impossible to exaggerate. The day might come when states wage "war" with each other through a competitive struggle in this realm.

Though denying that a dollar sign can be put accurately on the benefits of weather forecasting, the Weather Bureau sometimes succumbs to pressures to do so. It finds that in this country forecasts lead to preparedness that reduces losses from storms and bad weather by more than a billion dollars a year; "and it is reported that more definite forecasts longer in advance would double or treble the benefits." Note that there is no specific claim here that

[31] David I. Blumenstock, *The Ocean of Air,* as quoted in *Meteorological Satellites,* Senate, 1962, p. 123.

meteorological satellites will bring about the more definite forecasts that might double or treble the benefits; it is mentioned as a
possibility. The Weather Bureau goes on to indicate that the contribution to human welfare and national prestige would be incalcul-
able if the benefits of improved meteorological services could be
extended over the world.[32]

Miscellaneous Possibilities and Fantasies

Though the most promising of the economic benefits from the
application of space technologies are currently in the fields of communications and meteorology, there are other possibilities. The
Navy's work on a satellite navigation system may bring benefits to
merchant ships and perhaps to air lines. The Air Force's work on
photography from space may bring a variety of benefits to civilian
enterprises. At some point in the future, space ships might be used
to transport mail and other cargo, and even human passengers, between widely separated points on earth. Some have suggested,
along the same line, that we may sometime bring products to earth
from the heavens, whether by exploiting the resources of the moon
or the planets in their normal orbits or by capturing asteroids.
Lyndon B. Johnson speaks of the latter possibility, anticipating the
time when a space ship will intercept "an asteroid containing billions of dollars worth of critically needed metals" and bring it
"close to earth to provide a vast new source of mineral wealth for
our factories."[33] He does not say how or how soon this kind of thing
could be managed, and there are obvious reasons for skepticism.
But perhaps I should cite an astronautical engineer in the Missile
and Space Division of the General Electric Company who speaks
seriously of the possibility. "It's as reasonable to think now of
capturing asteroids in 15 years as it was in 1945 to think of manned
orbital flight. . . . Asteroid capture does offer the possibility of
eventually establishing highly profitable mining and manufacturing
endeavors in space."[34] For the foreseeable future, however, it will
surely be much cheaper to exploit the resources of the earth than

[32] "Economic Benefits to be Expected from Meteorological Satellite Input
into National Storm Warning System," in House Hearings, *1963 NASA
Authorization*, Part 5, p. 2201.
[33] Lyndon B. Johnson, "The New World of Space," in *Seattle Proceedings*,
p. 30.
[34] Dandridge M. Cole, "Capturing the Asteroid," *Astronautics and Aerospace Engineering*, 1 (March, 1963), 93.

to attempt to bring heavy materials in from an asteroid, or from the moon or Mars. "Lunar and planetary exploration cannot now, or for the foreseeable future, be justified on economic grounds. No commercially valuable materials now known, and likely to be found or 'produced' elsewhere in the solar system, can conceivably have a cost-per-pound on earth after a lunar or planetary trip which will be less than the cost-per-pound for the production of their equivalents on earth." [35]

One of the more remarkable expositions of the economic implications of space activities comes from a distinguished scientist-engineer. He figures that in the first three years after Sputnik I the Soviets gained more than $12 billion because of their achievement, and he does it in the following way. First, he thinks it can be taken for granted (*sic!*) that Soviet space successes "resulted in a few percentage points of the world market being transferred from the free world to the Communists," and that over the three years the few percentage points were "worth" $6 billion. Second, he thinks that because of the Sputniks the West had to increase its defense budget by a few percentage points; and to them he assigns a value of $5 billion. Third, he thinks that the Sputniks so increased national pride in the Soviet Union and popular support for the Communist Party that internal security costs—expenditures for the army and the secret police—could be reduced by $1 billion. He offers no evidence. But he adds six and five and one and gets twelve. It is as simple as that.

Expositions and predictions such as some of those given above call for two caveats. One is to beware of the man whose achievements and distinctions in his special field give him a sense of omniscience; sophistication in one field is no guarantee against naiveté in another. The second is that the miracles of the space age often do something to dim critical faculties. Once the seemingly impossible and incredible has been done and once thoughts are drawn toward a realm that is literally out of this world, the usual standards of discernment seem to weaken. Credulity and the inclination to play upon it both seem to increase. A warning from Dr. DuBridge is in point: "Just because many of the things about space which are true appear to be fantastic, it does not necessarily follow that everything fantastic is necessarily true."

---

[35] N. E. Golovin, Office of Science and Technology, "Space Science and Technology: The Near and Distant Future," speech of October 24, 1962, mimeo.

Social Effects

The title of this chapter refers to both economic and social progress. This is a pleonasm, for economic progress is also social. But implicit in the economic and other effects of the space program there are no doubt social effects beyond those mentioned above. A geographical redistribution of economic activities within the United States is occurring, partly because of the space program (though more because of changing military needs). Detroit and Pittsburgh are becoming relatively a little less important in the economy, and such states as California, Texas, and Florida are gaining. This is bound to have numerous further effects, e.g., on the distribution of the population, on problems of local government, on culture patterns. The demand for more and more scientists and engineers means a demand for more and more education, for a better quality in our schools, and perhaps more respect for intellectual activity as fruitful work and more respect for the intellectual as a person. Cultural interests and activities will necessarily be affected by such developments. What this may lead to is difficult to say.

Prospective social effects in the field of international relations are even more difficult to estimate. (I do not speak here of effects pertaining to military security or prestige, but of other kinds of effects stemming from new knowledge and technologies and the applications thereof.) On the one hand, to the extent that the space program produces the various benefits for the United States that some claim or anticipate, it will tend to accentuate the spread between nations in terms of their level of development. Whatever absolute progress the less developed make, in a relative sense they may be left farther and farther behind. The foreign aid program, and the program of international cooperation conducted by NASA itself, may or may not be enough to counteract this tendency. If you ask what difference it makes if the spread gets greater, I confess I do not know; but surely it would be a cause for concern. On the other hand, other aspects or effects of the space program may tend to bring nations together rather than increase the gulf between them. NASA's program of international cooperation, to be discussed in Chapter 14, is one of them. Further, it is quite possible that increases in the speed and reliability of transportation and communication resulting from the space program may have different effects than in the past. In the past, they have generally intensified intranational contacts more than international contacts, and so have presumably tended to strengthen a sense of national identity and unity more than a sense of membership in the world community. But the greatest advantages of a satellite communications system will apparently be in transoceanic and long-distance service, suggesting that the greatest relative increase in contacts may be in the international field.

Conclusion

With the available data it is impossible to determine clearly what the economic and social effects of the space program—or its various aspects—will be. But the most likely conclusion is similar to the one reached in the preceding chapter. The greatest prospect of beneficial economic effects attends instrumented flights in near-earth orbit. They are relatively inexpensive, but will no doubt produce some spill-over, and those used in communications and meteorological systems might turn out to be profitable. Nevertheless, even the instrumented flights are speculative, and this is all the more true of manned flight, including the lunar program. They enlist popular and congressional support, and for this reason can claim a share of the credit for whatever benefits any part of the space program brings. But if there were no reasons for a lunar program other than the prospect that it would produce economic and social benefits, it is safe to say that very few would consider it justifiable.

Among the various motives of the space program, national prestige is probably mentioned most frequently, but there is very little accompanying analysis. Our questions here concern the meaning and importance of prestige, the relative emphasis on it as a motive under Eisenhower and under Kennedy, and the extent to which the search for prestige seems to justify the different aspects of the space program.

The Meaning and Importance of "Prestige"

The prestige of a nation in world affairs is often thought of simply as its reputation for power, and for some purposes this conception is quite adequate. Charles Burton Marshall was evidently thinking of prestige in these terms when he said: "Prestige is the faculty enabling a great power to avoid final, miserable choices between surrender and war. Prestige is the ingredient of authority in international affairs. One may point up its meaning by an account of a geneticist who crossed a tiger and a parrot. When asked about the results of the experiment he replied: 'When it talks, I listen.' The quality which demands being listened to is prestige—and a nation suffers loss of it at great peril." [1]

For our purposes a somewhat more elaborate definition will prove useful. National prestige can be said to consist of a reputa-

---

[1] Charles Burton Marshall, "Cuba—Why the Russians Are There," *New Republic*, 147 (October 1, 1962), 9.

tion abroad for four qualities: (1) the pursuit of goals that are creditable and that respond to the challenges of the time; (2) the capacity to achieve the goals; (3) the necessary determination to achieve them, provided it can be done responsibly, i.e., by means that do not involve the undue sacrifice of other desirable goals; and (4) an assured future, in which the other qualities making for prestige will be preserved if not enhanced. Deference, as distinguished from prestige, can be obtained on the basis of the second and third qualities alone, and the proviso attached to the third can be dropped.

The record of the United States in space has raised questions about each of these four qualities. Has the United States responded adequately to the challenge of nature and the challenge of the Soviet Union? Is the response creditable—or should it be described as either adolescent or militaristic? Has the United States demonstrated a capacity to achieve goals so far, and does it have the capacity to achieve such goals as the lunar landing? Does it have the will? To what extent do others take the space achievements of the United States and the Soviet Union to be symbolic of the future of the two societies?

The Emphasis on Prestige Under Eisenhower

Eisenhower chose to deprecate prestige as a motive and to play it down. His inclination was to speak of only two kinds of reasons for going into space: military and "purely scientific." [2] The important thing was that the space program be "based on a systematic and technically sound approach to the complicated scientific and engineering problems involved." [3] He saw no reason to think in terms of competition with the Soviet Union, no reason to engage in a race. When asked at a news conference whether he didn't think our prestige was at stake in connection with space activities, he responded, "Not particularly, no." [4] This outlook dominated official statements concerning Project Mercury, as we have already noted. So far as Eisenhower was concerned—or, at least, so far as his public statements indicate—the man-in-space program was not

---

[2] U.S. President, *Public Papers of the Presidents of the United States, Dwight D. Eisenhower*, 1960-61 (Washington, 1961), p. 146 (hereafter cited as *Public Papers of the Presidents*).

[3] *Ibid.*, p. 66.

[4] *Ibid.*, p. 127.

motivated by military or prestige considerations, or any others of a competitive sort. It was a scientific effort, designed to "determine man's capabilities in a space environment." [5] Eisenhower continues to express the same general outlook since leaving office.

If we must compete with Soviet Russia for world "prestige," why not channel the struggle more along the lines in which we excel—and which means so much to the masses of ordinary citizens? Let's put some other items in this "prestige" race: our unique industrial accomplishments, our cars for almost everybody instead of just the favored few, our remarkable agricultural productivity, our supermarkets loaded with a profusion of appetizing foods. [6]

Obviously, Eisenhower wanted to stress the fact that prestige stems from a considerable variety of characteristics and achievements. And he claimed that it stood high, regardless of what we did in space.

At the same time, Eisenhower warmly endorsed the "Introduction to Outer Space," prepared by his Science Advisory Committee, of which James R. Killian, Jr., was Chairman; it listed four factors which gave "importance, urgency, and inevitability to the advancement of space technology," the third of which was "the factor of national prestige. To be strong and bold in space technology will enhance the prestige of the United States among the peoples of the world and create added confidence in our scientific, technological, industrial, and military strength." Dr. Killian's position was that in the long pull the soundest way to seek prestige is through a rich, varied, and balanced effort in science and technology rather than through an emphasis on the spectacular. "In the long run we can only weaken our science and technology and lower our international prestige by frantically indulging in unnecessary competition and prestige-motivated projects. . . . We shall build greater respect in the long run by ensuring the quality, vigor, and integrity of all our science and technology. We shall gain prestige by being better in more areas." [7]

The probability is that Eisenhower's position resulted from care-

[5] Cf. George M. Low, Chief, Manned Space Flight Programs, NASA, in U.S. Congress, House, Committee on Science and Astronautics, *Review of the Space Program,* Hearings, 86th Cong., 2d Sess., 1960, Part 2, p. 741 (hereafter cited as House Hearings, *Review of the Space Program,* 1960).

[6] Dwight D. Eisenhower, "Are We Headed in the Wrong Direction?" *Saturday Evening Post,* 235 (August 11-18, 1962), 24.

[7] James R. Killian, Jr., "Shaping a Public Policy for the Space Age," in Lincoln P. Bloomfield, ed., *Outer Space. Prospects for Man and Society,* The American Assembly (Englewood Cliffs: Prentice-Hall, 1962), p. 184.

ful deliberation. As noted in Chapter 3, Sputnik I was convincing evidence of a Soviet breakthrough in long-range missile power. If Eisenhower had shown great alarm or acknowledged a serious reduction of American prestige, he would have tended to undermine confidence at home in the security of the country and belief abroad in its power, and this would have tended to jeopardize efforts to deter the Soviet Union and might have been disconcerting to friends and allies. Moreover, Eisenhower would have made himself even more vulnerable to charges that he and his administration were at fault for not having pressed the development of missile and space capabilities sooner and more vigorously. It will probably be left to historians to determine the extent to which his stand reflected genuine conviction and the extent to which it reflected a conception of a desirable national and personal strategy in the face of difficult circumstances.

I noted above that Dr. Killian, Special Assistant to the President for Science and Technology, took a stand similar to Eisenhower's. In fact, the natural scientists have in general tended to shy away from an emphasis on a direct effort to enhance national prestige through space efforts. Dr. Lee A. DuBridge makes statements on the subject very similar to those of Dr. Killian.[8] Dr. Vannevar Bush grants that "we lost the first round" in terms of propaganda, but thinks that this has not

done us a great deal of injury in our relations with the hesitant nations of the world. They are going to look much more deeply into our strengths and intentions than the question of who first shoots the Moon, or puts a man into space. . . . Putting a man in space is a stunt. . . . There are far more serious things to do than to indulge in stunts. . . . I do not discard completely the value of demonstrating to the world our skills. Nor do I undervalue the effect on morale of the spectacular. But the present hullabaloo on the propaganda aspects of the program leaves me entirely cool.[9]

Dr. James A. Van Allen likewise rejects prestige as a motive. He prefers to seek "tangible achievements . . . with the confidence that such achievements will naturally lead to whatever level of

---

[8] U.S. Congress, House, Select Committee on Astronautics and Space Exploration, *Astronautics and Space Exploration,* Hearings . . . on H. Res. 11881, 85th Cong., 2d Sess., 1958, p. 778 (hereafter cited as House Hearings, *Astronautics and Space Exploration,* 1958); Lee A. DuBridge, "A Scientist Calls for Common Sense," *Reporter,* 24 (April 27, 1961), 23.

[9] U.S. Congress, House, Committee on Science and Astronautics, *To Amend the National Aeronautics and Space Act of 1958,* Hearings . . . on H. Res. 9675, 86th Cong., 2d Sess., 1960, p. 493. Statement of March 31, 1960.

prestige is appropriate." [10] This attitude toward the desirability of making the enhancement of prestige a deliberate purpose is curious, especially in the light of the willingness of some of the scientists to make world "leadership" a goal. I will take up this point in the next chapter. The rejection of prestige as a motive is not unanimous. Dr. Lloyd V. Berkner, for example, takes a contrary view.[11]

Some of those around Eisenhower clearly engaged in soul-searching on the question of the emphasis to put on the space effort as a source of prestige. T. Keith Glennan, the first NASA Administrator, was one of them. His personal perspective was similar to that of the scientists cited above, and he was an Eisenhower appointee. At the same time, he was exposed to pressures from people with different sets of values, and he was on the political firing line. Reluctantly but ineluctably he came to accept competition with the Soviet Union as "the principal factor which determines the pace at which we pursue our goals. . . ." Implicitly he seemed to say that Eisenhower's public view did not in fact prevail.

It is clear to me that, as of the present, the enhancement of national prestige in a divided world has been and continues to be uppermost in the minds of the majority of people who have bothered to think about the matter of competition in the space arena. And this principally because of the fear that the loss of prestige that we have experienced for a time somehow upsets our equanimity and probably means, in some vague way, that we are second-best in *everything*.[12]

Thought about prestige as a motive here gets intertwined with what in the next chapter I will call *pride*. I believe that ostensible concern for prestige is often, in reality, concern for pride, and that of the two motives pride has been, is, and should be the more influential.

Since leaving NASA Dr. Glennan maintains the same general outlook as the one expressed above. He thinks that "any difficulty in establishing tangible benefits to be derived from much of the space program is largely offset by a national desire to make progress in a space race. The elements of national prestige are

---

[10] House Hearings, *Astronautics and Space Exploration*, 1958, p. 883.

[11] U.S. Congress, Senate, Committee on Aeronautical and Space Sciences, *Scientists' Testimony on Space Goals*, Hearings, 88th Cong., 1st Sess., 1963, p. 108 (hereafter cited as Senate Hearings, *Scientists' Testimony on Space Goals*).

[12] T. Keith Glennan, speech at Yale Convocation, October 7, 1960, p. 17.

so obviously at stake that the current pressures are to increase our space effort." [13] He goes on to give at least a partial explanation of "the reluctance of top administration officials to state that we are in a space race with the Russians." The fear was that if the "race psychology" became dominant, spectaculars would have to be sought at the expense of a "technically sound program," and that this might lead to eventual failure. It was "hard to convince the general public that discovering the Van Allen Belt may have greater long-term significance than some of the Soviet Union's achievements"—hard to "translate solid technological achievement into prestige."

George V. Allen, Director of the U.S. Information Agency under Eisenhower, also faced a problem in dealing with the question of the implications of space efforts for national prestige, and his solution differed from Eisenhower's. He told the House Committee on Science and Astronautics that the Sputniks had greatly enhanced the prestige of the Soviet Union and that American prestige had suffered. "All space activities are now seen within the framework of Soviet-American competition. Regardless of how Americans may feel about it, the world sees the United States in a space race with the U.S.S.R." [14] A member of the committee asked Mr. Allen whether it was "a race in which we must win at all cost," evidently hoping for an affirmative answer, but Mr. Allen thought this too extreme. Other things were also important, such as military security and freedom. But to another question he gave the desired response in saying that he did not want to run second in the race. He believed that "space has become for many people the primary symbol of world leadership in all areas of science and technology." He spoke of the cockiness and arrogance that space successes had engendered in Soviet officials, and he feared the possible consequences. [15]

The members of the House committee made it abundantly clear that they themselves accepted the idea of a race, and that they were determined that the United States should win. Following the hearings at which Mr. Allen appeared they made a report in

---

[13] T. Keith Glennan, "The Task for Government," in Bloomfield, op. cit., p. 94.

[14] House Hearings, Review of the Space Program, 1960, Part 1, p. 38. Statement of January 22, 1960.

[15] Ibid., pp. 37-38, 61.

which they said that under the stimulus of such programs as the IGY "we have witnessed . . . the emergence of scientific achievement as a factor of great importance to world prestige and international influence." "The U.S. space program is joining the ranks of its defense program, foreign trade policy, mutual assistance, etc., as a prime force in world affairs. The committee expresses the strong belief that this and future administrations must emphasize and accelerate space research as a necessary element to the continued leadership of the United States." [16] Note that both Mr. Allen and the House committee simply took it for granted that "leadership" is good.

The Emphasis on Prestige Under Kennedy

The Kennedy Administration was quite explicitly concerned with prestige in relation to space, and quite willing to emphasize space exploits as a source of prestige.

Before taking office, Kennedy received a report from an Ad Hoc Advisory Committee on Space under the chairmanship of Dr. Jerome B. Wiesner, who became Chairman of Kennedy's Science Advisory Committee (PSAC). Among the motivations it listed for a space program the first was "the factor of national prestige." "Space exploration and exploits have captured the imagination of the peoples of the world. During the next few years, the prestige of the United States will in part be determined by the leadership we demonstrate in space activities." President Kennedy himself said that "there is no area where the United States received a greater setback to its prestige as the number one industrial country in the world than in being second in the field of space in the fifties." [17] In calling for the expanded and accelerated program in May, 1961, he cited the impact on the minds of men everywhere of the dramatic achievements of the Soviet Union in space; and concerning the proposed manned lunar landing he said that "no single space project in this [decade] will be more impressive to mankind."

NASA Administrator James E. Webb also stresses the enhance-

---

[16] U.S. Congress, House, Committee on Science and Astronautics, *Space, Missiles, and the Nation,* H. Rpt. No. 2092, 86th Cong., 2d Sess., 1960, pp. 4, 53.

[17] *Public Papers of the Presidents,* Kennedy, 1961, p. 734.

ment of prestige as a motive of the space program, usually associating it with other motives as well. (In the statements quoted below he also speaks implicitly on the question reputation for what and in whose minds. I will comment on this question later.)

Today prestige is one of the most important elements of international relations. . . . There is, without a doubt, a tendency to equate space and the future. Therefore, space is one of the fronts upon which President Kennedy and his Administration have chosen to act broadly, vigorously, and with continuous purpose. No other single field offers us the opportunity to gain more of what we need abroad and at the same time to achieve such a wealth of both practical and scientific results at home.[18]

On the question why the manned lunar expedition was selected "as the dominant goal of space exploration for this decade," he says that this is a natural and logical step following manned orbital flights and that the lunar landing is a task in which we can succeed if we try hard. Then he emphasizes an intensified space effort as a source of prestige.

How important is it for us, as a nation, to do this thing in the shortest possible time, recognizing that if we don't make the effort the Soviet Union undoubtedly will achieve this most impressive of all space exploration "firsts?" There is only one answer that the American people can give to such a question. Science and technology are rightly regarded by the world's peoples today as the keys to economic progress and military strength. . . . In the minds of millions, space achievements have become today's symbol of tomorrow's scientific and technical supremacy. The Soviet Union has recognized this. . . . We cannot afford to yield to them by default the next great prize in this competition. . . . When we can win, we must win.[19]

Mr. Webb points out that "we are in competition with just about every aspect of the Communist way of life and unless we compete strongly, ably, and successfully with the Soviet Union in space activities and the underlying technologies, our national prestige will suffer in the eyes of other nations."

It is important, as a device of foreign policy and diplomacy, to establish a definite position of leadership in order to increase the regard in which we are held internationally. In addition to the overall effects resulting from steady, continuous progress and achievements in our space efforts, there is the impact of dramatic "firsts." It is by these "firsts" that the relative progress of Russia and the United States is most often measured by the average person the world around. To some extent even specifically

---

[18] James E. Webb, address of September 27, 1961, NASA News Release No. 61-215, p. 8.

[19] James E. Webb, address of September 13, 1961, NASA News Release No. 61-205, pp. 9 ff.

trained scientific and technical minds are influenced by the often super-ficial but stimulating "firsts." [20]

Congressional sentiment on the point was clear at least until the spring of 1963. Even the Republican members of the House and Senate seem to have been unhappy with Eisenhower's restraint on space, and they and the Democrats went all the way with Kennedy and Webb in expanding and accelerating the program. Concern for national prestige was one of the major influencing factors. For example, the late Overton Brooks, Chairman of the House Committee on Science and Astronautics, reported in May, 1961, that every member of the committee was convinced "that a great deal more depends upon the success of our national space program than a simple race for scientific achievement between the United States and Russia. Right now the esteem in which the United States is held in the eyes of the world is dependent upon what we do in space as it is dependent upon few other areas of national endeavor." [21] Many other congressmen have expressed similar views. And, more recently, some have expressed doubts. In May, 1963, the Senate Republican Policy Committee issued "an examination of the budget and benefits of the moon shot in relation to other national problems," in which it deplored "the adolescent desire to beat the Russians" as a motive of the lunar program and asked whether the lunar landing in this decade was more important than a number of other needs and potential projects.[22] And Senator Fulbright has expressed doubts, recalling the question whether more might not be gained if only the money were spent in other ways:

Are there not other factors involved in our prestige and self-esteem, such as our capacity to employ and educate, to house and transport our own people? If, at the end of this decade, the Russians have reached the moon and we have not, but have instead succeeded in the renovation of our cities and of our transport, in the virtual elimination of slums and crime, in the creation of the best system of public education in the world, whose prestige would be higher, who more admired by the world? . . . The issue is one of priorities.[23]

As if to reinforce these questions came Kennedy's proposal in September, 1963, to make the lunar program a joint rather than

---

[20] James E. Webb, remarks of February 18, 1962, NASA News Release No. 62-34, pp. 10-11.

[21] *Congressional Record*, Vol. 107, No. 87 (May 24, 1961), 8233.

[22] *Ibid.*, Vol. 109, No. 71 (May 14, 1963), 7916-18.

[23] J. William Fulbright, "The American Agenda," *Saturday Review*, 46 (July 20, 1963), 15.

a competitive Soviet-American effort. But the prospect seems remote that it will be made a joint program in any very thorough sense, if at all.

Reputation for What? In Whose Minds?

Those who emphasize space activities as a source of prestige also emphasize them in connection with each of the elements comprising prestige: a reputation for significant and creditable goals, for the will and the capacity to achieve them, and for an assured future. They argue that the national competitive record in space is either indicative or symbolic of qualities relating to each kind of reputation.

Lyndon B. Johnson, Webb, and many others, like the late President Kennedy himself, put great stress on the claim that our goals in space are creditable. They stress the promotion of scientific and technological progress, economic development, and international cooperation. They deny that putting a man on the moon would be primarily a stunt. They emphasize the peaceful nature of our purposes. They endorse the decision made under Eisenhower that space activities should be preponderantly civilian. They insist that the military portion of the program is purely defensive, and that they do not want to extend the arms race into space. They cite the prospect of favorable reactions from abroad. A House committee report on the prospective communications satellite system pointed out that "if properly oriented to satisfy the communications requirements of all nations of the world, [the system] could . . . create the image of a nation sincerely dedicated to the improvement of the conditions of all mankind. . . ." [24] Another report made essentially the same statement concerning the meteorological satellite program. The use of meteorological satellites has been proposed not only for purposes of weather forecasting but also for locating and tracking "clouds" of locusts. "If successfully carried out, a new means of generating international good will and cooperation should result and America's overseas image accordingly strengthened." [25]

There is also stress on the importance to prestige of response

---

[24] U.S. Congress, House, Committee on Science and Astronautics, *Commercial Applications of Space Communications Systems,* H. Rpt. No. 1279, 87th Cong., 1st Sess., 1961, p. 21.

[25] U.S. President, Report to the Congress, *United States Aeronautics and Space Activities, 1962* (Washington: National Aeronautics and Space Council, 1963), p. 71.

to significant challenge. The general point is that if the United States did nothing in space while the Soviet Union went on from one triumph to another, American prestige would be seriously jeopardized. Mr. Webb has called attention to this point in deploring "a tendency in some quarters to belittle the psychological value of Project Apollo." "Think . . . what the reaction would be in this country if the Soviets made a successful landing on the moon and we had no plans and no potential for getting there. Certainly such a situation would be very damaging to our position throughout the world. The uproar after the first Sputnik would be mild indeed compared to the storm that would follow." [26]

Justifications of the space effort also include a stress on its utility as a means of demonstrating both a capacity and a will to achieve goals. In fact, one reason for the widespread dismay over our relatively bad showing in the first years of the space age was that it called the national capacity and will into question. As Mr. Webb says, "Essential to our prestige today is the belief of other nations that we have the capability and determination to carry out whatever we declare seriously that we intend to do. There is no denying that in the eyes of the world, during the past few years, our capability and determination have been brought into serious question." [27] Testifying to a House committee in 1962, Mr. Webb declared: ". . . some people doubt very much if the Russians would have moved as aggressively with respect to Berlin if they had not had such successes in space. You know, we had to add about $6 billion to our military effort per year to get in a position not to have our influence around the world eroded by what was happening in Berlin." In effect, Mr. Webb argued that we should use the space program to help create an "image for the Russians to keep in mind," seeking a reputation that would forestall the development of difficult problems.[28] After the Cuban crisis in October, 1962, he claimed that the support that Kennedy won around the world was to be attributed in part to "the image of the United States as a 'can-do' nation"—an image to which the

[26] James E. Webb, "National Goals in the Space Age," in NASA, Office of Scientific and Technical Information, *Proceedings of the Conference on Space-Age Planning*, Chicago, Illinois, May 6-9, 1963 (Washington, 1963), p. 4.

[27] James E. Webb, address of June 7, 1961, NASA News Release No. 61-124, p. 7.

[28] U.S. Congress, House, Committee on Appropriations, *Independent Offices Appropriations for 1963*, Hearings Before a Subcommittee . . ., 87th Cong., 2d Sess., 1962, Part 3, p. 424.

space program was contributing.[29] Secretary Rusk has notably
failed to make comparable statements,[30] and I suppose that there
is no way of either confirming or disconfirming such speculation
concerning the relationship between the behavior of other states
and the prestige that has been or may be acquired through space
activities. No doubt Mr. Webb himself would grant that reputations relating more immediately to military power are more important in the kind of context to which he referred.

A few who speak of the importance of demonstrating our capacities and will in space also speak, in effect, of the proviso that
there should be no undue sacrifice of other desirable goals. "We
have been internationally challenged in fields other than space—
for example, in our industrial efficiency as reflected in the ability
of our goods to compete in world markets, or by the rate of growth
in our per capita and over-all industrial productivity. Clearly these
challenges are no less vital, even if less visible, than primacy in
space."[31] The scientists and others who have questioned the
justifiability of the lunar landing program seem to have done so
mainly for other reasons, but there have been mentions of the
potentially adverse effect on our prestige of an unbalanced program and an effort to stage spectaculars.

Those stressing prestige as a motive for the space program have
given considerable emphasis to the fourth element too—a reputation for an assured future, in which the qualities making for prestige will be preserved if not enhanced. George V. Allen believed
that the people of other countries might regard our space program
"as a measure of our vitality and our ability to compete with a
formidable rival, and as a criterion of our ability to maintain
technological eminence worthy of emulation by other peoples."[32]
James E. Webb, as indicated above, says, "In the minds of millions,
dramatic space achievements have become today's symbol of
tomorrow's scientific and technical supremacy. There is, without
a doubt, a tendency to equate space and the future." Similarly As-

[29] U.S. Congress, House, Committee on Science and Astronautics, *Space
Posture*, Hearings, 88th Cong., 1st Sess., 1963, pp. 8-10.

[30] U.S. Congress, Senate, Committee on Aeronautical and Space Sciences,
*Documents on International Aspects of the Exploration and Use of Outer
Space, 1954-1962*, Staff Report, S. Doc. No. 18, 88th Cong., 1st Sess., 1963,
pp. 290-91.

[31] N. E. Golovin, "Space Science and Technology: The Near and Distant
Future," speech of October 24, 1962, mimeo., p. 10.

[32] House Hearings, *Review of the Space Program*, 1960, Part 1, p. 39.

sistant Secretary of Defense Rubel says that "science has become a principal concern of major states, and prowess in science or in the technology equated to it become a symbol of their real or potential military power." And he thinks that for the average man everywhere, spectacular achievements in new fields, such as space, are the indices of potentials for the future.[33]

It is in this context that the outcome of certain public opinion polls abroad acquires special significance. In 1960, people in a number of countries were asked, "Looking ahead ten years, which country do you think will have the leading position in the field of science?" The following gave Russia the lead: France, Britain, India, Holland, Uruguay, Switzerland, Norway, and West Germany. Only Greece placed its bet on the United States.[34] Polls taken a year later in Britain, France, West Germany, and Italy showed a series of interesting correlations.[35] In general, those who believed that the United States was ahead of the Soviet Union in space were much more inclined than the others to think that the United States was ahead in science in general, and the same holds true regarding anticipations about the situation 10 years hence. Moreover, those who thought that the United States was and would continue to be ahead in science were much more inclined than the others to think that the interests of their country were in agreement with those of the United States, and that their country should side with the United States. For example, on the average in the four countries named, of those who thought that the Soviet Union would be ahead in science 10 years hence, only 38 per cent wanted their country to side with the United States; and of those who thought that the United States would be ahead in science, 65 per cent favored siding with the United States. These are correlations, not causal relations. It is possible that the desire to side with the United States influenced the other opinions, rather than vice versa; or perhaps there was a two-way flow of influence. Still, though the polls do not prove that attitudes toward space

[33] John H. Rubel, address of December 30, 1962, Department of Defense, Office of Public Affairs, News Release No. 2105-62, p. 3.

[34] Hazel G. Erskine, ed., "The Polls: Defense, Peace, and Space," *Public Opinion Quarterly*, 25 (Fall, 1961), 486.

[35] USIA, Research and Reference Service, Survey Research Studies, "The Image of U.S. Versus Soviet Science in West European Public Opinion. A Survey in Four West European Countries," WE-3, October, 1961, pp. 23, 28-31.

achievements tend to shape the other attitudes, there is some likelihood that they do.

Concern about the national reputation for an assured future is also reflected in statements that competition in space is symbolic of competition between two ways of life. Webb and many others stress the thought that "we are in competition with the Soviet Union to prove the merits of our social, economic, and political system." Several years ago Marshall Shulman expressed the view that the Soviet challenge in space "implies that their system of organizing the human and material resources of their society is more rational in technological purpose than ours. . . . We cannot evade this critical question whether our kind of society can provide means for stressing some sense of national purpose, using our resources, and doing this in terms that are consistent with our political values." [36]

Such statements, it might be noted, have their counterpart in Soviet attitudes. A review of Soviet propaganda on the subject reveals various themes, among them persistent assertions that "Soviet successes in space provided concrete evidence that the Soviet communist system was superior to Western capitalism." [37] I might note, too, that efforts to shore up our national reputation in the categories identified above have a counterpart in rejections of similar Soviet claims. There is an obvious attempt to rob Soviet achievements of their prestige value through stressing the allegedly greater role of the military in the Soviet space effort and thus suggesting that it has a menacing character; further, there is stress on the secrecy with which the Soviet Union proceeds, in contrast to American openness, the implication being that what is done in secret must somehow be evil or dangerous. The current capacity of the Soviet Union to achieve goals in space, and its will, are conceded. But we repeatedly claim that in the future we will be first.

Implicit in the above answers to the question reputation for what is the fact that American spokesmen, especially since the beginning of the Kennedy-Johnson Administration, make claims

---

[36] Joseph M. Goldsen, Chairman, *International Political Implications of Activities in Outer Space*, report of a conference, October 22-23, 1959 (Santa Monica: RAND, 1960), p. 63.

[37] U.S. Congress, Senate, Committee on Aeronautical and Space Sciences, *Soviet Space Programs: Organization, Plans, Goals, and International Implications*, Staff Report, 87th Cong., 2d Sess., 1962, p. 42.

for the symbolic significance of space achievements that go far beyond what they intrinsically indicate. The Russians made this choice first, of course. Given their early triumphs, they tried to make the most of them. Eisenhower's efforts to restrict the significance attached to space achievements were not very successful, and as a practical matter Kennedy and Webb probably did not have much choice but to go in the other direction. At the same time, there are dangers in making space the acid test of all our virtues.

Answers to the question in whose minds we seek prestige are not at all clear-cut. In fact, they are almost always quite undiscriminating. The references are to "the minds of millions," "the world's peoples," the "belief of other nations," "the public mind," "the world at large," and so on. Concern for the attitude of "uncommitted peoples" is especially common. Thus T. Keith Glennan once commented that "the Soviet Union has been able to create in the minds of the people of a very large portion of the world's uncommitted areas the belief that success in space research is the principal measure of the scientific and technological efforts of a nation, and hence, the real measure of the worth of a culture." [38] And President Kennedy said: "I think the fact that the Soviet Union was ahead first in space in the Fifties had a tremendous impact upon a good many people who were attempting to make a determination as to whether they could meet their economic problems without engaging in a Marxist form of government. . . ." [39]

Some Limits on Our Knowledge

Given the importance attached to prestige it is surprising that more effort is not made to determine its conditions and consequences. In connection with the other objectives of the space program, NASA, DOD, and other agencies spend a great deal of money to get relevant knowledge. But none of them, so far as I know, spends anything to learn more about the process by which opinions and attitudes get formed. Politically the subject is, of course, very sensitive and delicate. A government agency that

[38] T. Keith Glennan, "My True Security," statement of July 21, 1959, mimeo., pp. 4-5.

[39] Department of Defense, Office of the Secretary of the Air Force, Director of Information, *Air Force Information Policy Letter*, Supplement for Commanders, Special Issue: Military Mission in Space, Number 110, p. 11.

announced a research program designed to show how to manipulate attitudes more effectively would undoubtedly arouse public wrath. But the fact is that we hope to influence attitudes, and we are attempting to do it not simply through space shots but also through publicity concerning them. In this situation surely it would be possible to arrange for appropriate studies to be made and to justify them both intellectually and politically.

The questions raised by Eisenhower and Senator Fulbright—concerning the relative importance to our prestige of achievements in various different fields—also call for more investigation. As Dr. DuBridge says, "We do not know whether $1 billion will buy more prestige if invested in space or in housing or in education or medicine or military power or foreign aid programs, or in what combination of all these things, and a dozen others." [40] For various reasons—including reports from American observers abroad, surveys of the foreign press, opinion polls, and intuitive expectations —I am inclined to think that space exploits have a very special effect on the relative prestige of the Soviet Union and the United States in third countries. But the available hard evidence is inconclusive. And it is quite possible—in fact likely—that the factors contributing to American prestige abroad differ in the different countries and in different groups. Governmental leaders in France and governmental leaders in Indonesia are not likely to be impressed in the same way by the different kinds of activities in which the United States is engaged.

Apart from the question how opinions get formed and what the opinions actually are, there is also the question of the consequences. Here again there is little evidence of serious inquiry.[41] In connection with Soviet-American competition in space, the assumption is that the behavior of foreign governments is affected by the beliefs of their officials or their citizens on such questions as whether the United States is ahead or behind and whether it is gaining or losing. Whether this is true, or true only in marginal circumstances, is not the point for the moment. The point is that the assumption seems to rest on nothing more than impression and intuition. Empirically based theory on predictable relationships

---

[40] Senate Hearings, *Scientists' Testimony on Space Goals*, p. 139.

[41] See, however, Gabriel A. Almond, "Public Opinion and the Development of Space Technology," *Public Opinion Quarterly*, 24 (Winter, 1960), 553-72; and Donald N. Michael, "Beginning of the Space Age and American Public Opinion," *Public Opinion Quarterly*, 24 (Winter, 1960), 573-82.

between the reputations that we gain by space activities and the behavior of other governments toward us do not exist, so far as I know.[42] Surely it would be dangerous to assume that the reputations gained in this way are more important than reputations gained in other ways, e.g., through our military power and posture, through our productive capacities, and through the preservation of a desirable political and social order. Big and important as the space program is, it is not, and should not be looked upon as, our only claim to fame.

Conclusion

The considerations advanced in the preceding chapters have led uniformly to the conclusion that more could be said in justification of near-earth space activities than in justification of the lunar program. That conclusion does not hold for the present chapter. Certainly the search for prestige was one of the major considerations leading President Kennedy to call for a lunar landing. Certainly, too, though instrumented flight has prestige value, the attention and interest of the world are captured much more by manned flight. It is arguable (though doubtful) that we could gain deference more surely by stressing the development of capabilities in near space—especially military capabilities—than by stressing a lunar landing. It is also arguable that other goals are more important than the attempt to enhance national prestige by beating the Russians to the moon. But for prestige purposes it is hard to imagine any national achievement in space that would have a value comparable to a successful manned lunar landing and return to earth—unless it be a manned exploration of Mars.

[42] Cf. Donald N. Michael, "Peaceful Uses," in Bloomfield, *op. cit.*, p. 61; Klaus Knorr, "On the International Implications of Outer Space," *World Politics*, 12 (July, 1960), 564-84; William H. Meckling, "The Economic Importance of Space Technology," in NASA, Office of Scientific and Technical Information, *Proceedings of the Second National Conference on the Peaceful Uses of Space*, Seattle, Washington, May 8-10, 1962 (Washington, 1962), p. 201.

NATIONAL PRIDE: THE ACHIEVEMENT MOTIVE

9

   I do not mean anything invidious in saying that national pride is an important factor motivating the space effort. I do not mean that the country is guilty of one of the seven deadly sins, or of conceit or inordinate self-esteem. There is an alternative dictionary meaning: "a reasonable delight in one's position, achievements, possessions, etc."; "pleasure or satisfaction taken in something done by or belonging to oneself or conceived as reflecting credit upon oneself." National pride, as I am using the term, is the "just pride" to which Washington referred in his Farewell Address. It is associated with a need for national achievement and with national morale. It designates gratification stemming from actual or confidently anticipated achievement. It is a counterpart of prestige, and the same constituent elements—identified in the preceding chapter—are involved: belief that the country is achieving or pursuing creditable goals, goals that are responsive to the opportunities and challenges of the time; belief that it is demonstrating the necessary will and capacity to achieve these goals; and belief that the future is assured. To the extent that our beliefs about these matters coincide with our reputation in the minds of people abroad, pride and prestige go together.

   The goals whose pursuit and achievement are a cause of pride fall into two categories: those associated with challenges posed by man and those associated with challenges posed by nature; and this distinction is important to what follows. The challenge posed by man is, of course, posed by the Soviet Union, and the search for a basis for pride necessarily calls for a competitive effort. The challenges posed by nature are of a different sort, demanding struggle for achievement but not necessarily for competition with human rivals.

In speaking of national pride, I may seem to reify the nation—to treat it as a Being with beliefs about itself. But I do not intend this. The statement that pride is a factor motivating the space effort of the United States translates itself into other statements, including the following: that a number of persons who make or influence decisions relating to the space program identify themselves with the United States to such an extent that its failures and successes affect their self-esteem; that such persons have in mind one or more standards for judging the performance of the United States in space; that they regard these standards as difficult to achieve or maintain; that they are gratified when the standards are met, and disappointed or mortified when they are not met; and that they influence decisions in such a way as to maintain or increase their gratification and to reduce or eliminate disappointment or mortification. The standards, the belief that they are difficult, and the judgment that they have been met are all subjective, though inevitably influenced by objective conditions and the attitudes of others.

The literature of political science, and more particularly literature on foreign policies and international politics, includes remarkably little on pride as a motivating factor. Undoubtedly there would be general acceptance of the view that those who identify themselves with an entity ordinarily like to be proud of its status and achievements, but the influence of this factor on behavior—especially in the field of foreign affairs—is rarely discussed or acknowledged. Harold Lasswell's writings contain numerous references to the importance of self-esteem, but his stress is on welfare and deference values. In the early part of *The American People and Foreign Policy*, Gabriel Almond notes the prevalence of extreme competitiveness among Americans and of a need for achievement and success. But he does not relate this characteristic directly to attitudes concerning relationshps with other states; and he apparently had little or no specific reason to do so, for the characteristic does not seem to have shown up explicitly in the attitudes on foreign policy of the groups that he analyzed—even in the patriotic-nationalist groups. Almond concludes that American competitiveness has been concerned "with 'private' values, as distinguished from social-group, political, or religious-moral values." [1] He points out that nationalist groups have tended to be advocates of free enterprise and isolationism. One would not expect from his book that competition with the Soviet Union, and success relative to that of the Soviet Union, would be among the compelling motives of the space effort.

The literature dealing specifically with the space program gives some attention to pride as a motive, but the record is spotty. President Eisenhower's Science Advisory Committee spoke of responding to the challenges of nature (". . . the compelling urge of man to explore and to discover, the thrust of curiosity that leads men to try to go where no one has gone before"), but not of responding to the challenge of the Soviet Union. The Ad Hoc Committee under Jerome B. Wiesner that advised Kennedy at the time of his inauguration found five major reasons for a space program without showing concern for pride. It has until recently been the exception rather than the rule among those describing the motives behind the space program to include mention of what I am calling pride; on many occasions, however, after a speaker or writer has listed motives without referring to pride, he has gone on to give implicit evidence that he was stirred by concern for it. Several years ago Professor Raymond A. Bauer of the Harvard Business School conducted a poll concerning attitudes toward the space program. His questions acknowledge the element of competition. He invited respondents to agree or disagree with the proposition that the idea of competing with Russia in a race for space is nonsense, and his list of "possible objectives" of the space program included "winning the prestige race with the Soviet Union." But there is little to suggest recognition of the possibility that we might be competing essentially for our own self-satisfaction, out of pride. [2] When I made up my own early list of the apparent motives of the space effort, it did not occur to me to include pride. But I found unexpected evidence on the point, crying to be recognized.

What kinds of evidence? Though the answer will come out more fully below, perhaps I should give a preliminary indication. There is some explicit discussion of the question whether pride is or

---

[1] Gabriel A. Almond, *The American People and Foreign Policy* (New York: Praeger, 1960), p. 48.

[2] Raymond A. Bauer, "Executives Probe Space," *Harvard Business Review*, 38 (September-October, 1960), 14, 178.

should be a motive. Even more, there are expressions of humiliation and of pride following space failures and successes, expressions that clearly reveal deep emotional involvement and that clearly indicate a yearning for achievements giving basis for pride. There is abundant evidence of a desire to beat the Russians, to win, to be preeminent, to possess leadership, to be first, to avoid being second-rate, and so on. Sometimes, of course, these are instrumental values; for example, preeminence is sometimes desired as a means of reinforcing military security. But at least as often these seem to be goal values, desired for their own sake. We want preeminence, leadership, etc., as good in themselves. We can't stand being second, let alone second-rate.

Apart from the response to the Soviet challenge, there is also evidence of a search for pride by responding to the challenges of nature. As Dr. Glennan said, "There is man's unwillingness to leave unconquered any new and adventurous frontier."

I will present evidence along the above lines in the pages that follow. Dealing first with the Soviet challenge, I propose to demonstrate that hurt to American pride, and a corresponding desire to regain and maintain pride, has been a vitally important factor in the space effort—above all a vitally important factor in the decision of 1961 to expand and accelerate the effort. And, given the role of pride in this connection, I wonder whether it does not play a much more important role than has been recognized in other aspects of American political behavior, in both domestic and international affairs. Toward the end of the chapter, I will deal with the search for pride through responding to the challenges of nature.

Humiliation and Pride Under Eisenhower

Understandably, President Eisenhower gave no public evidence of a feeling of humiliation because the Russians got into space first and so impressively. As we have seen in the preceding chapter, he rejected the notion that we were competing in a race. It follows, so far as he was concerned, that pride was not much involved, though he departed slightly from this view in one or two instances to be noted below.

Outside the White House, however, the prevailing attitude was very different. Speaking of the Sputniks, Secretary of State Dulles struck a key note.

No doubt the Communist rulers gained a success. They have an opportunity to gloat, an opportunity that they have not neglected. But Sputnik, mocking the American people with its "beep-beep," may go down in history as Mr. Khrushchev's boomerang.

It jolted the American people. . . . A wave of mortification, anger, and fresh determination swept the country.[3]

Obviously, a people mocked and mortified by a gloating opponent is not going to be very happy about the situation.

NASA Administrator Glennan spoke explicitly of the impact of the Sputniks on American pride. "The blow to our national pride in this unexpected achievement of Soviet science was tremendous." [4] The Sputniks "finally shocked our people into a state of real concern about our standing in the race for technological leadership in the world." [5]

Most of us were torn between desire to applaud a great scientific and technological accomplishment and a troubled concern over having been bested, even temporarily, in a field where we had assumed, complacently, that we held at least a comfortable lead.

Our reaction . . . was to mobilize our resources for a concerted effort to secure the position which we had thought we held.[6]

Dr. Glennan once commented to the House Committee on Science and Astronautics that the Russians were no doubt motivated by a desire to "beat America," and that he in turn was motivated by a desire not to be beaten. When a member of the committee asked whether he wouldn't change the statement to indicate in a positive way that we were determined to win, he agreed. "Yes, absolutely." [7] In another connection he declared that "when, as in the space program, the United States is made to look second-best, there is an outpouring of public opinion in this country demanding that we regain first place." [8]

The desire to regain and maintain basis for pride was even more evident in the pages of the *Congressional Record*. Senator Johnston

---

[3] John Foster Dulles, "The Role of Negotiation," *Department of State Bulletin*, 38 (February 3, 1958), 159.

[4] T. Keith Glennan, "My True Security," statement of July 21, 1959, mimeo., p. 4.

[5] T. Keith Glennan, address of December 17, 1958, mimeo., p. 3.

[6] T. Keith Glennan, address of May 7, 1959, mimeo., pp. 2-3.

[7] U.S. Congress, House, Committee on Science and Astronautics, *To Amend the National Aeronautics and Space Act of 1958*, Hearings . . . on H. Res. 9675, 86th Cong., 2d Sess., 1960, pp. 519, 522.

[8] T. Keith Glennan, "The Task for Government," in Lincoln P. Bloomfield, ed., *Outer Space. Prospects for Man and Society*, The American Assembly (Englewood Cliffs: Prentice-Hall, 1962), p. 99.

of South Carolina was disturbed by the thought that the Vanguard failures were getting "scornful and ridiculing headlines all over the world," and he believed that the poor showing of the United States was "not only humiliating but dangerous." Representative John W. McCormack was mortified to think that America was becoming "the butt of foreign jokes." After the Army got Explorer I into orbit, editorials on the event were reprinted in the *Congressional Record*. According to the *Washington Post*: "Americans and their colleagues in the free world can once more lift their heads. The successful launching of the first American earth satellite . . . is a tremendously welcome achievement. It will help revitalize the sorely buffeted self-confidence of the free peoples." [9] And the *Portland Oregonian* said: "The technical achievement of putting a satellite of earth into orbit caused a great sigh of relief to go up among Americans. It was not that anyone really doubted that our scientists and military men could, in time, match the Russian experiments in outer space. It was more that Americans, a prideful people, do not like to accept the idea that others can do some things better than we; that others may lead in any field." [10] Representative George Miller cited the view that "we can't be ahead in everything," and he denounced it. This indicated that "we are going to be second-best in some things. I don't subscribe to that." [11]

In the spring of 1958 President Eisenhower recommended the establishment of NASA. The list of the purposes of the proposed organization included "the preservation [*sic!*] of the role of the United States as a leader in aeronautical and space science and technology," and Congress included these words in the National Aeronautics and Space Act of 1958. Mr. Glennan endorsed them and in effect changed "a leader" to "the leader." "I believe, with the utmost conviction, that we have a national—yes, an international—responsibility to lead in the exploration of space." [12] "I never envisioned my assignment as one where I would always be driving the second place entry in this race. . . . I have faith that we will win this contest." [13] "The preservation of this nation's role

---

[9] *Congressional Record*, Vol. 104, Pt. 2 (February 3, 1958), 1198. The quotation contains an interesting assumption concerning the extent to which "the free world" and "the free peoples" identify themselves with the United States.

[10] *Ibid.*, Vol. 104, Pt. 2 (February 5, 1958), 1728.

[11] U.S. Congress, House, Committee on Science and Astronautics, *International Control of Outer Space*, Hearings, 86th Cong., 1st Sess., 1959, p. 10.

[12] T. Keith Glennan, address of December 17, 1958, mimeo., pp. 10-11.

[13] T. Keith Glennan, address of November 19, 1959, mimeo., p. 3.

as a leader in this field in which there is only one other real contender does not permit us to run second." [14]

When Representative McCormack reported on the text of the above act as agreed on in conference committee, he described the goal as "leapfrogging" Soviet accomplishments. "Leapfrogging" was one of the favorite words of the House Committee on Science and Astronautics. "A great many of us are tired of playing tag with the Russians; we would like to jump ahead of them." [15] A report of a House committee later indicated that after Sputnik "the United States had no alternative" to committing itself to a major space program. "There was the painful fact of hurt national pride to overcome." [16]

Of course, pride was not the only factor. Getting ahead of the Russians was also thought to have implications for military power and for prestige. Moreover, Democrats sought political advantage, especially in election years, by scoring the Republican Administration for failings in space as well as in other realms. Nevertheless, concern for pride, demonstrated by both Democrats and Republicans, was clearly a powerful force.

In 1960 the House committee examined a 10-year space plan developed by NASA, a major question being whether through it we would "catch up with and surpass the Soviet Union." Most of the members of the committee were dissatisfied. The plan was good as far as it went, but it did not go far enough. "The space program is not being pushed with sufficient urgency." The Chairman of the committee, Overton Brooks, seemed scornful of the plan on the ground that it was inadequate "to wrest space leadership from the U.S.S.R." [17] The committee called for its expansion and acceleration, including a change in the timing of a manned lunar landing from "beyond 1970" to "this decade." [18]

[14] T. Keith Glennan, address of September 28, 1959, NASA News Release No. 59-225, p. 12.

[15] U.S. Congress, House, Select Committee on Astronautics and Space Exploration, *Astronautics and Space Exploration*, Hearings . . . on H. Res. 11881, 85th Cong., 2d Sess., 1958, p. 512 (hereafter cited as House Hearings, *Astronautics and Space Exploration*, 1958).

[16] U.S. Congress, House, Committee on Government Operations, Eleventh Report, *Organization and Management of Missile Programs*, H. Rpt. No. 1121, 86th Cong., 1st Sess., 1959, pp. 1-2.

[17] Overton Brooks, "The Place of Government in the Utilization of Space," in Simon Ramo, ed., *Peacetime Uses of Outer Space* (New York: McGraw-Hill, 1961), p. 204.

[18] U.S. Congress, House, Committee on Science and Astronautics, *Space, Missiles, and the Nation*, H. Rpt. No. 2092, 86th Cong., 2d Sess., 1960, p. 55.

General Medaris' *Countdown for Decision*—concerned largely with the development of launching vehicles for missiles and satellites at the Army's Ballistic Missile Agency in Huntsville— is implicitly a curious commentary on attitudes toward space competition. Formally the General adhered to the Eisenhower line: "We are not in competition with anyone in the satellite program." But less formally the book pictures its author as an aggressive, highly competitive person who views life as an unremitting battle, bitter and joyous, for achievement and success; and it is full of evidence of his burning zeal to beat not only the Air Force but also the Russians. He speaks of Sputnik I beeping "derisively" overhead and of begging DOD to give the Army a chance to put up a satellite and "restore some measure of the Free World's damaged pride." [19]

Wernher von Braun also comments on the impact of the Sputniks. "The reaction to these events has been profound. They triggered a period of self-appraisal rarely equaled in modern times. Overnight it became popular to question the bulwarks of our society: our public educational system, our industrial strength, international policy, defense strategy and forces, the capabilities of our science and technology. Even the moral fiber of our people came under searching examination." [20] A British author refers to the "chagrin and dismay" in the United States after Sputnik I. "The Americans are crestfallen because it shakes their confidence in their technological supremacy." [21] Several years later, after the Shepard flight, the London *Times* spoke of "the demon of inferiority which, since October 4, 1957 . . . has disturbed American well-being." [22]

It would not be correct to leave the impression that after Sputnik all Americans felt as the above statements suggest. Donald N. Michael points out that the results of public opinion polls "did not indicate unanimous psychological shock or national loin-girding." [23] But the fact that, in February, 1958, almost half

---

[19] Major General John B. Medaris, USA (Ret.), *Countdown for Decision* (New York: Putnam, 1960), pp. 155-57.

[20] Wernher von Braun, "Can We Withstand the Acid Test?" *Chemical and Engineering News*, 36 (March 3, 1958), 52.

[21] Ritchie Calder, in Richard Witkin, ed., *The Challenge of the Sputniks* (Garden City: Doubleday, 1958), pp. 12, 14.

[22] London *Times*, May 6, 1961, p. 9B.

[23] Donald N. Michael, "Beginning of the Space Age and American Public Opinion," *Public Opinion Quarterly*, 24 (Winter, 1960), 578-79.

did admit to shock is of considerable significance. Moreover, some of the indifference was due to a confident expectation that the United States would soon match Soviet space achievements, an expectation that gradually crumbled away in mortifying fashion. Further, if members of Congress and others in Washington believed that the American people demanded preeminence in space, that is probably more significant than the actual state of public opinion, especially when they themselves seemed to endorse the demand. My impression is that the wound inflicted by the Sputniks on our pride came to smart more and more as the months went by, becoming unbearable in the spring of 1961 when Kennedy—also influenced by other motives—recommended the expansion and acceleration of the program.

The Demand for Achievement Under Kennedy

The evidence is abundant that the complex of values here identified with pride was a powerful factor in influencing President Kennedy and Congress to expand and accelerate the space program in the spring of 1961, and that it has remained an important factor ever since.

Deputy Secretary of Defense Roswell L. Gilpatric says, "The United States was stung into further action by the Soviet space successes." [24] The late Overton Brooks commented in April, 1961: "My objective, and this is speaking individually, is to beat the Russians," which led a member of the committee, Mr. Fulton, to say, "May I just join you in that. That is fine." Mr. Fulton was "darned tired of being second." [25] According to Mr. Brooks "every member of the committee" felt that there was "no room for thinking of second place for the U.S.A. in any part of the space program." [26] The House majority leader, Mr. McCormack, declared that the committee "stands not for catching up—but for surpassing." Representative Bell, though not sure of all the reasons for the space program, was sure of one: "Whether we see our space program as a matter of national defense, as a matter of scientific research

[24] Roswell L. Gilpatric, remarks of May 16, 1962, Department of Defense, Office of Public Affairs, News Release No. 774-62, p. 4.

[25] U.S. Congress, House, Committee on Science and Astronautics, *1962 NASA Authorization*, Hearings . . . on H. Res. 3238 and H. Res. 6029, 87th Cong., 1st Sess., 1961, Part 1, p. 380; Part 2, p. 828 (hereafter cited as House Hearings, *1962 NASA Authorization*).

[26] *Congressional Record*, Vol. 107, No. 87 (May 24, 1961), 8234.

and development, as a matter of national prestige, or as the great
adventure of our age, we know that the people of the United
States are demanding that this country pass Russia and become
No. 1 in space." [27] Representative Daddario called for "a new
sense of dedication to the goal of being first in space." Representative King felt "a lump of lead in my heart" when it became
clear that Russia had beaten the United States to a manned
orbital flight—the Gagarin flight. "Who ever heard of the name
of the second man to fly nonstop from New York to Paris?" He
favored "any program, regardless of the cost, that would put us
definitely in the race to reach the moon first." [28] To Senator Dodd
the various Soviet "firsts" were "devastating humiliations." Representative Randall said that "people were not simply shocked and
awed, they were literally stunned" by Sputnik I, and that after
the Gagarin flight they were "downright hurt that we must again
take second place."

President Kennedy was publicly restrained about the space
program in the early weeks after his inauguration. In his State
of the Union message in January, 1961, he explicitly acknowledged a space race, but it is not at all clear that he gloried in it.
"Today this country is ahead in the science and technology of
space, while the Soviet Union is ahead in the capacity to lift
large vehicles into orbit. Both nations would help themselves
as well as other nations by removing these endeavors from the
bitter and wasteful competition of the cold war." In April he
seemed restrained less by a tendency to deplore competition
than by purely practical considerations. He wondered whether
the country was so far behind, in terms of boosters, that we were
going to be second for the rest of the decade, regardless of what
we might do—whether any program offered us "hope of being
pioneers." But however tired Mr. Fulton might be of being second, "no one is more tired than I am." "If we can get to the
moon before the Russians, we should." In signing legislation pertaining to the National Aeronautics and Space Council he described it as "a key step toward moving the United States into
its proper place in the space race," and he did not feel it neces-

[27] *Ibid.*, p. 8243.
[28] *Ibid.*, Vol. 107, No. 62 (April 13, 1961), 5382; House Hearings, *1962
NASA Authorization*, Part 1, p. 375; U.S. Congress, House, Committee on
Science and Astronautics, *Discussion of Soviet Man-in-Space Shot*, Hearings,
87th Cong., 1st Sess., 1961, pp. 3, 4, 7, 13, 14.

sary to specify what he meant by the country's "proper place." [29] Others have spoken of the country's "rightful place," equally confident that everyone would know what they meant.

A description of Kennedy's recommendation of May 25, 1961, for an expansion and acceleration of the space program is given in Chapter 2. In making it, Kennedy cited the terms of the legislation creating NASA, calling for the preservation of America's role as "a leader," and he called this "a great responsibility." But he made it clear implicitly then and explicitly later that a role as "a leader" was not enough. We must be "the leader." In his Rice University address in 1962 he said that we would "become the world's leading spacefaring nation." "No nation which expects to be the leader of other nations can expect to stay behind in this race for space. . . . This generation does not intend to founder in the backwash of the coming age of space. We mean to be a part of it—we mean to lead it." "Before the end of this decade, the United States will be ahead." [30]

NASA spokesmen and others testify to the importance of a spirit of competitiveness—of a desire to be first—in influencing the decision that Kennedy made. Webb points to the fact that "within two months and four days after [Kennedy's] inauguration, the United States launched five satellites. In the same period, the Russians launched three satellites and a Venus probe." One of the Soviet satellites weighed more than four times as much as our heaviest, and one of them contained Gagarin. "In the face of these demonstrations, it became obvious that the United States could not do less than its best in space if we were to remain a first-class Nation. . . . Space activity was coming to the forefront as never before as an element of international competition." [31]

The factor of competition was also very influential in the selection of a manned lunar landing rather than some other goal as the number one feature of the Kennedy program. Given the Gagarin flight, the American response had to be in the form of manned flight rather than instrumented flight; but the man could

[29] U.S. President, *Public Papers of the Presidents of the United States*, John F. Kennedy . . . January 20 to December 31, 1961 (Washington, 1962), pp. 262, 309-10, 321-22 (hereafter cited as *Public Papers of the Presidents*).
[30] News conference of August 22, 1962.
[31] James E. Webb, "What's Next in Space," address of April 2, 1962, NASA News Release No. 62-79, pp. 5-6.

have been sent around the moon and back, or to Mars. Boosters were apparently the crucial factor here. The Russians had boosters that gave them a good chance of staging a manned circumlunar flight before we could, making it too risky for us to fix this as the key event in the space Olympics. Even their boosters, however, were not large enough for a prudent attempt at a manned lunar landing, so in relation to this event their lead was problematical, if it existed at all. Mr. Webb made this line of thought clear later in explaining that the decision to make a manned lunar landing the main goal had depended, among other things,

upon a judgment concerning our relative position vis-à-vis the Soviet Union and our chances of winning such a competition. We want to be first; and if there were not a good chance of being first, the whole enterprise would take on a different hue. It is the combined judgment of those responsible for this decision that we are not under any overall disadvantage as we set our sights on sending men on a round trip to the moon at the earliest possible date. . . . Both the Soviet Union and ourselves must develop propulsion systems vastly different from anything in our inventories today in order to undertake manned expeditions to the moon. . . . We believe that we can win.[32]

Congress endorsed Kennedy's recommendations of May 25, 1961, with near unanimity and practically without debate. Senator Cooper of Kentucky was a bit plaintive. He thought that the President had "not made it clear to the country, the basic reasons why the United States should embark on a program to send a man to the moon." The President's statement had "emphasized too much the feat, rather than the broad purposes and advantages." "Much more must be done to explain to the Congress and the people of the United States, the reasons which demand the program." [33] But Senator Cooper did not oppose the recommendation.

Concern for pride continues. John Glenn's flight—the first American manned orbital flight—released a veritable orgy of self-congratulation in Congress. The flight inspired "a feeling of deep pride and quiet jubilation." It was "a monumental achievement of which America can be justly proud." It "revived in all of us our pride and self-confidence." "This is the day when a proud government pays tribute. . . ." "Our spirits soared with the rocket.

[32] James E. Webb, address of September 27, 1961, NASA News Release No. 61-215, p. 11. Cf. the statement by Hugh L. Dryden, NASA's Deputy Administrator, in "News Conference on Russian Space Shot," NASA News Release, August 15, 1962, p. 19.

[33] Congressional Record, Vol. 107, No. 106 (June 26, 1961), 10,494.

We enjoyed a surge of pride." Editorials that congressmen entered in the *Congressional Record* likewise stress pride in Glenn's feat. "Tuesday millions of Americans figuratively held their breath. Today they are holding their heads high. They have reason to be proud. . . . We did it. We proved it. . . . Americans have good cause today to look the rest of the world in the eye and be proud." Glenn himself was invited to speak to a joint session of Congress, and among other things said:

I am certainly glad to see that pride in our country and its accomplishments is not a thing of the past.

I still get a hard-to-define feeling inside when the flag goes by—and I know that all of you do, too. Today as we rode up Pennsylvania Avenue from the White House and saw the tremendous outpouring of feeling on the part of so many thousands of our people I got this same feeling all over again. Let us hope that none of us ever loses it.

A few weeks later Senator Gore spoke of the "gnawing doubts" that had been felt after Sputnik "as to the ability of a democracy to meet the challenge of an organized, monolithic society," but the Glenn flight gave "a much-needed shot in the arm . . . to the pride of the American people." "The acclamation of the world poured in; the Nation was jubilant." [34]

Those involved in implementing the program and those in Congress primarily responsible for it continue to speak repeatedly of pride and the immediately related values. According to Victor L. Anfuso, a former member of the House space committee: "By far the most important bonus from this adventure [in space] will be its effect on the human spirit. We can look for Americans to walk with a quicker step and to hold their heads higher. A people who have become a little satiated by the greatest standard of living the world has ever known will be refreshed by the new frontiers we will open. Vaulting ambition will be restored, the kind of ambition that made us great in the first place.[35] Mr. Anfuso spoke of America's "rightful supremacy and leadership in space." Mr. Webb says, "We want to give the American people something in modern terms that they can be as proud of as the heroic march of the settlers who came West over the Oregon Trail. . . ." He expresses confidence that "we will make the

[34] U.S. Congress, Joint Committee on Atomic Energy, Subcommittee on Research, Development, and Radiation, *Space Nuclear Power Applications*, Hearings, 87th Cong., 2d Sess., 1962, p. 352.

[35] *Congressional Record*, Vol. 108, No. 172 (September 24, 1962), A7063.

manned lunar landing and return before they do." He thinks that preeminence is already virtually assured: "In my view, we are entering a period when our national decision and the debates which accompany them will not so much relate to whether and when we can achieve pre-eminence in space, but the rate at which we should proceed beyond the time when this pre-eminence is achieved—beyond the time when we have begun manned exploration of the moon." [36] Dr. Edward C. Welsh, Executive Secretary of the National Space Council, says that "we did not have any sensible choice as to whether we would or would not enter the race to win. Second place for the U.S. is unacceptable. Our goal is space leadership." [37] Like others, he stresses additional goals as well. On the occasion of another Russian first—the twin flights and near rendezvous of August, 1962—Representative George P. Miller, Chairman of the House Committee on Science and Astronautics, voiced reassurances: "Our program . . . will give this nation the leadership in space exploration. . . . In the long run this Nation will overtake the competition with accomplishments second to none in the field of manned space flight as we have already done in space science, in communication satellites, and in weather satellites." [38]

Dr. George L. Haller, Vice President of the General Electric Company, points to a latent function of the space program that is implicit in what is said above:

One of the added values of the manned space flight program is its ability to marshal the spirit of the American people in support of a rather magnanimous national effort. In my lifetime I have only seen this attitude manifested in the grim determination to defeat our enemies on the battlefield. . . .

One of our objectives must be to nurture this dedication and to make it grow into a strong influence on the American spirit. [39]

D. Brainerd Holmes, former Director of Manned Space Flight in NASA, makes statements similar to those that in earlier times went with imperialism. He thinks that response to "the challenge

[36] James E. Webb, address of November 14, 1962, NASA News Release.

[37] Edward C. Welsh, "Economic Aspects of Space Program," address of June 12, 1962, mimeo., p. 7.

[38] *Congressional Record,* Vol. 108, No. 142 (August 13, 1962), 15,242.

[39] U.S. Congress, House, Committee on Science and Astronautics, Subcommittee on Manned Space Flight, *1963 NASA Authorization,* Hearings . . . on H. Res. 10100, 87th Cong., 2d Sess., 1962, Part 2, p. 427 (hereafter cited as House Hearings, *1963 NASA Authorization*).

of the unknown . . . has been a measure of society's vitality, and, ultimately, has determined the course of civilization." Project Apollo "exemplifies our urge to act, to discover, and to excel."[40] Reaching the moon has become "a matter of America's pride."

Great nations cannot mark time. . . . The study of history discloses that the lives of nations and civilizations are filled with change. They do not stand still. They grow or they shrink. . . .

If we do not make these efforts, we will not be first on the moon, we will not be first in space and, one day soon, we will not be first on earth.

With the support of the American people, and with the help of God, we will not be second.[41]

To be sure, as noted in the preceding chapter, there are dissident voices. Those who doubt whether the manned space flight program is justified by its contribution to national prestige tend to raise the same question with regard to pride or self-esteem. The Senate Republican Policy Committee, for example, not only deplores "the adolescent desire to beat the Russians in a space race"; it goes on to say, "The United States has been committed to a race for the moon, partly at least due to our own emotional drive always to be first, always to be best in whatever we try. For momentary transcendence over the Soviet Union we have pledged our wealth, national talent, and our honor."

Scientists and the Soviet Challenge

I pointed out in the last chapter that the natural scientists are not much inclined to mention the search for national prestige as an appropriate, deliberate motive of the space effort. And, in truth, not many of them mention response to the Soviet challenge —to the challenge posed by man—as important; they are more concerned, as we will shortly see, with the challenges of nature. But some mention the Soviet challenge, and their attitudes are worth notice. Lloyd V. Berkner, former Chairman of the Space Science Board of the National Academy of Sciences, is prominent among them. He speaks of "our intellectual deterioration as an

---

[40] U.S. Congress, House, Committee on Science and Astronautics, Subcommittee on Manned Space Flight, *1964 NASA Authorization*, Hearings, 88th Cong., 1st Sess., 1963, Part 2, pp. 888-89.

[41] Foreword by D. Brainerd Holmes to Walter Sullivan, ed., *America's Race for the Moon. The New York Times Story of Project Apollo* (New York: Random House, 1962); D. Brainerd Holmes, address of March 21, 1963, NASA News Release, pp. 5, 15.

advanced nation in the pre-Sputnik days," and goes on as follows:
The Sputnik has demonstrated that we are engaged in more than a military contest; it is a total contest in which intellectual leadership plays a major role. The contest requires that the victor demonstrate the ability of his system to provide opportunity to accomplish easily those things that men want and admire. Promise of individual freedom and dignity, and mere material welfare, are not enough. To these essential ingredients peoples expect of a nation that would be great, the added opportunities to challenge the frontiers of mind and nature—opportunities that man has treasured in his rise to civilization. The world's recognition of the challenge of space is but a symbol of this need.[42]

I might cavil at this statement on the ground that it does not recognize clearly enough that the desired intellectual leadership should include leadership of a political sort, e.g., the identification of a coherent set of values that will be attractive at home and abroad, and an effective strategy for promoting them. But a predisposition toward the natural sciences on the part of a natural scientist is not surprising.

In another context Dr. Berkner says: "The United States with her leadership in advancing man's welfare—a leadership triggered by a superb science and technology—has become the standard that must be surpassed by any other nation if that nation is also to claim the distinction of leadership." [43] Dr. Berkner does not say how he determined that science and technology "triggered" American leadership in advancing man's welfare. A political scientist would be more likely to refer to the principles of the Declaration of Independence and of the Constitution, and he might mention the Truman Doctrine and the Marshall Plan. But the main point is Dr. Berkner's assumption that leadership is good.

"Man," says Dr. Berkner, "prizes the idea of escape from the earth as the highest symbol of progress." "Therefore, the nation that can capture and hold that symbol will carry the banner of world leadership. Consequently, leadership in space exploration has a real political meaning. Failure in that leadership means inevitably falling into the status of a second-class nation with the heavy costs to our way of free enterprise which subjugation to

[42] U.S. Congress, House, Committee on Appropriations, National Science Foundation, National Academy of Sciences, *Report on the International Geophysical Year* (February, 1959), Hearings Before the Subcommittee . . ., 86th Cong., 1st Sess., pp. 192-93.

[43] Lloyd V. Berkner, "Space Research—A Permanent Peacetime Activity," in Ramo, *op. cit.*, p. 7.

others would involve." [44] To a political scientist such generaliza-
tions are breath-taking, and one wonders what scientific method
led to them. But again the significant point is that Dr. Berkner
accepts world leadership as a value for which to strive.

Some other scientists also regard Soviet achievements as a
challenge either to their pride as scientists or to their pride as
patriots. In 1958 Dr. W. H. Pickering, Director of Caltech's Jet
Propulsion Laboratory, described the Sputniks as a "remarkable
achievement," and said that it "behooves us to either accept second-
class status or demonstrate to all the world that we are capable
of an even more dynamic development." [45] Also in 1958 a proposal
by the American Rocket Society and the Rocket and Satellite
Research Panel, with James A. Van Allen signing for the latter,
declared it "imperative that the United States establish and maintain scientific and technological leadership in outer space research
in the interests of long-term human progress and national survival. . . . It is already clear that international leadership hinges,
to a very great extent, on preeminence in scientific and technological matters." [46] Testifying before the House Select Committee
on Astronautics and Space Exploration, Dr. Van Allen expressed
general sympathy with a statement by someone else that we were
involved in "an intellectual race," a "race for intellectual preeminence," and he thought it "quite easy to visualize, if we don't
get cracking in this field, that my young son, for example, will
want to go to Russia to study physics. By the time that he is of
college age, it may well be that this is the best place to do so.
I think that we are strongly in danger of losing intellectual leadership. . . . I think we will become a second-rate nation if we do
not support our best talent in basic research." [47] These statements
assume that leadership is desirable, both as an instrumental value
and as a goal value; and the final statement seems to make it a goal
value that the nation be first-rate rather than second-rate.

In 1957 Dr. Edward Teller expressed the conviction that in 10
years the best scientists would be found in Russia. "If one looks
at this situation realistically, one must not say that we ought to
retain leadership in science, but rather, that we should do every-

---

[44] *Ibid.*
[45] House Hearings, *Astronautics and Space Exploration,* 1958, p. 804.
[46] *Ibid.,* pp. 820-22.
[47] *Ibid.,* p. 868.

thing in our power to regain that leadership." [48] Five years later, "emphatically" supporting the space program, he said: "I believe that we should be, and could be, in the first place, and that in the long run it will be of great importance in many ways, most of which cannot be foreseen at present, to continue or rather to recapture leadership in this extremely important field." [49]

That the United States should not strive for world leadership seems unthinkable even to some of the scientists who have doubts about the various kinds of seeming distortions of emphasis that the space program has brought. For example, Dr. George B. Kistiakowsky, after a critical appraisal, feels bound to deny, twice, that he is suggesting a secondary role for the United States. "To repeat, we cannot accept a secondary role in future outerspace exploration. But true leadership must be seen in the context of far broader efforts. We must be constantly aware that our strength lies in excellence spread over a wide scientific and technological base. . . . We must continue to move across the entire broad front of scientific and technological advance. Thus, as a nation, we will remain a world leader." [50]

At the same time, some scientists and others dwell on the point that we cannot be first in everything. For example, President J. C. Warner of the Carnegie Institute of Technology emphasizes this view: "The United States does not have a monopoly on creativity in science and engineering any more than it does in art, music, and literature. To pursue a national policy that attempts to create the impression that it does and to pour our national wealth and national talent recklessly into the preservation of such a myth, is both silly and dangerous." [51] No doubt everyone shares the view that in fact we cannot be first in everything. But Dr. Warner does not say, nor, I think, would anyone else, that we should be satisfied to be second in everything; and he does not suggest the criteria for determining in what areas to seek to be first and in what areas to accept a secondary position. In any event, the recognition of the fact that we cannot be first in everything does

[48] U.S. Congress, Senate, Committee on Armed Services, Preparedness Investigating Subcommittee, *Inquiry into Satellite and Missile Programs,* Hearings, 85th Cong., 1st Sess., 1957, Part 1, p. 43.

[49] House Hearings, *1963 NASA Authorization,* Part 3, p. 1615.

[50] George B. Kistiakowsky, "Science and Foreign Affairs," *Science,* 131 (April 8, 1960), 1020.

[51] J. C. Warner, "National Goals and the University," commencement address at Duquesne University, June 3, 1963, mimeo., p. 6.

not necessarily call for a renunciation of the ideal. David Mc-Clelland's *The Achieving Society* is in point here. Certainly the achievement motive is a powerful factor in our society. We want to get ahead, to do things, to make progress. We put great emphasis on virtuosity in almost every imaginable field of activity. In sports, in the arts, and in the sciences, we applaud and reward the man who excels. We speak deprecatingly of those who do not strive to achieve up to the level of their ability, and sometimes actually penalize them. Conversely, we praise those who do their best, and acclaim those who set new and higher standards. The competition and the comparisons occur within many frames of reference, including a world-wide frame of reference. Sometimes expression of the motive verges on megalomania, as when we speak of winning the "World Series" even though all of the teams are American—and even though, for many years, they all came from the small northeastern section of the country.

Now people obviously differ in selecting the kind of activity in which they think it important to excel. Moreover, the choice is normally private and decentralized, and for the most part it remains so. There has been no governmental decision to seek to be first in everything—only in space. And for a variety of obvious reasons competition in this sphere, if it was to occur at all, could not be left in private hands. The shift of the locus of decision may or may not portend much for the future. Conceivably the selection of one national goal may lead to the selection of another. If it does, the effect on American life may well be profound.

Responding to the Challenge of Nature

The challenge of Moscow has undoubtedly been a far more important factor than the challenge of nature in goading the United States into an extensive space program, and, though there is some reason for doubt on the point, this seems likely to continue to be the case. Nevertheless, the challenge of nature is there, and it is of some interest to assess reactions to it.

I have already noted that President Eisenhower's Science Advisory Committee gave as the first reason for a space program "the compelling urge of man to explore and to discover, the thrust of curiosity that leads men to try to go where no one has gone before." Many others play on this theme. Mr. Webb speaks of "the spiritual awakening which accompanies the pursuit of a new, vast and enormously challenging goal." Jerome B. Wiesner, former Chairman of the President's Science Advisory Committee, thinks of space exploration "as one of the really great adventures of this century. This is enough of a human motivation to want to do it— just because it is challenging." [52] President Kennedy himself spoke of space as "one of the great adventures of all time." Moreover, like many others, he explained the desire to get to the moon in the same way as George Mallory explained the desire to climb Mount Everest: "Because it is there." [53] Getting there becomes an end in itself. And getting there becomes the task of government, not an activity left in the private domain.

Natural scientists seem especially inclined to stress response to the challenges of nature. The theme appears again and again in the testimony that a number of them gave to the Senate space committee in June, 1963. Harold C. Urey's testimony was especially eloquent on the point.[54] He said that five or six years earlier, when interviewed by a reporter, he had taken a rather negative stand about proposals being made for the exploration of space, feeling "that the expense of the program would be out of all proportion to the scientific knowledge to be gained." But before the report of the interview could be published, he changed his mind.

The reason for the change in point of view was that overnight it had occurred to me that when men are able to do a striking bit of discovery, such as going above the atmosphere of the Earth or to the Moon, men somewhere would do this regardless of whether I thought that it was a sensible idea or not. All of history shows that men have this characteristic. Therefore, it seemed to me that the proper attitude for a scientist was to aid the program and especially to try to see that good science was done during such explorations.

Dr. Urey went on to elaborate on this theme in various ways. The "real reason" for undertaking the space program, he thought, was "some curious drive to try to do what might be thought to be the impossible—to try to excel in one way or another—to try to do what has never been done before." But why not build more

[52] "Thinking Ahead with Jerome Wiesner," *International Science and Technology*, February, 1962, p. 32.

[53] *Public Papers of the Presidents*, Kennedy, 1962, p. 671.

[54] U.S. Congress, Senate, Committee on Aeronautical and Space Sciences, *Scientists' Testimony on Space Goals*, Hearings, 88th Cong., 1st Sess., 1963, pp. 51-53 (hereafter cited as Senate Hearings, *Scientists' Testimony on Space Goals*).

houses? Why not cure more diseases? Why not provide better
education? He responded to these questions by saying that the
fraction of the population "interested in doing these daring things"
in space is the same fraction "interested in doing more in regard
to these other problems." He thought that "if we should decide
not to do the space program we will probably do less for education than we would otherwise." "There is nothing so deadly as not
to hold up to people the opportunity to do great and wonderful
things, if we wish to stimulate them in an active way." He pointed
to the contrast between Athens and Corinth. "Athens built the
Acropolis. Corinth was a commercial city, interested in purely
materialistic things. Today we admire Athens, visit it, preserve
the old temples, yet we hardly ever set foot in Corinth." We
could "choose to be a fat cat, merely be wealthy, rich, comfortable,
and not take a dare," but if we did it would indicate that "something has gone out of this country."

The space program is fundamentally a great adventure for all of us. . . .
When the first man sets off to the moon, all of us will watch the news
that day. I fear none of us will work if we can possibly avoid it. We will
admire the men who dare to go. We will be pleased if we have been able
to make a small contribution to the event and will take a great pride in
the fact that we of this century have been able to do such a remarkable
thing. The space program in our way is our cathedral which we are
building.

Pervading Dr. Urey's testimony is a recognition of a need for
achievement as a powerful motive. "Creative men do not work on
tasks merely for their salaries. They work because they get a
sense of accomplishment." The implication of his testimony was
that building more houses or curing more diseases or providing
more and better education are not terribly inspiring because we
already have had so much experience along these lines. To focus
on them would be relatively dull and boring. But to focus on the
great and exciting challenges of space would in some way release
energies in other areas as well. Dr. Urey's thought seemed to be
that this would happen through encouraging in the country a
spirit of creative daring that would come to pervade fields of
activity in addition to space. And he may have had the thought
in mind that a full response to the challenges of space would
indicate that political control is held by those who will favor responding to other challenges too.

Several of the other scientists based their support for the space
program on about the same case. Martin Schwarzschild, Professor

of Astronomy at Princeton, spoke as follows: "The idea of man leaving this earth and flying to another celestial body and landing there and stepping out and walking over that body has a fascination and a driving force that can get the country to a level of energy, ambition, and will that I do not see in any other undertaking. I think if we are honest with ourselves, we must admit that we needed that impetus extremely strongly." [55] He thought that the staggering effort required for the flight to the moon is worthwhile only if the fascination and historic uniqueness of this undertaking fire the energies of all of us in this country back to those heights that were characteristic of the great periods in the past. . . . I sincerely believe that the space program, with its manned landing on the moon, if wisely executed, will become the spearhead for a broad front of courageous and energetic activities in all the fields of endeavor of the human mind—activities which could not be carried out except in a mental climate of ambition and confidence which such a spearhead can give.

In his eyes the issue was not between other worthwhile activities and space but rather between "relaxing back into the lethargic state of the early fifties" and going ahead in space competition "with gaiety and vision," consciously using its stimulus to get things done on a broad front of activity.[56]

Lloyd V. Berkner has expressed a similar thought: "Human society—man in a group—rises out of its lethargy to new levels of productivity only under the stimulus of deeply inspiring and commonly appreciated goals. A lethargic world serves no cause well; a spirited world working diligently toward earnestly desired goals provides the means and the strength toward which many ends can be satisfied." [57] Dr. Berkner describes "the aspiration of men to reach out to the stars, to accomplish what men have not accomplished before" as a "very deep, driving force within man . . . that has caused him to rise to unparalleled social accomplishment." [58] Dr. Frederick Seitz, President of the National Academy of Sciences, considers the general goals of the space program "a natural continuation of the human adventure. It is unthinkable that our society, particularly Western society, can ignore this challenge." [59] Dr. Colin S. Pittendrigh, Professor of Biology at Princeton, favors the Apollo program "largely because it is so

[55] *Ibid.*, p. 155.

[56] *Ibid.*, pp. 164-65.

[57] Lloyd V. Berkner, "The Compelling Horizon," *Bulletin of the Atomic Scientists*, 19 (May, 1963), 8-9.

[58] Senate Hearings, *Scientists' Testimony on Space Goals*, p. 108.

[59] *Ibid.*, p. 93.

tangible and exciting a program and as such will serve to keep alive the interest and enthusiasm of the whole spectrum of society. . . . It is justified because . . . the program can give a sense of shared adventure and achievement to the society at large." [60]

Along the same general line, but apart from the testimony of scientists to the Senate space committee, I might cite a British scientist, Sir Bernard Lovell, who believes that the United States should spend its money on space:

The challenge of space exploration and particularly of landing men on the moon represents the greatest challenge which has ever faced the human race. Even if there were no clear scientific or other arguments for proceeding with this task, the whole history of our civilization would still impel men toward the goal. In fact, the assembly of the scientific and military with these human arguments creates such an overwhelming case that it can be ignored only by those who are blind to the teachings of history, or who wish to suspend the development of civilization at its moment of greatest opportunity and drama.[61]

At the risk of appearing trivial, let me recall that we are brought up reciting "Twinkle, twinkle, little star, how I wonder. . . ." One of the Psalms tells us that "the heavens declare the glory of God." In contrast to earth, which is mundane, we think of the moon and the planets as celestial bodies, and of space as heaven, implying a region of purity and goodness and grandeur. How much the outlook may have influenced decisions, I do not know. It is reflected facetiously by the official who left Procter & Gamble to join NASA and who spoke of it as a natural step: cleanliness was next to godliness.

The scientists testifying to the Senate committee were not all of one mind, but those who rejected the above general line of thought were in a minority. Dr. Polykarp Kusch, Professor of Physics at Columbia, took an interesting position. He agreed with all of the above except the conclusion that the space program should have a high priority now. He suggested "a possible national goal that outweights in its importance the space effort: the preservation and repair of our continent. The water table in substantial areas of America has fallen drastically. . . ." [62] Dr. Philip H. Abelson naturally took a position like the one that he had

---

[60] *Ibid.*, p. 84.

[61] Bernard Lovell, " 'The Greatest Challenge' to Man," *New York Times Magazine*, April 21, 1963, p. 48.

[62] Senate Hearings, *Scientists' Testimony on Space Goals*, p. 67.

already expressed in the journal he edits, Science: [63] "man's spirit of adventure—his desire to conquer the inanimate" was a transient and insubstantial basis for the space program; the great excitement that attended earlier exploits had dissipated soon after their achievement. "The first lunar landing will be a great occasion; subsequent boredom is inevitable." He apparently felt that since people no longer get excited about flying the Atlantic, it wasn't worth Lindbergh's while to go.

In the nature of things there is no way of knowing to what extent the national government would respond to the challenges of nature if there were no concomitant Soviet challenge. President Kennedy acknowledged the motive, and so has President Johnson, Mr. Webb, and a number of others in addition to the scientists quoted, but members of Congress do not often speak of it. Dr. James A. Van Allen thinks that "the sheer human achievement" in space exploits "has a great appeal to a substantial segment of our population." But he goes on to say that "without the concomitant aspect of international competition it is doubtful that the peaceful space effort could command 20% of its present tax support." [64]

A Joint Soviet-American Lunar Program?

When Kennedy met Khrushchev in Vienna in June, 1961, he is said to have suggested a joint expedition to the moon. "Let's go to the moon together." [65] He can scarcely have expected agreement, but even so the proposal was inconsistent with the concern for pride and prestige that dominated American decisions on space at the time. The cooperative arrangements later made with the Soviet Union, to be described in Chapter 14, had nothing to do with the lunar program and did little or nothing to modify the egoistic concerns that largely inspired American behavior. In September, 1963, as we have noted in Chapter 1, Kennedy suddenly proposed "further joint efforts in the regulation and exploration of space," and he specifically included among the possibilities a joint expedition to the moon. He professed to see no reason why the lunar

---

[63] Philip H. Abelson, "Manned Lunar Landing," Science, 140 (April 19, 1963), 267.

[64] U.S. Congress, House, Committee on Science and Astronautics, Panel on Science and Technology. Fifth Meeting, 88th Cong., 1st Sess., 1963, p. 25.

[65] New York Times, September 22, 1963, 1:2.

project should be competitive. Thus he seemed ostensibly to be responding favorably to informal suggestions from Moscow that the manned lunar program be made cooperative.[66] But it seems highly unlikely that he expected or even wanted agreement. At a press conference a month earlier he had spoken of Soviet attitudes that would preclude collaboration, and at another press conference a few weeks afterward he took the same view again. Had he genuinely sought agreement, he would presumably have explored possibilities more fully behind the scenes. His dramatic treatment of the question suggested that his proposal was itself a competitive move, perhaps preemptive, designed mainly for propaganda purposes. Moreover, though he implicitly professed willingness to give up the idea of winning a race to the moon, he did not suggest accepting a position second to that of the Soviet Union. Even so, his proposal called into question the importance of pursuing space achievements on an urgent basis in the search for pride, prestige, and security.

Concluding Comments

The *Washington Post* ran an editorial on space in the spring of 1963, when Congress was considering NASA's appropriations for the forthcoming year, which took a seemingly mystical view of the decision-making process concerning the lunar program. Enterprises of this sort, it said, "are not to be weighted on the balance against some other more practical and more appropriate or more feasible endeavor." "Such heroic enterprises move by their own laws, abide by their own rules and set their own precedents and when they are over, leave humanity with its knowledge multiplied, its future expanded, its horizons widened, its outlook sharpened and its hopes uplifted by a new sense of man's unending and unlimited possibilities." [67] This suggests that we are like chips on the stream of history carried this way and that, without choice, by forces beyond our control and perhaps beyond our knowledge. And the results are happy! In a similar category are most of the attempts to justify the space program by reference to the voyages of exploration and discovery in the fifteenth and sixteenth centuries. The references are almost always optimistic, which is to be expected of those who are achievement-oriented. Voyages of discovery that led to failure or death, or to the discovery of bleak

---

[66] Cf. *Congressional Record*, Vol. 109, No. 123 (August 9, 1963), 13,093.
[67] *Ibid.*, Vol. 109, No. 68 (May 8, 1963), 7491.

and barren regions, are rarely recalled; and if difficulties are acknowledged, it is usually with a view to magnifying the glory when success is achieved. The example of Queen Isabella and Columbus is practically the only one that counts. All voyages of discovery and exploration lead to America—to really great results that transform the course of history! Actually, everything we know indicates that the moon and the planets will be infinitely less hospitable to man, and infinitely more difficult of access, than Antarctica. They will probably be so viciously hostile as to make Antarctica seem like a South Sea island by comparison. In these circumstances it is not surprising that mysticism should show up in the attempts to explain the space effort.

But quite apart from the reasons for the effort analyzed in preceding chapters, consideration of pride and the achievement motive do much to eliminate the need for mysticism. The competitive spirit and the desire to excel are important and integral parts of American life. Sputnik was so sharp a challenge that it could not be ignored. To reinforce the Soviet challenge was the challenge of nature which, even if secondary in its influence, is not to be dismissed. By its very nature the achievement motive rests on an emotional commitment—on the postulate that it is good to excel, that it is good to test one's mettle against significant challenges. Such motives—laden with affect—are commonly much more powerful than those brought into play by detached and cold calculation. The idea that we should have a space program to advance knowledge, to stimulate technological development, or to promote economic progress involves some people emotionally, but not many—especially in political circles. Emotional involvement shows up very commonly, however, when people speak of national security, prestige, and the factors here identified as making for pride.

Alfred North Whitehead once made an observation that is relevant here. "The vigour of civilized societies is preserved by the widespread sense that high aims are worth-while. Vigorous societies harbour a certain extravagance of objectives, so that men wander beyond the safe provision of personal gratifications. All strong interests easily become impersonal, the love of a good job well done. There is a sense of harmony about such an accomplishment, the Peace brought by something worth-while." [68] Neither

---

[68] Alfred North Whitehead, *Adventure of Ideas* (New York: Macmillan, 1933), p. 371.

this statement nor what precedes it in this chapter proves that we should have a space program or that we should go to the moon. But they help to explain the choices that have been made.

Commentators on American foreign aid programs have remarked —sometimes patronizingly—on the desire of many backward and underdeveloped countries to have their own steel mill or their own national air line, or both; and they have no difficulty detecting the influence of pride in this connection. My suggestion is that we are not much different; it simply takes a different kind of achievement to make us proud. After a trip to the Soviet Union Dr. Glennan concluded that "the really important ingredient that Soviet young people—indeed, people of all ages in the Soviet Union—possess is the pride they have in their present achievements." [69] No doubt pride might take on the character of wasteful vanity, a pursuit of frills rather than substance; and it might be self-destructive. The space program involves this danger. But there are also dangers in a complacent neglect of challenge.

---

[69] T. Keith Glennan, "My True Security," statement of July 21, 1959, mimeo., p. 6.

SPECIAL INTERESTS AND ULTERIOR MOTIVES

10

The motives discussed in the preceding chapters relate directly to the presumed national interest rather than to special interests. That is, they concern instrumental and goal values that are talked about openly and commended for the benefit of the country as a whole. In principle, everyone might share them and be moved by them in the same direction. They are public rather than private. They are all socially acceptable and even admirable. They do not appear, prima facie, to be the self-serving interests of persons or entities within the nation.

But obviously not all motives are in this broad category. Special interests (i.e., the distinctive instrumental and goal values of parts of the assumed whole) necessarily get involved in group activities. NASA itself has special interests, and so do most persons and entities that have anything to do with the space program. Private interests are at stake as well as the public interest. Ulterior motives operate as well as those that are open and manifest.

By the very nature of the situation little evidence concerning special interests and ulterior motives is obtainable through ordinary methods of scholarship, and I do not have much. But we ought to recognize the category and identify pigeonholes into which data could be placed if only we had it. This makes for logical symmetry, and perhaps contributes a little toward a philosophy of interests and their interrelationships. Moreover, it may make us more alert to evidence of special interests and ulterior motives when it appears.

Common observation and experience point to several types of special interests and ulterior motives that involve an extreme and perhaps exclusive emphasis on accepted principles.

It is to be taken for granted that most of those involved in the space program, like almost everybody else, seek some kind of private advantage or satisfaction. Within limits, this is in line with the principle that it is desirable to offer personal incentives (e.g., honor, profit) to get the public good served.

It is also to be taken for granted that those in government seek to serve their constituents. Everybody is in some sense beholden. Members of Congress are to look out for the welfare and interests of the people who elect them. Members of the Executive, especially the responsible appointed officials, must in some degree cater to the wishes of others in the political system, e.g., to powerful members of Congress and to the President. At every level there is a tendency to do good turns for one's friends, and to entrust jobs and responsibilities to those with whom one is familiar. The President himself owes much to many.

It is further to be taken for granted that going concerns like to keep going. Institutions ordinarily want to preserve themselves. Responsible officials ordinarily believe in the importance of the activities and programs that they conduct, and seek to inspire those on their staffs with similar beliefs. Almost everyone, especially at the higher levels, wants to do a good job; this usually means a desire to control virtually everything pertaining to the job and a desire to handle relationships with outside agencies in such a way as to preserve and promote internal loyalty and morale.

Finally, it is to be taken for granted that in our system leaders and parties seek to promote their political fortunes. The "ins" champion policies (goals, and rules and methods for achieving them) with an eye to the next election—and perhaps some subsequent elections too. The "outs" look for weaknesses and failings, and try to devise alternative policies with electoral appeal.

So long as these principles are pursued responsibly—with due regard to other social values—there is no problem. But problems begin to arise when special interests are pursued at the expense of the general interest, or when the likelihood of a "conflict of interest" is so clear-cut that actions of the person involved are especially suspect, or when someone assumes (however innocently) that what is good for General Motors is good for the United States. Almost all good principles lead in certain circumstances to what is considered socially undesirable. Remember the boy who justified seduction by quoting the Golden Rule.

Personal Incentives and the Search for Private Advantage

The principle that it is desirable to offer personal incentives to get the public good served leads inevitably into problems. There is a built-in contradiction. If we glory in a competitive, achieving society in which individuals are urged to seek their own good, it is almost automatic that some will make this the supreme end, seeking their good at the expense of others as individuals and at the expense of what is regarded as the public good. Struggles are inevitable over the question where the search for private advantage begins to conflict with the public interest—where what was good becomes bad. And, assuming that the limits of acceptable self-serving are identified, great vigilance, determination, and skill are required to see to it that they are respected. It is easier to induce people to seek their fortunes than to contain this kind of motivation once it is aroused.

Obviously the search for private advantage occurs in connection with the space program. And there is something in it for so many. The scientist who stands to get research funds, the university that anticipates grants, the nonprofit research organization that wants contracts out of which it can pay very high salaries, the trade union that wants to keep up employment, the business concern that wants profits, the trade journal that caters to the military-industrial complex, the congressman who seeks re-election, the promoter (perhaps himself a congressman) who wants to bring more wealth to his state or region, and others—perhaps including a president who, as the freshman says, wants immortal fame for many years—are all suspect. They all have private reasons that may influence their public stand regarding the space program. It would be surprising if in a number of cases the private reason were not the dominant one. Moreover, the space program is of such a nature that it does not call up much of a specific counterweight to pressures from those who stand to gain; that is, few stand to lose in any direct and crucial way. Few significant vested interests are trampled on, if any. Thus the dangers of abuse—of what someone has called a "moondoggle"—are very real. The main safeguards against those who would carry the pursuit of private advantage beyond acceptable limits are the usual ones: the integrity and intelligence of public officials and the open scrutiny of proposals and policies. The upright man is said to be the man who is held in that posture by pressures from all sides.

Possibilities of serving private purposes through the space program are so obvious that I need not dwell on them, especially in the absence of concrete data. But a speculative question should be raised about one specific matter: did the fiasco at the Bay of Pigs in April, 1961, have any influence on the recommendation made a month later to expand and accelerate the space program? Many in the United States, as we have seen, were already smarting under the relatively bad showing of the country in space. NASA officials have cited the Gagarin flight as a factor that helped to sting the country into action. The Cuban failure came about a week later, carrying American prestige and pride to a very low point; and it may well have had a sharp impact on the new President personally, because responsibility for the miserable episode was his. Certainly it would not be surprising if his advisers thought that in such circumstances he might be especially likely to respond to proposals of a bold and dramatic sort, with considerable potential appeal, and if in fact the circumstances did affect his attitudes. Such speculation may or may not ever be confirmed.

We should not speak of the search for private advantage as a motive without recognizing the fact that some people accept positions in NASA, as in other governmental organizations, at a financial sacrifice. This does not necessarily mean that they are neglectful of private satisfactions; they may look upon service with NASA as an interlude that will be materially helpful to their later careers; or they may be in search of nonmaterial satisfactions, e.g., public honor, new and challenging experience, or pleasure in duty done.

Catering to Constituencies

In many cases there is no sharp dividing line between the search for private advantage and the effort to serve constituencies, but it is convenient to take the points up separately.

There is, I believe, general agreement on several propositions concerning efforts of members of Congress to serve their constituencies. (1) It is part of their job. It is simply to be taken for granted that they will try to look after the welfare and interests of people in their districts and in their states. (2) At the same time, there are limits beyond which members of Congress should not go in trying to serve their constituencies. They must also have the national welfare and the presumed national interest in mind. (3) The limits beyond which congressmen should not go in pressing the cause of their constituencies are not clearly defined, and congressmen differ in fixing them. Most congressmen are honest and conscientious, but their consciences instruct them somewhat differently; a very few are scoundrels. In pressing their claims, they may use either open arguments or threats, or a combination of the two.

In connection with NASA the question of the special interests or ulterior motives of members of Congress has arisen mainly in connection with the choice of locations for NASA installations —most particularly, the choice of the Houston area for the Manned Spacecraft Center and the choice of the Greater Boston area for the electronics center proposed after the 1962 election. In a more general way, the question has also arisen in connection with NASA's procurement policies—the distribution of its contracts and expenditures among the states. These choices are made in NASA itself, not in Congress. But in varying degrees members of Congress have opportunities to influence them.

So far as I have been able to discover, there is very little in the public record about the choice of the Houston area for the Manned Spacecraft Center. The most obvious fact is that Representative Albert Thomas comes from Houston, and holds a crucial position in connection with appropriations for NASA. He is (and has for some time been) on the House Committee on Appropriations, and Chairman of the Independent Offices Subcommittee, which recommends the amounts to be appropriated for NASA. It would have been a very simple matter for him to convey the thought to Glennan and Webb—however subtly or brutally—that a major NASA installation must be located in the Houston area if NASA was to get good treatment from his subcommittee. Moreover, Olin Teague and Bob Casey from Texas were both on the House space committee, and Lyndon B. Johnson was in a powerful position in the Senate, and later on in the National Aeronautics and Space Council. Had Houston been a totally unsuitable location for the Manned Spacecraft Center, it presumably would not have been placed there; administrative officials—or other congressmen—can always make it a public issue if a congressman pushes a bad case too hard. But I am told that Houston was listed among the acceptable sites by a special committee that assessed the most likely possibilities. And in these circumstances almost any NASA administrator might well have decided that political prudence required the selection of Houston.

In contrast to the choice of Houston, NASA's request for appropriations permitting the establishment of an electronics center in the Greater Boston area has come under considerable public scrutiny, two questions being raised: whether NASA really needs such a center and, if so, what considerations led to the choice of Boston. The possibility existed that the recommendations had been made to please the Kennedys, including Teddy Kennedy, who had just been elected to the Senate after claiming that he would be able to do more for Massachusetts; and the fact is that the Speaker of the House, Mr. McCormack, together with the venerable Republican leader, Joseph W. Martin (himself a member of the space committee) also come from Massachusetts. The questions were accentuated by seemingly widespread discontent in Congress with the geographical distribution of NASA's expenditures. We will consider this matter in more detail in Chapter 13. Suffice it to say here that in the fiscal year ending in June, 1962, almost half of NASA's procurement dollars were spent in California, and about 87 per cent were spent in coastal states; and of the 13 per cent going to the vast interior of the country, 8 per cent went to Missouri.

Discussions of these issues in Congress in 1963 included the pointed advocacy of the cause of specific states and districts and also the championship of general principles in the name of the presumed national interest. Senator Dodd of Connecticut objected to any specification that the electronics center should be placed in the "Boston area," but he had no objection to "Greater Boston" if its borders extended as far as Willimantic, Connecticut; he was perhaps indulging in satire, but others were deadly serious in indicating that they wanted their constituencies to be taken care of. The general principles championed to bring about a more widespread geographical distribution of NASA's expenditures were that it was undesirable to create "a one-industry, or almost one-industry, economy in any area," and, conversely, that it was desirable as a matter of public policy both to develop and to utilize the resources and talents available over the whole country. The general principle to which NASA appealed was that it had a "duty to carry out the civil space program in a timely, efficient and economical manner," and that the success of the program depended "on placing contracts with companies which are found best qualified to perform the work."[1] It was this, NASA claimed, and not favoritism of any sort, that led to the concentration of NASA's procurement in California, in other coastal states, and in the state of Senator Symington and of Representative Clarence Cannon (Chairman of the House Appropriations Committee). So far as the electronics center was concerned, the main point was that the Greater Boston area was already a major center for electronics research and related intellectual and cultural activities and that NASA wanted to build on strength. Political motivations were denied.[2]

Though many members of Congress made it clear that they wanted more NASA dollars coming into their states, they could not and did not champion the principle that political considerations should control the placing of installations and contracts. In fact, Mr. Wydler, a member of the House space committee from New York, said, "If I ever found that any judgment was used in awarding any of these contracts, except on the basis of the standard of excellence, really meaning the standard of excellence, I personally would object to it, and would make it public."[3] Another member of the committee, Mr. Rumsfeld of Illinois, challenged the custom followed by NASA and other executive agencies in inviting a congressman to announce the letting of contracts and other actions that would be of substantial economic interest to the congressman's constituents. "The implication might be that he was instrumental in getting that contract," and "for the most part" this was not the case.[4] Mr. Morris of New Mexico addressed himself to the question whether Teddy Kennedy was doing more for Massachusetts.

Most of us are not exactly modest when we speak of what we can do for the country and, in particular, what we can do for our own area when we face the people of our State.

I'm reasonably sure that the Democratic candidate for the Senate from Massachusetts was not being modest, either. . . .

[1] U.S. Congress, House, Committee on Science and Astronautics, *1964 NASA Authorization*, Hearings, 88th Cong., 1st Sess., 1963, Part 3, p. 1756.

[2] *Ibid.*, Part 3, pp. 2207, 2223.

[3] *Ibid.*, Part 4, pp. 3353-54.

[4] *Ibid.*, Part 4, p. 3369.

But, by and large, I think that most projects are placed where it will be in the national interest, even though some of us like to think that we have something to do with getting them.[5]

The question of the role of ulterior political motives is thus a complex one, full of subtleties. To add to them, I might note that congressmen do not necessarily have to say anything to get attention for their home areas; their very presence on the space committees or in other positions of political power automatically gives assurance that alert administrators will try, at least within the limits of propriety, to anticipate their wishes. Surely this fact has something to do with the desire of some representatives and senators to have seats on the space committees.[6] In a political system it would plainly be absurd to say that political power has nothing to do with the important decisions that are made, and naive even to hope that this might be the rule. But in view of the cross-pressures that operate—including the cross-pressures within the consciences of many of the powerful—it would be wrong to think that decisions are always governed by the grasping selfishness of a few who are on top.

As already suggested, members of Congress are not the only ones who have constituents, if the term is used in a broad sense. Everyone in public life has a circle of friends and supporters to whom he owes something and on whom he is likely both to confer favors and to rely for effective service. Mr. Teague of the House space committee speaks of a university professor who told him that when you know who in NASA makes the university contracts you can tell, because of the friends the man has, where they are going. The very suggestion that NASA places installations and contracts on the basis of political considerations implies that it has a constituency to please. And so on. But, by and large, the effort to please constituents is only one of many motives that operate in connection with the space program.

Keeping Going Concerns Going

Dynamic and capable people need to believe, and do commonly believe, in the importance of what they are doing. This means that

[5] *Ibid.*, Part 3, p. 2208.

[6] D. S. Greenberg, "News and Comment," *Science,* 139 (March 8, 1963), 891; John Walsh, "Congress: Senator Anderson Brings Activist Record, Some Definite Views, to Space Committee Helm," *Science,* 139 (March 15, 1963), 1037.

they want to maintain and perhaps to expand the activity or institution in which they are involved—to keep the going concern
going.

In a sense this is the converse of the point just made. If the leaders of NASA were indifferent about its fate, they would not have
to respond to congressional or other pressures. They could shrug
and do as they pleased. But given the fact that they care, they must
adopt strategies that permit them to keep going; they must seek to
maintain support for their organization, if not to enhance it. They
can do this in part, perhaps, by quite open methods, e.g., by giving
persuasive testimony and making persuasive speeches. And they
can do it in part through a prudent distribution of benefits. In
many cases, perhaps in most, when NASA has a contract to let or
an installation to locate, publicly declared principles will leave little
or no room for choice. But in many other cases that will not be
true. There will be some freedom of choice within the limits of
declared principles; and in such cases other principles no doubt
come to the fore. All the requirements of law and propriety being
met, what choice stands the best chance of providing a political
pay-off some time in the future? What kinds of legitimate activities
will contribute most to grass-roots support? What can properly be
done that will promote good will toward NASA in different parts
of the country and in different segments of the population? Which
representatives and which senators will be pleased or displeased by
this or that choice? How much power do they have over the future
of NASA?

The Air Force no doubt has similar motivations. Technological
change threatens it in a very special way. The manned bomber seems
obsolescent; at least, in unrestricted war among great powers its
future is highly questionable. It was thus important to the Air Force
that it get primary responsibility for long-range missiles, but even
this assignment is not necessarily an entirely satisfying one, especially in view of the fact that missiles are, in the main, placed
underground. The jibe that Air Force personnel are destined to become the "silent silo sitters of the '70s" must surely be a little disturbing. The natural, human reaction is for the Air Force to try to
develop a role for itself in space, and so it adopts the word *aerospace* and chafes under restrictions placed upon it. The nature of
the restrictions does not necessarily matter, for under any circumstances the Air Force would probably chafe as a matter of principle.
But in fact the restrictions are imposed both by DOD—in the rule

that there must be a definable military mission before major development programs are financed—and by the principle that the civilian and "peaceful" aspects of the space effort are to be emphasized.
Now the Air Force has even more largesse to distribute than NASA.
It quite naturally attracts the support of trade journals, and of lobbyists employed by firms with which it might do business. Within
the limits of quite respectable rules and principles it has some freedom of choice in locating its facilities, letting its contracts, and
selecting programs and projects for financing. It knows which
senators and representatives are especially powerful. It would be
surprising in this situation if the special interests of the Air Force
did not somehow exert influence. Moreover, the Air Force is among
the agencies that has an intelligence service whose mission relates
to the identification and assessment of foreign dangers, and surely
there would be no temptation to minimize the dangers.

Within limits it is no doubt desirable that responsible officials in
the Air Force and elsewhere should believe in the importance of
what they are doing. Up to a point the pursuit of special Air Force
interests no doubt also serves what is generally regarded as the national interest. Wherever that point is (and it would be very difficult to locate reliably) I have no evidence that the Air Force has
crossed it in its efforts to build up a military space program. At the
same time, it is obviously of some importance to be alert to the
possibility.

Serving Partisan Interests

The very proper desires of political parties to find suitable issues,
and to find policies with electoral appeal, also involve the danger
of abuse. The line between proper and improper partisanship, between responsible and irresponsible criticism, between action that
is responsive to accepted values and action that is subversive of
them, is difficult to draw, and it may or may not have been crossed
in connection with the space program. Obviously in the period leading up to the 1960 elections the Democrats made what capital they
could out of an alleged Republican fault at the fringe of the space
program, i.e., in connection with the disputed "missile gap." Beginning in 1963 some Republicans have made attempts to turn
tables, but there has been no general agreement on the line to
take. In January, 1963, the National Republican Congressional
Committee released a "Preliminary Work Report on the Military

Space Lag." The report declared that "the Kennedy Administration's failure to build up a strong military space capability is perhaps the most disastrous blunder by any government since the last World War," and it urged that a military space build-up should have priority; at the same time, the military build-up "should not hamper or slow down our current civilian program." [7] The call was thus apparently for a bigger total space program. In apparent contrast, the Senate Republican Policy Committee, under the chairmanship of Bourke B. Hickenlooper, released a statement in May, 1963, called "A Matter of Priority." I have quoted from it in preceding chapters. Though the statement contained a number of ambiguities, it constituted an attack upon the "crash" lunar program and a hesitant suggestion that "greater emphasis might be placed on the multitude of human problems we face here on earth." Subject to the requirements of "our vital security," the report suggested "a less ambitious program." At the same time, the ranking Republican on the Senate space committee, Margaret Chase Smith, declared that she did not regard NASA's budget a partisan matter.[8] In July, 1963, the House space committee voted unanimously on NASA's authorizations for the fiscal year ending a year later, and the Chairman of the committee, Mr. Miller, declared that "at no time did partisanship or party interests play any part in influencing committee decision." [9] In subsequent voting in both the House and Senate on NASA's budget for FY1964, however, partisanship clearly appeared. Republicans were much more inclined than Democrats to cut the authorization and the appropriation; and some of them showed increasing concern for an even fuller development of a military space program.

In sum, it is obvious that most of those who are active in relationship to the space program are inspired to some extent by special interests and ulterior motives. If there were no opportunity to pursue such interests and motives, NASA would very probably collapse, just as every other organization would. It is imperative that personal incentives be provided if the job is to be done, that responsible officials should believe in the importance of their agency

[7] National Republican Congressional Committee, Bob Wilson, Chairman, News Release, January 4, 1963, together with "Preliminary Work Report on the Military Space Lag by the Republican Advisory Committee for Space and Aeronautics to the Chairmen of the GOP National, Senatorial, and Congressional Committees," mimeo.

[8] *Congressional Record*, Vol. 109, No. 70 (May 13, 1963), 7803.

[9] *Ibid.*, Vol. 109, No. 108 (July 17, 1963), A4507.

and their work, and that in a democracy parties should pursue the voters; and it is inevitable that in a political system major decisions will be influenced by political considerations. The question is not whether special interests and ulterior motives are pursued but to what extent, if at all, they are the "real" motives, for which the public interests and manifest motives discussed in the preceding chapters are covers, and to what extent, if at all, they are pursued at the expense of these public interests and manifest motives. Given the magnitude of the space effort and the number of people involved, it is a foregone conclusion that for many the publicly expressed motives are rationalizations and that sometimes private advantage is pursued at the expense of the public good. But this kind of thing is surely the exception rather than the rule.

THE RELATIVE IMPORTANCE OF DIFFERENT MOTIVES

The motives for developing the space program have varied in importance in the minds of different persons and groups and at different times. This general proposition is worth elaborating on, and a few more specific propositions can be made. I will speak on the basis of what is better described as an informed impression than as hard evidence.

From the very beginning motives were mixed. The urge to try it, to find out, to discover and explore, to do the new and the challenging lay back of the increasing interest in space in the decades and years leading up to Explorer I and Vanguard. Specifically scientific purposes were no doubt dominant in the minds of those planning the IGY. Those within the military structure concerned with the development of missiles (e.g., the Wernher von Braun group and some of those above it in the chain of command) shared these motives and also had some thoughts about the military potentialities of space and, perhaps, the implications of space exploits for national prestige. But prior to Sputnik the military and political leadership were not greatly impressed by these latter considerations, as is demonstrated by the meagerness of the funding provided for the Vanguard program.

For many of the natural scientists—especially those critical of the lunar program—the desire to enhance knowledge has remained the dominant reason for a space program; in truth, these scientists seem to find it difficult to grasp the fact that other reasons really count. For other natural scientists and for those outside the natural sciences the scientific reasons for a space program have much less relative significance. Mr. Webb makes a formal distinction between scientific objectives, on the one hand, and the commitment to a lunar landing, on the other; and he clearly attaches much greater importance to the lunar landing. Of course, the distinction does not have as much practical significance as might be the case, for preparations for the lunar landing necessitate considerable scientific inquiry. Spokesmen for the military rarely stress the purely scientific purposes of the space program. When members of Congress do, they give the impression as often as not that they are rationalizing, e.g., that having decided to support a space program out of national pride, they justify it in the name of contributions to science. They would vote only a small fraction of current appropriations for a space effort if the enhancement of scientific knowledge were the only object.

The desire to enhance military security through a space program is influential in governmental circles—emphasized primarily by the military, by certain members of Congress whose general outlook calls for great stress on the armed forces and military preparedness, and to a much lesser extent by NASA officials. Concern for military security in relation to space seemed most intense in Congress in the first two or three years of the space age. To some extent this appears to have been a partisan matter, with Democrats looking very hard for Republican faults. To some extent it appears to have reflected confusion between space power and missile power. Soviet missiles have fundamentally transformed America's strategic position. How much the transformation is accentuated by actual or potential Soviet space power is as yet uncertain. Despite the fact of uncertainty, there have been many assertions that national survival is at stake in the space race, and fears for security (whether in the short or long run) have clearly had a very substantial influence in Congress. Gilbert Burck goes so far as to describe the whole space program as "para-military," but this is scarcely justified. True, the Air Force has an extensive space program, and there are potential military implications in most of what NASA does, even in the "purely scientific" investigations. But it was not the Air Force that induced Kennedy to go for the moon. If concern for military security were dominant, there would be no Project Apollo; there would instead be an emphasis on the development of various kinds of capabilities in terrestrial space. Thus, though the security motive has been powerful, whether for good reasons or bad, it has been one among others, and probably not the most influential one. I will comment more on this below.

To some extent the emphasis on the military aspects of the space program has been restrained by a desire to stress peaceful purposes. In Chapter 5 I have noted the confusion of thought attending the word *peaceful,* concluding that the general intent seems to be to avoid creating alarm, to avoid the appearance of threatening anyone, to avoid contributing to a frame of mind in which thoughts of war are in the foreground. Peaceful purposes in this sense are emphasized mainly by political leaders in Congress and in the Administration, and not so much by others. Emphasis on the point has been fairly constant in time.

In political circles since Sputnik I concern for national prestige and pride has been the most powerful of the motives associated with the space program. And though prestige is more commonly named, more stress should go to pride. Signs of both motives, especially concern for prestige, show in the planning of the Vanguard program. Sputnik I brought them, along with the security motive, into the foreground, though they did not gain great strength as long as it was more or less complacently assumed that the United States would duplicate Soviet feats with some speed. But when successive Soviet firsts were matched by so much ignominy at Cape Canaveral, thoughts of lost prestige began to rankle, and the hurt to pride became galling. Eisenhower resisted the attitude. At the same time, he may inadvertently have strengthened it. He took a very restricted view of the role of the President, failing to provide exciting and dynamic leadership. Moreover, the forced cancellation of his trip to Japan, the blundering associated with the U-2 affair, and the indignities suffered by Vice President Nixon in Venezuela all raised distressing questions about both respect abroad and self-respect at home. Republicans as well as Democrats in Congress became increasingly disturbed, and when the Kennedy Administration came in, all were ready to join in an effort to recoup the situation, without much regard to cost.

The very act of adopting a bold and challenging program probably did something to relieve the psychological pressures that led to it. Further, even before Kennedy's inauguration, Cape Canaveral was producing a much greater measure of satisfaction than earlier in terms of successful launches and the acquisition of scientific

knowledge; and successes were also being scored from the Vanden-
berg Air Force Base in California. After the inauguration came the
suborbital flights of Shepard and Grissom, and a year later the
Glenn flight that did so much to purge the country of feelings of
inferiority and doubt and to restore prestige and pride. Moreover,
as if to compensate for the miseries of the Bay of Pigs came the
confrontation with the Soviet Union over Cuba in October, 1962,
and the tremendous surge of national confidence that success
brought.

With national morale restored, however, concern for prestige and
pride has lost some of its force as a motive for the space program.
The change began to show in Congress in the spring of 1962, after
the Glenn flight, and it has become increasingly apparent. Though
many in Congress are no doubt still moved by a desire to beat the
Russians, others have come to express scorn for this motive; and
some favor making even the lunar program a cooperative enterprise. Thus a motive that once was so obsessive has declined significantly in its appeal. Whether or not Kennedy's proposal of September, 1963, reflected a genuine desire for cooperation with the
Russians, it was logically inconsistent with the principal motives of
the expanded program that he had championed two years earlier.

Speaking figuratively, the developments raise the question
whether America knows its own mind. The question has been raised
many times before. Time and again the country has demonstrated
either an unawareness of values that turned out to matter very
much or an inconstancy in pursuing them. We went into the
Spanish-American War at the end of the last century without a consensus on the values being pursued and thus without a coherent
conception of the strategy to employ and the terms of peace to insist upon when victory was won. In the years prior to World War I
there was substantial unawareness of the importance to American
values of averting such a conflict; and when the disaster engulfed
Europe, Wilson declared our neutrality—only later to ask for a
declaration of war in the name of goals that had nothing to do with
those that he had been proclaiming up to that time. And there was
no consensus on goals when victory came, with the result that we
left it largely to others to determine what would or would not in
the longer run be achieved. Then what were our goals between the
wars and down to Pearl Harbor? Not knowing what we wanted, we
got the appalling blight of Nazism and the tragedy of World War

II. For half a century each crisis that came upon the country found it without a clear conception of goals and how to achieve them, compelling improvisation that usually had dismal results.

The record in diplomatic affairs looks better since World War II, but previous failures warn against assuming too much. So far as space is concerned, there was an obvious general failure before Sputnik to identify values that soon come to seem so important. Even after Sputnik, many of those who were clearly motivated by pride gave other reasons for wanting to develop a major space program. Not until 1963 did it become more or less common for those analyzing the reasons for the space program to mention concern for pride or self-esteem among the major factors. And doubt about the justifiability of the program, particularly the projected manned lunar landing, became prominent at about the same time.

In part, the shift in attitudes may be due to increasing awareness of the influence of pride and to a genuine belief that the desire to bolster it through a lunar landing does not justify the great expenses involved. In part, the explanation is to be found in an analysis of human motivation by A. H. Maslow.[1] He speaks of motivation in terms of needs, suggesting a number of categories: physiological needs, safety needs, love needs, esteem needs, etc. People have motives in a number of such categories, but are rarely conscious of them all. When their physiological interests are threatened, concern for them is likely to be a controlling guide to behavior; for a man threatened with suffocation, a breath of air is the paramount motive. But when a reasonable degree of satisfaction for the physiological needs is assured, they are more or less taken for granted, and attention is directed to, e.g., safety needs. When satisfaction for these can also be taken for granted, they are more or less forgotten and attention shifts to another category. Maslow suggests that, in principle, there is an endless set of categories of motives or needs (goals, values, interests), and that men shift their attention back and forth among the categories depending on circumstances. Changes in circumstances may call attention to values that hitherto were ignored or may lead to the development of totally new values.

In other words, a value provides motivation mainly when it is in jeopardy. When there is no problem about it, no one gives it any

---

[1] A. H. Maslow, "A Dynamic Theory of Human Motivation," in Chalmers L. Stacey and Manford F. DeMartino, eds., *Understanding Human Motivation* (Cleveland: Howard Allen, 1958), pp. 28 ff.

thought. Thus people may not become aware of a value until a threat to it develops; and if the threat recedes, concern for the value may abate. This is precisely what seems to have happened in connection with the space program. It took Sputnik to awaken the American people, and Congress, to some precious values—especially to the importance of pride; and with the restoration of pride, concern for it diminishes. Concomitantly, there is an increasing tendency to cite military security as a major motive, whether because of a genuine Soviet threat in space or because this kind of appeal usually elicits a favorable response.

PART  METHODS

Though labeled "Motivations," Part II also dealt in part with methods, e.g., with the question of the extent to which space R&D and various uses of satellites are likely to be effective methods of promoting the various goals.

The chapters of Part III concern methods exclusively: how the federal government has organized itself for the implementation of the space program; the principles and the strategies that NASA employs in mobilizing the necessary resources; and international cooperation and the dissemination of information at home and abroad as methods of promoting security, peace, the enhancement of scientific knowledge, and the other goals.

The treatment of methods is incomplete. Scientific research and the development of hardware are important methods in the pursuit of space goals, but I must leave it to others to describe and appraise activities in these fields. And I do not propose to examine the recruitment and assignment of administrative personnel in NASA, or detailed management policies, even though what is done in these fields may have vital significance.

12

The organizational arrangements for implementing a space program were already largely made before the space age began. The Constitution dictated that the President and Congress should play key roles. The rule that DOD has primary responsibility for military power and military security—as well as the fact that it had taken the lead in developing launching vehicles—virtually dictated that it should be heavily involved. It was also a part of the logic of the situation that such agencies as the Bureau of the Budget, the Weather Bureau, the U.S. Information Agency, and the Department of State should play the roles in connection with the space program that fell more or less naturally into their usual sphere of activity. Even so, a number of choices had to be made. Should the space program continue to be managed by DOD? If it was transferred in whole or in part to a civilian agency, how should that agency be organized? Within DOD, how should responsibilities be allocated? How should Congress organize itself to handle problems relating to space, and what kind of special assistance, if any, should the President have? What kinds of relationships do NASA and DOD have with each other, and how are differences between them resolved?

Civilian vs. Military Control

Had DOD beaten the Russians into space and assured American preeminence from the first, many subsequent developments would surely have been vastly different. Perhaps the greatest difference would be in the magnitude and urgency of the space program in the United States and the Soviet Union, for a competitive race of serious proportions might not have developed. So far as organizational arrangements within the United States are concerned, DOD would have strengthened its claim to the continued management of the space program, perhaps sufficiently to make the question of management a real issue. But, given the failure of DOD, the question was not seriously debated. There was, from the first, overwhelming endorsement of the principle that the space activities of the country should, in the main, be managed by a civilian agency.

President Eisenhower took the lead in this matter. "The President's insistence on this distinction [between *civilian* and *military*] has been fanatic, his one piece of enthusiasm in the whole space picture." [1] Opening the Senate hearings on space legislation in 1958, Lyndon B. Johnson pointed out that twelve years earlier, when legislation for the development of atomic energy was being considered, "much of our attention was dedicated to choosing between civilian or military control." But, he said, "I believe that choice is not really before us now." He took it for granted that the control would be civilian. And the committee report declared that "the essentiality of civilian control is so clear as to be no longer a point of discussion."

Various reasons inspired the attitude, including some relating to the motivations analyzed in preceding chapters. As we have seen, there was early agreement on the principle that the United States would stress peaceful purposes in space and a desire for international cooperation, and these considerations called for civilian control. Similarly, according to the American style, exploration and the promotion of scientific knowledge, technological development, and economic progress are all essentially civilian pursuits, and there was an expectation that scientists would cooperate more fully and readily with a civilian than with a military effort. We might possibly have gained more prestige or deference in Moscow had we made space the domain of the military (though the fact that, as it is, Moscow regards our space program as military makes this doubtful), but in connection with space developments we seemed more concerned with the attitudes of peoples

---

[1] Frank Gibney, "The Missile Mess," *Harper's*, 220 (January, 1960), 43.

elsewhere, e.g., the uncommitted peoples of the world who, it was assumed, tend to be repelled by emphasis on the military and on the possibility of war. Very probably, too, there was a feeling that we had a better chance to beat the Russians and so restore our pride if the main thrust of the space effort was civilian. Moreover, the National Advisory Committee for Aeronautics (NACA) was already in existence as a civilian organization, with scientists, engineers, and various facilities that would be useful in a space effort. Furthermore, the identifiable military uses of space vehicles are few enough and remote or uncertain enough that it is hard to make a really good case for military control.

Nevertheless, despite general acceptance of the principle that the space effort should be predominantly civilian, sharp issues have accompanied the principle from the first. At a very early point, it came to be assumed that NACA would be the nucleus of the space agency, but what functions and powers would the new agency have? Would the military be excluded from space research and development entirely? This had occurred in the field of atomic energy, and the precedent was frequently cited. But the circumstances were different. In the field of atomic energy there were fewer crucial materials and a rather coherent and distinctive technology; moreover, nuclear weapons had been developed in the Manhattan Project, set apart from other activities. But research and development pertaining to space had not been similarly set apart and really could not be; too many kinds of materials and technologies were involved. Moreover, a number of military agencies were already active in the field, e.g., in developing launching vehicles, guidance mechanisms for missiles, and tracking facilities. The result was that when the AEC precedent was cited and examined, it was regularly dropped as inapplicable.

Even so, the legislation that Eisenhower recommended to Congress in April, 1958, created some alarm in DOD. As expected, it provided for the transformation of NACA into NASA. But its language was rather unclear on the question of the freedom of DOD to engage in space research and operations. Vigorous pressures to clarify the wording were quickly exerted. Some of the departmental spokesmen hoped for a division of functions between DOD and NASA analogous to that which had prevailed between DOD and NACA; that is, they hoped that the civilian space agency would confine itself largely to laboratory research

and scientific testing, leaving the management of space operations to the military.[2] Earlier, NACA itself seems to have anticipated this kind of a division, and it had carried self-abnegation
even further in suggesting a substantial role for the National
Academy of Sciences and the National Science Foundation.[3] Other
spokesmen from DOD anticipated an arrangement under which
DOD and NASA would each engage in space research and each
go into space "without domination of either over the other," and
as a variation on this there was talk of a three-way split, DOD
undertaking those activities primarily designed to meet military
requirements, NASA undertaking those primarily scientific and
exploratory, and the two engaging jointly in activities cutting
across the two categories, e.g., man-in-space.[4]

As finally enacted, the National Aeronautics and Space Act of
1958 does not clearly resolve the issue. It reflects an intention that
the space program should in the main be under NASA, but it provides an exception that could become more important than the
rule. In the Act Congress declares that aeronautical and space
activities

shall be the responsibility of, and shall be directed by, a civilian agency
. . . except that activities peculiar to or primarily associated with the
development of weapons systems, military operations, or the defense of
the United States (including the research and development necessary
to make effective provision for the defense of the United States) shall be
the responsibility of, and shall be directed by, the Department of Defense.

Whether the tail will ever wag the dog remains to be seen.

Paradoxical as it may seem, the assignment to DOD of responsibility for military pursuits in space may turn out to be a
good way of reinforcing the desire for primary emphasis on
civilian, scientific, exploratory, and political pursuits. T. Keith
Glennan took this view. He did not want complete control over
all space activities, nor did he want to concede it to DOD. He
believed that if military and nonmilitary space projects had to
compete for funds within any one agency, the decision-makers
would be so impressed by the overwhelming importance of national security and survival that they would play it safe by stress-

[2] U.S. Congress, Senate, Special Committee on Space and Astronautics,
National Aeronautics and Space Act, Hearings . . . on S. 3609, 85th Cong.,
2d Sess., 1958, Part 1, pp. 74, 165, 168 (hereafter cited as Senate, *Hearings
on 3609,* 1958).

[3] *Congressional Record,* Vol. 104 (daily edition), (March 3, 1958), A1902-4.

[4] Senate, *Hearings on 3609,* 1958, Part 1, pp. 180, 193.

ing the military. In effect, he was saying that no one at his general level in the hierarchy should be asked to decide on the relative emphasis to be placed on military and nonmilitary space activities —that this decision should be made at higher levels.

Glennan's argument had another aspect. Within each of the military services, space projects have to compete with other defense projects for endorsement. For example, the Department of the Air Force, in which most of the military space projects are located, is also responsible for air power and long-range missile power; it cannot concentrate on space alone. The Office of the Secretary of the Air Force must weigh the recommendations of space enthusiasts against the recommendations of those more immediately concerned with aircraft and missiles. In turn, his recommendations go through the same kind of scrutiny in the Office of the Secretary of Defense, where the askings and recommendations of the Air Force are weighed against those of the Army and Navy. Thus the first competition of military space projects is with other defense projects, and not with the space projects of NASA. Glennan's comment on this situation was that "the competition for funds between military programs utilizing the space environment and other military programs designed to achieve the same or similar end results is one of the best assurances that military use of space will continue to be realistic." [5] The comment is quite plausible. And it is especially plausible in view of the emphasis in recent years on preparations for limited (conventional) and guerrilla warfare. This calls for stress on the Army and, to a lesser extent, on the Navy; and if the budget is to be limited it therefore also requires a very careful scrutiny of Air Force proposals.

From another point of view, Glennan's comment raises the question whether any comparable arrangement operates to keep the nonmilitary uses of space "realistic." I will comment on this below.

Organizational Arrangements Within NASA

When legislation leading to the establishment of NASA was being discussed, some favored placing the organization under a

---

[5] U.S. Congress, House, Committee on Science and Astronautics, *To Amend the National Aeronautics and Space Act of 1958*, Hearings . . . on H. Res. 9675, 86th Cong., 2d Sess., 1960, p. 73 (hereafter cited as House, *Hearings on 9675, 1960*).

commission—like the Atomic Energy Commission, NACA (a committee, acting through a Director), and the National Science Foundation (under a Board and a Director). But contrary views prevailed. The Administration thought of NASA not simply as a research organization but also as one that would manage more or less extensive space operations and develop more or less extensive relationships with business firms through contracts. For this purpose it wanted to follow the "normal" rule, "which is to place one man in the position where the President and the Congress can clearly and without any doubt hold him fully responsible, not only for such successes as his Agency might have, but for any failures which may occur. . . . The traditional American way of organizing any large operating enterprise, be it public or private, is to head it up with a single executive." [6] From the Administration's point of view, the Atomic Energy Commission was an anomaly, a commission-type organization having been accepted regardless of the question of "efficiency" because of the awesome responsibilities involved and because the responsibilities had to be exercised to a considerable extent behind a cloak of secrecy. The Administration view prevailed. Dryden, among others, shifted his position. And Congress provided for an Administrator.

The first Administrator and those around him faced a fundamental decision about the nature of the organization that they were to build. On the one hand, they might have chosen to develop and use "in-house" capabilities to the maximum. That is, they might have attempted to do all of the necessary research in government laboratories, expanding the NASA staff and facilities to the extent required; and they might have tried to develop the necessary technologies and even produce the necessary hardware within government plants. The old Army system of producing matériel in government arsenals gave some measure of precedent for this kind of choice. On the other hand, the NASA leadership could choose to rely to the maximum on external capabilities —on business firms, universities, and other private agencies. In this event, the principal functions of the NASA staff would be to plan and administer the program, arranging to let contracts to private agencies to get the actual research and development work done. Among other agencies, the Air Force gave precedent for this kind

---

[6] William F. Finan, Bureau of the Budget, in Senate, *Hearings on 3609,* 1958, Part 2, p. 304.

of choice, for it let contracts to private concerns for most of its research and development work, and even for some managerial services.

The decision that NASA made came closer to the second of these alternatives than to the first. To be sure, the agency was born with a considerable "in-house" competence. The fact that it absorbed NACA meant that it took over various laboratories and research centers together with their 8,000 employees. Moreover, in fairly short order it took over additional scientific and engineering expertise from other governmental agencies: the Vanguard Office of the Naval Research Laboratory, a substantial portion of the Army Ballistic Missile Agency, and the Jet Propulsion Laboratory, which Caltech had operated under contract with the Army. According to General Medaris, when the von Braun group in the Army Ballistic Missile Agency felt compelled to choose between a transfer to the Air Force and a transfer to NASA, it was tempted to go to the Air Force but was deterred by "some very dangerous possibilities in that course of action." "We recognized the dependence of the Air Force on the aircraft industry, and we had seen those interests continuously attack the concept of government-operated in-house major activities in the missile and space field. With, I believe, some justice, we were afraid that if the Air Force did take the von Braun organization, it would be under continual pressure to get it out of the hardware business and restrict it to engineering." [7] So the von Braun organization went to NASA, and NASA has expanded its in-house capabilities still further. By the end of 1962 it consisted of eleven major field centers or stations, two regional field offices, and a Washington headquarters. Almost 26,000 were on its payroll, of whom over 9,000 were professionally trained scientists and engineers. An additional field center, to focus on electronics, is proposed. But Webb and others repeatedly make it a point to claim that more than 90 cents out of every NASA dollar go to private agencies for their services or products.

The official statement is that NASA seeks to maintain "an exceptionally strong technical competence within its own laboratories." Its own staff—"government representatives, rather than contractors"—must "make the basic determinations of what is to be done with public funds." The staff must be "sufficient to ac-

[7] Major General John B. Medaris, USA (Ret.), *Countdown for Decision* (New York: Putnam, 1960), p. 267.

cept full responsibility for any specification for the hardware work
done outside NASA and sufficient to assure effective performance
under such specifications." [8] For these purposes the staff must engage directly in some research and development activity not only
to get it done but also to keep abreast of relevant problems and
possibilities. But most of the work is to be farmed out. Even in
the field of scientific research, "it is expected, and intended, that
the majority of the experiments and experimenters in the NASA
satellite and space probes will come from outside of NASA.
Counting past, present, and definitely planned missions 60% of the
experimenters are from outside NASA, 40% from inside." [9]

Both expediency and principle no doubt contributed to the
choice. Building an organization is at best a slow and difficult
process. NASA could get its job done much more speedily if it
obtained services and products more through contracts than
through recruiting employees and expanding government facilities.
Political expediency may or may not have influenced the decision
in NASA's formative period, but from hindsight it well might have.
Through its contracts and grants, NASA builds up a kind of political constituency; firms and persons benefited are likely to be
favorably disposed, and their favorable attitudes surely have—
or may in the future have—something to do with the amount of
popular and congressional support that NASA obtains. Dr. George
Wright of the Brookings Institution speaks of "the belief which
over the past decade has captured the imagination of top administrators in Washington . . . that, other things being the same,
a program with substantial contracting out has more chance for
budgetary support in the Congress than does a comparable in-
house program." For many, reliance on private enterprise is a
matter of principle. The most powerful figures in American economic and political life would undoubtedly have been alienated
if NASA had attempted to make the space program a government
activity to the maximum extent. Concern for "creeping socialism"
would certainly have become more intense. Even as it is, some are
dubious and skeptical about the wisdom of channeling additional
billions through the U.S. Treasury.

[8] Albert F. Siepert, "The NASA Organization," in NASA, Office of Scientific
and Technical Information, *Proceedings of the Second NASA-Industry Conference*, Washington, D.C., February 11-12, 1963 (Washington, 1963), pp.
15-16.
[9] Homer E. Newell, "NASA and Space," in Hugh Odishaw, ed., *The Challenges of Space* (Chicago: University of Chicago Press, 1962), p. 180.

NASA's organizational structure follows a common pattern, and its details need not concern us. Two points that are made elsewhere, however, ought to be noted here. One is that NASA's projects are executed through the various centers, stations, and field offices referred to above; and the other is that, as we will see in the next chapter, some of NASA's management functions are contracted out to private agencies.

Organizational Arrangements Within DOD

In the early years of the space age the Army, Navy, and Air Force all had space projects under way. The Army launched the first American satellite, Explorer I. The Navy, through the Naval Research Laboratory, managed Vanguard. The Air Force developed the Atlas and Thor boosters which, though designed primarily for missiles, became important to the space effort. At the DOD level two additional offices were created after Sputnik I, the Advanced Research Projects Agency (ARPA) and the Office of the Director of Defense Research and Engineering. Obviously, this all meant that a vague and confusing administrative situation existed, and it suggests that vigorous in-fighting was in progress.

In September, 1959, DOD announced a step in the direction of greater clarity, indicating that space projects were to be transferred from ARPA to the military departments and, further, that the development, production, and launching of military space boosters would eventually be assigned to the Air Force, payloads being developed by the several departments according to their primary interest or special competence. Nevertheless, more than a year later, President-elect Kennedy's Ad Hoc Committee on Space, under Jerome B. Wiesner, found that "each of the military services has begun to create its own independent space program," and suggested that "if the responsibility of all military space developments were to be assigned to one agency or military service within the Department of Defense, the Secretary of Defense would then be able to maintain control of the scope and direction of the program. . . ."

To the considerable anguish of personnel in the Army and Navy, Secretary McNamara in March, 1961, announced his decision "to assign space development programs and projects to the Department of the Air Force, except under unusual circumstances." All departments might continue to conduct "preliminary research" relating to space, and the fact that "development" was to be at the hands of the Air Force did not automatically mean that operational responsibilities would be assigned to it once development was complete. Even so, the practical import of the decision was to reinforce the already powerful position of the Air Force with regard to the military aspects of the space program. (It is said that "the Air Force was already responsible for over 90% of the total defense effort in space development activities, either by direct assignment or in support of other programs.") [10] ARPA is no longer responsible for space projects, except in connection with the Vela Hotel program for the detection of nuclear explosions in space.[11] The navigation satellite program (Transit) has been assigned to the Navy, and ground stations for a communications satellite system have been made the responsibility of the Army. I am told that other assignments have also been made to the Navy and Army without public announcement. But, for the most part, military space projects are under the Air Force.

The National Aeronautics and Space Council

The Space Act of 1958 provided for a National Aeronautics and Space Council. It was to consist both of statutory members (the President himself, as Chairman; and the Secretary of State, the Secretary of Defense, the Administrator of NASA, and the Chairman of the Atomic Energy Commission) and of not more than four others appointed by the President. Its formal purpose was to advise and assist the President, as he might request. Actually, Eisenhower chose to make very little use of it. He convened it only eight times; and he did not create a staff for it, allowing other agencies (NASA and the Office of the Special Assistant to the President for Science and Technology) to provide successive acting executive secretaries.[12] In January, 1960, he recommended to Congress that it be abolished. The House passed a bill to accomplish this, but Lyndon B. Johnson, majority leader and Chairman of the Committee on Astronautical and Space Sciences, blocked it in the Senate.

---

[10] U.S. Congress, House, Committee on Science and Astronautics, *Defense Space Interests,* Hearings, 87th Cong., 1st Sess., 1961, pp. 2-4, 37.

[11] Willis H. Shapley, "United States Space Program," in Odishaw, *op. cit.,* p. 165.

[12] House, *Hearings on 9675,* 1960, pp. 249-50.

In the Kennedy Administration, Lyndon B. Johnson was apparently very influential in several decisions, including those relating to the Space Council. As we have seen in Chapter 2, he was heavily involved in the selection of James E. Webb as the new NASA Administrator. No doubt Johnson also influenced the selection of the new regular Executive Secretary for the Space Council —a man who had been on the staff of Senator Symington; and along with the new Executive Secretary he has built up a Council staff consisting of some 28 persons, about half of whom can be considered professional. Clearly Johnson took the lead (with Kennedy's approval) in revising the part of the Space Act providing for the Council. The revision removed the President from membership and replaced him with the Vice President, i.e., with Johnson. It eliminated the nonstatutory members; among others, this meant the elimination of the President of the National Academy of Sciences and the Director of the National Science Foundation, whom President Eisenhower had appointed. But the revision did not significantly alter the legal powers or functions of the Council. It remains advisory only, meaning that the President can utilize and rely on it as much or as little as he chooses. What Johnson, as President, will do concerning the chairmanship of the Council is uncertain at the time of writing.

Public evidence of the activities of the Council is meager. It does not put satellites in orbit or place contracts for hardware or manage other operations of a visible sort. The chapter concerning the Council in the Annual Report of the President to Congress indicates that it meets without saying how often; and the chapter lists activities without always differentiating between those of the Council as such and those of its staff. In part, at least, the vagueness may be the inevitable result of the fact that the Council lacks the power of decision and the fact that the advice it gives to the President is considered privileged. Even if the Council met every day, it could not claim to have decided anything, and under present practice information concerning its recommendations would not be available. The relevant statement in the President's report to Congress concerning space activities in 1962 is as follows:

The Space Council held formal meetings on such subjects as the comparison of U.S. and Soviet space programs, review of space budget plans and requests, impact of our space program on foreign relations, examination of the role of nuclear propulsion and nuclear power devices in the space program, assignment of priorities for major space programs, evaluation of defense plans for space activities, aspects of astronaut recruitment and training, examination of schedules and methods for the lunar project, and public information aspects of the national space program.

The staff of the Council appears to be quite active. Much of what it does is apparently related only indirectly to the formal task of advising the President. Its members have contacts in NASA, DOD, and other relevant agencies, based both on formal status and on personal ties, and become involved in discussions of the various problems that arise. They have informal opportunities to provide leadership in planning the space effort, which is perhaps their most significant function. And they are sometimes able to ward off or help resolve interagency disputes before they reach a critical stage. More formally, before matters come to the Council itself, the staff must conduct preliminary discussions with personnel in the agencies involved, perhaps disposing of issues in this way and perhaps getting them—and alternative ways of dealing with them—identified with sufficient sharpness to permit effective Council action.

Other Executive Agencies

Earlier in this chapter I noted Dr. Glennan's argument that competition for funds within DOD helps keep the military use of space "realistic," and I raised the question whether anything comparable operates in connection with the nonmilitary uses. The Bureau of the Budget is in point in this connection, for it regularly sits in judgment of the recommendations made to it by the various departments and agencies. In fact, James R. Kerr quotes an unnamed NASA official as saying, "With an agency like ours, the Budget Bureau is where the battle for funds takes place, not before congressional committees. The Budget Bureau puts the budget together as a whole, and once the battle has been won there, there is no real battle elsewhere." [13] The official granted that the relative importance of Congress and its committees might increase, as it has. The point is, though, that there is competition for funds in the proceedings of the Bureau of the Budget, and the question is whether this competition is comparable to that within DOD. It can scarcely be, for DOD has a much narrower range of ends and means to consider. It is one thing to weigh the relative

[13] James R. Kerr, *Congressmen as Overseers: Surveillance of the Space Program* (Ph.D. dissertation, Stanford University, 1963), p. 173.

merits of an ICBM system and an orbital bombing system as contributors to deterrent power, and quite another thing to weigh the varied ends and means relating to scientific and technological progress, farm prosperity, social security, foreign aid, education, health, prestige, pride, etc. If NASA's program were purely scientific or purely military or purely anything else, there would presumably be a suitable context in which to judge it. But in fact no one suitable context exists, and the criteria of judgment are necessarily vague. Moreover, Kennedy's commitment to the lunar program gave funds for it a major advantage in the competition, and the advantage seems likely to continue under Johnson. To be sure, NASA's budget is carefully scrutinized in the Bureau of the Budget, and this has significance. But the test is different from the one to which military space proposals are currently subject within DOD.

Other executive agencies should also be mentioned. The Weather Bureau of the Department of Commerce is active in the meteorological satellite program. In principle, NASA finances the research and development phase of the program and the Weather Bureau finances the operational phase. But close coordination must be maintained in both phases. The Weather Bureau specifies the kind of data it needs and processes the data once they are obtained. NASA develops the satellites, launches them, obtains the data, then feeds them to the Weather Bureau.

The Atomic Energy Commission is responsible for developing the technology of nuclear propulsion, and nuclear sources of energy for in-flight use. The Department of State works with NASA in arranging for international cooperation. The U.S. Information Agency disseminates information abroad concerning the space program. The Space Science Board of the National Academy of Sciences serves as a source of advice for NASA, and its efforts to enhance scientific knowledge through the Committee on Space Research (COSPAR) serve also to enhance international cooperation among scientists on a private basis. And a number of other executive agencies perform functions that relate in one way or another to the space program.

Congressional Arrangements for Legislation on Space

We noted in Chapter 2 that the special and select committees established in 1958 by the Senate and House gave way to permanent standing committees. In the Senate, Johnson became Chairman of the new standing committee, and other powerful members of the Senate became members. In the House, events took a different turn. Overton Brooks became Chairman of the new committee, having been offered the post to get him off the Armed Services Committee and so to make sure that he did not become its Chairman.[14] Subsequently Nicholas A. Masters interviewed a number of members of the House, and reports as follows:

There was surprising agreement among those interviewed that Democratic transfers to the newly created Science and Astronautics Committee —not taken seriously by the House—were made in order to provide some of the transferees with sinecures, and so to remove some of the less qualified members from other committees. The transfer offers were made attractive to senior members by promises that they would receive subcommittee chairmanships, which would provide them opportunities to build their niches within the legislative bureaucracy.[15]

Democratic practice was such that members of "exclusive" or of "semi-exclusive" ("major") committees had to withdraw from them if they accepted seats on the new space committee—which itself was "semi-exclusive" ("major")—and not many wanted to give up good assignments for a new committee with an uncertain future. Partly as a result of this, a considerable portion of the members of the first committee were junior congressmen.

The standing of the committee, and the attractiveness of service on it, have increased. This follows almost inevitably after the increase in the space budget. Moreover, in the case of NASA Congress follows the unusual rule that it will make appropriations only after authorizing legislation has been enacted; the rule applies in only a few other instances, e.g., in relation to foreign aid and in relation to the procurement of aircraft, missiles, and naval vessels.[16] The authorizing legislation must be cleared through the space committee, thus enhancing its importance. At the beginning of the 87th Congress in 1961, the Republican Committee on Committees decided that the work load of members of the space committee was heavy enough that they should not serve simultaneously on other committees with work loads that were comparable

---

[14] Neil McNeil, *Forge of Democracy, The House of Representatives* (New York: McKay, 1963), p. 159.

[15] Nicholas A. Masters, "Committee Assignments in the House of Representatives," *American Political Science Review*, 55 (June, 1961), 356.

[16] Raymond H. Dawson, "Congressional Innovation and Intervention in Defense Policy: Legislative Authorization of Weapons Systems," *American Political Science Review*, 56 (March, 1962), 42; Kerr, *op. cit.*, pp. 161, 377-78.

or greater; the decision obliged four members to choose between their committee assignments, and two chose for space. In September, 1961, on the death of Brooks, George P. Miller became Chairman, and has handled his responsibilities in such a way as to win the committee increased respect. Among other things, he has made considerable use of standing subcommittees, which Brooks had declined to do. Even so, the number of junior congressmen on the committee remains large. Of the nine vacancies at the beginning of the 88th Congress in 1963, eight went to first-term congressmen, and the ninth to the majority leader, Albert. Five other seats were held by congressmen in their second term, and nine by congressmen in their third term. In sum, 22 members out of 31 were in their first, second, or third terms.[17]

The House committee holds very extensive hearings not only on authorizing legislation but also on other matters. In 1962, according to Chairman Miller, it

conducted 26 investigations, issued 16 reports, held 124 days of hearings, and heard 236 witnesses.

Indicative of the committee's activity is the more than 2,175,000 words of testimony taken this year, incorporated into approximately 3,860 pages of printed hearings.

Since its formation in 1959, the committee has conducted 108 investigations, issued 88 reports, held 498 days of hearings, and heard 1193 witnesses.[18]

Other House committees and subcommittees also hold hearings relating to space, particularly the Armed Services Committee, which has jurisdiction over the primarily military aspects of the space program, and the Committee on Appropriations and its subcommittees. A comparable committee structure exists in the Senate, though Senate hearings tend to be briefer if for no other reason than that there are fewer senators to man the various committees. The Joint Committee on Atomic Energy holds hearings for both houses of Congress on matters having to do with the utilization of nuclear energy in space. Mr. Webb says that from February 27, 1961, to April 17, 1962, he made "31 separate appearances before 12 different committees and subcommittees of the two houses of Congress." Probably no other person in NASA appeared as frequently, but the total number of man-hours devoted to hearings is immense.

---

[17] I am indebted to James R. Kerr for these data.
[18] *Congressional Record,* Vol. 108, No. 176 (September 28, 1962), 19,987.

Each committee also has a small staff at its disposal, assisting with the hearings and preparing studies and reports as directed. And the Legislative Reference Service includes one person with a special interest in the space program.

The hearings have shortcomings. They are grossly one-sided. Though industry witnesses sometimes appear, and though the Senate committee gave two days to a number of natural scientists in June, 1963, the rule is that witnesses come from NASA and DOD; and, in the main, they agree with each other. There is, in general, no presentation of the negative, nothing to resemble an adversary proceeding in court, with contending lawyers trying to establish opposite cases. Members of the committee, and sometimes a member of its staff, question the witnesses, but rarely in a fundamentally challenging way.

In the printed record of the hearings there are odd disproportions in the allocation of space. An inordinate number of pages are devoted to scientific and technical reports that can scarcely be of much use to a layman in assessing the space program and in deciding on the amount to be appropriated. This is perhaps a vestigial reminder of the fact that the space program was once primarily scientific. In contrast, some other purposes of the space effort are entirely neglected, or nearly so. Most notably, though almost everyone who tries to justify the space program mentions the enhancement of national prestige as one of the factors, the committees do not probe into the question at all. The Chairman of the House committee, Mr. Miller, says that he "can speak from firsthand knowledge gained from personal contact with scientific and technical leaders both here and in Europe that world respect for American technology, as a direct result of our space program, has been enhanced many times over." [19] Perhaps so. But Mr. Miller has to rely on his limited personal contacts. His committee hearings do not provide evidence one way or another, save for the fact that the question repeatedly arises whether we are ahead of the Russians or how soon we will be. Neither is there any probing into the question of the influence that pride and the achievement motive do and should have. So far as the alleged contribution of the space program to economic progress is concerned, the hearings have been pretty much confined to (1) reports from NASA officials on what they are doing to stimulate

[19] *Ibid.*, Vol. 109, No. 108 (July 17, 1963), 4508.

progress, (2) the examination of patent policies, and (3) comments on the potential benefits of meteorological and communications satellites. No real scrutiny is given to the question of the value of the potential "spill-over." Much more attention is given to the question of potential economic benefits at the local level, e.g., to the geographical distribution of NASA's installations and contracts; even in this connection there is no real effort to debate and clarify questions of principle, and to get satisfactory principles established. As for promoting peace and limiting ourselves to peaceful purposes, the congressional committees have joined everyone else in missing opportunities to get the question clarified. Though, as indicated, a tremendous number of pages are devoted to scientific and technical reports from NASA officials, scarcely any consideration is given to the conditions and procedures that most fully assure scientific and technological progress. Finally, so far as the record shows, the committees make no attempt whatsoever to compare the prospective benefits of expenditures for space with the prospective benefits of devoting the same money to some other purpose; the question is yes or no for space, with no consideration of possible alternatives, even within the area of the committee's jurisdiction. Moreover, the hearings do little or nothing directly to indicate whether the appropriation for the year should be $2 billion or $10 billion; they simply argue for a project or program or goal, and if the committee accepts the argument it also accepts the price tag attached, perhaps with minor modifications.

James B. Conant once suggested that healthy skepticism is in order when an expert speaks, especially if he speaks with enthusiasm. Referring to enthusiasms for research that developed in DOD after World War II, he suggested a more or less formal arrangement under which an expert "devil's advocate" would present reasoned opposition to whatever was proposed.[20] The suggestion also applies to the proceedings of the space committees in Congress. Another possibility has also been mentioned: that Congress might imitate such agencies as the Air Force and NASA, which make contracts with especially established corporations for various kinds of studies and other services. By so doing, Congress might obtain appraisals and recommendations inde-

---

[20] James B. Conant, *Modern Science and Modern Man* (Garden City: Doubleday Anchor, 1952), pp. 115-18.

pendent of those made in the Executive branch. Whatever the merit of such proposals, their chances of adoption do not seem good.

The shortcomings of the hearings are no doubt related not only to the influence of congressional tradition but also to the attitude of committee members toward the space program. As is clear from the chapters of Part II, they have been overwhelmingly committed to the urgent development of possibilities in space, pushing from the first for a competitive effort to outdo the Russians. Given this attitude, it followed that they would urge the Eisenhower Administration to spend more, and that they would not be disposed to question seriously the larger appropriations that Kennedy recommended. Had the chairman of the space committee in either house been skeptical of the space program or of the projected manned lunar landing, the hearings would no doubt have taken on a rather different complexion. They may yet do so, for skepticism about the feasibility of a lunar landing, about its timing, and about the competitive motivations for it is obviously increasing.

If there are some shortcomings in the way in which Congress handles its portion of the processes of legislating and exercising oversight, it should not be forgotten that there are other portions. The President and various agencies in the Executive branch—especially the Space Council, the Bureau of the Budget, NASA, and DOD—are heavily involved and indeed have the lead. It might well be that if the negative were presented at congressional hearings, or if Congress had "desirability studies" made by private agencies under contract, the outcome would be the same. Presumably the negative has already lost the argument within the Executive branch, and quite possibly disinterested studies made by private agencies for Congress might lead to the same result that the Executive branch has already reached.

NASA-DOD Relationships

Given the above survey of the principal agencies concerned with the space program, we should now revert to the question of relationships between NASA and DOD, the two that actually launch vehicles into space. These relationships are both cooperative and competitive, both harmonious and strife-ridden. The purpose here is to note both kinds of relationships and, more particularly, to identify the types of issues that arise and the types of methods and bargaining counters used in their resolution.

As a preliminary, we should recall that there is also cooperation and competition within DOD. The Army, Navy, and Air Force are all active in space in some degree; they cooperate with each other, and at the same time they engage in intense and bitter rivalry in the search for greater roles. With the manned bomber obsolescent, at least as a major weapon in nuclear war, the course of the struggle is of especially great significance to the Air Force. I have not heard it suggested that any of the services has employed poisonous drugs or physical violence in its struggles against the others, but few other weapons are neglected. I am even told of one case of the employment of a woman to seduce a member of another service and worm information from him. Over the three services is the Office of the Secretary of Defense (OSD), which has endorsed a very substantial military space program but which, under McNamara as well as under his predecessors, has resisted the more extreme pressures from below (as well as from certain senators). Thus, much of the struggle over the nature and size of the military space program is not a struggle between NASA and DOD, but rather a struggle within DOD. As the Chairman of the House space committee has put it: "The real cause of all this squabble about the military-in-space stems from an inhouse difference of opinion within the military establishment. . . . The problem is that the military space enthusiasts have not been able to obtain all the green lights they want from their bosses." [21] The fact that OSD is resistant to the more extreme demands of the services is a safeguard for NASA. It is difficult to say what Congress would do if Mr. McMamara were to recommend a doubling or tripling of appropriations for the military space program, or if he were to say that it is vital to national security that the Air Force be permitted to go ahead with a full-fledged man-in-space program. So far, his refusal to take such stands has left NASA clearly in the leading role.

When the Space Act was enacted, Congress tried forlornly to facilitate bilateral liaison between NASA and DOD by providing for a Civilian-Military Liaison Committee (CMLC), consisting of representatives of NASA and DOD plus a Chairman who was to be an independent third party. But Congress did not grant the Chairman (or the committee) any power. The committee

---

[21] *Congressional Record*, Vol. 108, No. 160 (September 6, 1962), 17,588.

could thus be bypassed with impunity, and this is what happened. Apparently DOD used the chairmanship as a kind of cushion on which to drop an employee whose services it no longer wished to retain, and then DOD ignored him. He soon resigned, and the CMLC dissolved.

The function that the CMLC was supposed to serve has been taken over to some extent by the Aeronautics and Astronautics Coordinating Board (AACB), created in 1960 by an administrative agreement between NASA and DOD. The agreement lays down the principle that liaison should be maintained "in the most direct manner possible" at the various bureaucratic levels. Where policy issues and management decisions are not involved, project-level personnel in the two agencies deal directly with each other. "Where policy issues and management decisions are involved, it is important that the planning and coordination of activities, the identification of problems, and the exchange of information be facilitated between officials having the authority and responsibility for decisions within their respective offices." No longer is there a third-party chairman without responsibility or power. Instead, at least on the basis of the original plan, the members of the Board are officials who have considerable authority in their own organizations, and so can themselves execute whatever agreements are reached. At first, the Deputy Administrator of NASA and the Director of Defense Research and Engineering served as Co-Chairmen, presiding in turn; but each side has come to be represented by persons somewhat lower in the hierarchy. The Board has six panels, dealing with the following subjects: (1) manned space flight, (2) unmanned spacecraft, (3) launch vehicles, (4) space flight ground environment, (5) supporting space research and technology, and (6) aeronautics. These panels and the Board itself serve as forums for the exchange of information and for the discussion and resolution of problems. Secretary McNamara testified in February, 1963 (29 months after the establishment of the Board), that it had met 18 times. According to him, "the functions and work of this Board provide one of the best examples of continuing and effective cooperation between Government agencies engaged in parallel and interacting fields of activity." [22]

[22] U.S. Congress, Senate, Committee on Armed Services, *Military Procurement Authorization for Fiscal Year 1964*, Hearings, 88th Cong., 1st Sess., 1963, p. 247.

When issues come up that are "too hot for the AACB to handle," according to the Director of Defense Research and Engineering, "we solicit advice and we sometimes perform a study to help the AACB, but we don't go through the procedure of failing to reach agreement with the panel and then failing to reach agreement in the AACB; we take them to the Administrator and the Secretary." The Director went on to say that "there has never been a disagreement that could not be resolved by the Administrator and the Secretary of Defense." [23] He must have been thinking only of a restricted range of issues, for some kinds (such as DOD's part in manned space flight) necessarily go to third parties. The statement does, however, suggest that NASA and DOD want to settle issues between themselves insofar as possible. Where issues are entirely within their jurisdiction, a failure to settle them bilaterally would surely be somewhat embarrassing; it would place third parties— perhaps the President himself—in an unwelcome position; and NASA and DOD would risk getting a worse settlement than they might reach on their own.

In fact, NASA and DOD cooperate in many ways. Almost all of the astronauts selected so far come from the armed services. The Navy recovers astronauts landing in the sea. The Air Force gives NASA substantial support in the realm of bioastronautics (space medicine). All of the services respond to requests from NASA to assign personnel to NASA headquarters and centers; nearly 300 were so assigned as of the spring of 1963, mainly by the Army and Air Force. [24] In addition, cooperation is no doubt facilitated by the fact that many civilians who formerly worked in DOD, as well as a number of retired officers, now work for NASA. Early in 1963 the position of Deputy Associate Administrator for Defense Affairs was established in NASA, and a retired admiral was appointed to it. A deputy commander of the Air Force Systems Command has an office at NASA headquarters; and, according to the Air Force, "he can and does call upon the full resources of the Systems Command in support of NASA." [25]

---

[23] U.S. Congress, House, Committee on Science and Astronautics, *1963 NASA Authorization*, Hearings . . . on H. Res. 10100, 87th Cong., 2d Sess., 1962, Part 2, pp. 593, 611.

[24] U.S. Congress, House, Committee on Science and Astronautics, *Posture of the National Space Program*, Report, 88th Cong., 1st Sess., 1963, Appendix C, pp. 55-63.

[25] Lieutenant General James G. Ferguson, USAF, in U.S. Congress, House, Committee on Science and Astronautics, *Space Posture*, Hearings, 88th Cong., 1st Sess., 1963, p. 225.

NASA uses the Atlantic and Pacific missile ranges, operated by DOD and its contractors. Each agency sometimes provides scientific payloads for launching by the other. NASA has launched a satellite for the Air Force from its Wallops Island station. Considerable "cross-servicing" occurs. For example, when NASA does business with firms heavily involved in DOD contracts, it makes "extensive use of the in-plant contract administration and audit services of the Army, Navy, and Air Force." [26] A spokesman for NASA said in the fall of 1962 that about 25 per cent of its business was handled through DOD. Many of the boosters that NASA uses are ordered through the Air Force. In its new construction, NASA utilizes the Army engineers and personnel from the Navy's Bureau of Yards and Docks as well as personnel from the General Services Administration. The rule is that NASA reimburses DOD and other agencies for their services; e.g., it reimburses DOD for the salaries of the officers detailed to it and for the costs of recovering astronauts from the sea. DOD's ground stations are employed in connection with NASA's Syncom project—the synchronous communications satellite—and there is substantial cooperation in the X-15 and X-20 (Dyna-Soar) projects.

Much of the cooperation between NASA and DOD occurs on the basis of formal written agreements, somewhat suggestive of treaties between sovereign powers. An agreement concerning the National Launch Vehicle Program stipulates that neither DOD nor NASA will initiate the development of a new launch vehicle without the concurrence of the other, and subsequent agreements have been made concerning specific new vehicles. A 1962 agreement calls for the exchange of five-year plans; "and each of us will look over the other's plans, and we will make sure between us and with the help of the Bureau of the Budget that we are not duplicating or overlapping but we are using each other's technology." [27] Each year, when DOD and NASA formulate their budgetary requests for the construction of new facilities—and before these requests go to Congress—the AACB has been providing for a joint review to check on possible duplications; in the preparation of the 1964

[26] Albert F. Siepert, "Organization and Funding of NASA," in NASA, Office of Scientific and Technical Information, *Proceedings of the NASA-University Conference on the Science and Technology of Space Exploration,* Chicago, Illinois, November 1-3, 1962 (Washington, 1962), I, 32-33.

[27] Roswell L. Gilpatric, in U.S. Congress, Senate, Committee on Aeronautical and Space Sciences, *NASA Authorization for Fiscal Year 1963,* Hearings, 87th Cong., 2d Sess., 1962, p. 18.

budget, at least, the joint review led to the signing of an agreement indicating that both parties were satisfied.[28] In 1963, as we noted in Chapter 3, agreements were reached concerning Air Force participation in the Gemini program and concerning a possible new program in the area of manned earth orbital research and development vehicles. NASA has representatives on nearly 100 interagency committees and working groups, on most of which DOD is also represented, e.g., the "Gas Lubricated Bearing Advisory Group" with the following membership: NASA, Army, Navy, Air Force, Atomic Energy Commission, and Bureau of Standards.

The fact of cooperation says something, but not much, about the extent to which NASA-DOD relationships are characterized by friendly good feeling and to what extent bitter in-fighting occurs. The public pronouncements of the leaders of both sides are to the effect that very good relationships exist and that they go out of their way to be responsive to each other's needs. But it is inevitable that more or less serious conflicts would arise both over the ends to pursue and the means to employ, and it is scarcely credible that this would not lead to intense struggles, especially when those involved are aggressive, success-oriented men dedicated to the achievement of goals that they consider very important. Evidence of in-fighting has appeared in several connections. The House Committee on Science and Astronautics found it desirable early in 1961 to probe into what seemed to be a kind of Air Force imperialism aimed at NASA, and one of the conclusions stated in the committee's report went as follows:

Witnesses from the Department of Defense have disavowed any designs on NASA, and have renewed promises to work in full cooperation with NASA. The committee is happy to have these assurances from the proper officials in DOD. However, the committee has a large bulk of printed material which derogates NASA in relation to the Department of Defense. This would seem to throw the responsibility for slurring remarks about the importance or the efficacy of NASA on nongovernmental sources; but whatever the source, the committee regrets such attacks as unwise.[29]

[28] U.S. Congress, Senate, Committee on Aeronautical and Space Sciences, *NASA Authorization for Fiscal Year 1964,* Hearings, 88th Cong., 1st Sess., 1963, Part 1, p. 92; U.S. Congress, House, Committee on Science and Astronautics, *1964 NASA Authorization,* Hearings, 88th Cong., 1st Sess., 1963, Part 4, p. 3285.

[29] U.S. Congress, House, Committee on Science and Astronautics, *Military Astronautics* (Preliminary Report), H. Rpt. No. 360, 87th Cong., 1st Sess., 1961, p. 36.

Strong feeling also showed up on the question of the extent to which NASA should rely on the Air Force for research in bioastronautics and the extent to which it should develop a program of its own. A visitor at Cape Canaveral speaks of "the ill-concealed antagonism between NASA and the Air Force at the working level. . . . The frictions at the Cape cannot help but slow down space progress. Crossing from Air Force installations into NASA's celebrated Mercury control center is like going from one country to another." [30] The very fact that so many agreements have been reached between NASA and DOD on important issues suggests prior struggles and negotiations.

Though the relevant information about issues is obviously incomplete, logically they must fall into three categories. In the first category are issues concerning the respective roles to be played in the space program by NASA and DOD. For example, as we noted in Chapter 3, rival claims are being made for the management of the manned orbital laboratory or station that will presumably be the major space project following Apollo. In the second category are issues arising when the agency managing an activity is not fully responsive to the desires of the other concerning it. For example, NASA manages the Gemini project, and DOD has wanted it implemented in such a way as to produce a maximum amount of militarily useful knowledge and experience. The issue has led to an agreement referred to above. In the third category are issues of a subordinate sort, arising over the actual execution of agreements reached. For example, given an agreement that DOD and NASA will share facilities at Canaveral, what will the precise terms and arrangements be?

In principle, disputes in each of the above categories might be settled either through direct bilateral negotiations or with the aid of third parties. Direct bilateral negotiations may be conducted in personal meetings of top officials or through such agencies as the AACB and the Gemini Program Planning Board. The major available third parties have been mentioned above: the Space Council and its staff, the Bureau of the Budget, the National Security Council, the Vice President and the President personally, and Congress. Depending on circumstances, the third parties may see it as their function either to lead the disputants to agreement or to impose a settlement.

---

[30] Richard A. Smith, "Canaveral, Industry's Trial by Fire," *Fortune*, 65 (June, 1962), 204.

What factors count in resolving issues? What leverage does each side have—what weapons—in dealing with the other?

So far as bilateral settlement is concerned, there are a number of possibilities. Some issues are settled simply on the basis of discussion and argument. Perhaps it is simply a question of providing fuller information about activities or plans, or clarifying meanings. For example, given the agreement that neither side will initiate the development of a new launch vehicle without the concurrence of the other, just what does the agreement mean? Settlement by discussion and argument might also turn on the establishment of scientific fact or technological feasibility, or on logical inferences from agreed premises. A considerable portion of the matters that come before the AACB, for example, are settled on the basis of persuasion. Alternatively, when issues cannot be resolved through persuasion, they can be the subject of a bargain, each side making certain concessions and gaining certain *quid pro quos*. Still another basis for settlement—the one apparently used in connection with the agreement of January, 1963, for Air Force participation in the Gemini program—is financial: the Air Force may have its way, within limits, if it pays for what it gets.

The more difficult a bilateral settlement is, the more each side must consider the probable outcome if one or more third parties become involved. And here the relevant factors may be very complex. If the third party is within the Executive branch, the question that is ultimately crucial is the probable attitude of the President. If either side can count on his support (for whatever relevant or irrelevant reason), its power to persuade is likely to be irresistible! If his attitude is not predictable, or if it seems impolitic to draw on credit with him, then other attitudes gain in importance: the attitudes of members of the Space Council and its staff, the attitudes of personnel in the Bureau of the Budget, etc. Similarly, if the third party is to be Congress or a congressional agency, the probable attitudes of certain subcommittee and committee chairmen may well be of crucial importance. In struggles at Cape Canaveral the "cost-conscious Air Force" is said on occasion to have threatened "to bring the General Accounting Office clucking down on NASA for extravagance." [31] Subordinates in either agency can always leak information to the press if they think some purpose would be served thereby. This is apparently what happened in

---

[31] *Ibid.*

the spring of 1963 when an Air Force document was published alleging that NASA's askings called for the duplication of Air Force facilities whose use would save the government $77 million.

Given the fact that third parties are involved in the space program, both NASA and DOD must be solicitous of them. Depending somewhat on the relative importance of individuals and the offices they hold, their slightest wishes must get attention and, if possible, be anticipated. For DOD, the space program simply gives an additional reason to look after the happiness and welfare of congressmen, especially the more influential congressmen on the key committees and subcommittees. The Air Force, for example, can arrange interesting and pleasant inspection trips or, fortuitously, can have a flight scheduled that will permit the congressman to get to his home district for the weekend. If a member of the congressman's staff or a committee staff is in the reserves, he can be called up at a suitable time and given an attractive assignment, perhaps abroad. As indicated above, congressmen may be given the opportunity to announce developments that will presumably add to their popularity. And, within limits, contracts can be placed and facilities located in such a way as to cultivate the support of congressmen in key positions. NASA also can employ some of these devices—as is suggested by the decision to locate the Manned Spacecraft Center near Houston. Similarly, both DOD and NASA can be attentive to the wishes and interests of third parties within the Executive branch. Neither can go too far beyond the limits of propriety in cultivating favor, but most congressmen have a very indulgent conception of propriety where benefit to colleagues is concerned.

Discussions of relationships among the Army, Navy, and Air Force frequently include the statement that their rivalries are predominantly beneficial, stimulating each to excel. Possibly this is true, and possibly the same is true of the rivalry that exists between NASA and DOD. Not enough evidence is available to permit a judgment.

Lest I leave the impression that organizational relationships associated with the space program are all strained and unsavory, let me recall the account of cooperation, given above. Moreover, the highest officials of NASA and DOD have on various occasions expressed pleasure and satisfaction concerning the relationships that exist among them, and Mr. Webb commonly cites a contribution to military security as one of the justifications of the space program, which suggests quite voluntary concern for the problem on his part; contributions toward meeting military needs do not always have to be wrung from him unwillingly. Secretary of the Air Force Zuckert has testified that "NASA is ready to respond. Jim Webb . . . harbors no illusions about NASA's responsibilities in support of national defense requirements." [32] Common goals can provide a basis for cooperation, even if there is conflict over the terms on which it will occur.

Concluding Comments

This chapter deals with a series of rather discrete questions, and thus does not lead to any one general conclusion. We have examined (1) the reasons for putting the major portion of the space program under civilian management; (2) NASA's administrative arrangements and policies, especially its reliance on contractual arrangements with private firms and agencies; (3) the allocation of responsibilities for space within DOD; (4) the work of the National Aeronautics and Space Council and of other executive agencies dealing with space; (5) congressional arrangements for legislation on space, with special reference to the adequacy of the committee hearings; and (6) NASA-DOD relationships, with special reference to the cooperation between the two organizations and the means available to them in settling differences that arise. Obviously, nothing about the organizational arrangements surveyed here precludes the development of a space program that will promote the various purposes described in the chapters of Part II.

---

[32] *Congressional Record*, Vol. 109, No. 55 (April 15, 1963), 6174.

MOBILIZING RESOURCES

13

To give effect to the motives analyzed in the chapters of Part II it is necessary not only to adopt appropriate organizational arrangements within the government but also to mobilize resources outside the government. For this purpose, governmental agencies have developed relationships with business firms, with the universities, and with a relatively new kind of organization that in some ways is a cross between the two, i.e., corporations established especially to provide research and other specialized services to the federal government.

As in every other field of activity, the process of mobilizing resources involves problems and choices. How does or should an additional vast governmental program fit with traditional notions of free enterprise and private profit-seeking? How do political considerations impinge on the administrative and technical implementation of the program? How are NASA's dollars allocated among different parts of the country? How does small business fare? Suppose that a private firm makes a patentable innovation in the course of research financed by the government, who does or should get the patent rights? What are the advantages and disadvantages of using especially established private corporations rather than civil service personnel or regular business firms for research and other specialized services? What kinds of relationships does or should NASA have with the universities? Does or should it assume responsibilities for helping to develop the trained manpower that the space program (and the country) will require in the future?

These problems are big and complex, and some of them are new enough that the relevant literature is rather scant. The main object here is to describe, and hopefully to clarify, both the problems and some salient actions and attitudes relating to them.

NASA and the Business World

SPACE AS AN ADDITION TO THE PUBLIC SECTOR

In a formal sense the space program is an addition to the public rather than the private sector of the American economy. Government takes the initiative. It selects the goals and the methods, fixes the schedules and priorities, and provides the funds. It does the planning. Given the motivations identified in the chapters of Part II—in particular, the desire to promote military security, national prestige, and national pride—it was virtually inevitable that this would be the case. Moreover, though some predict economic benefits from the space program, the prospect of profits from activities in space is not such as to attract private investments on any great scale. Investors may be quite venturesome in their efforts to get government contracts for space work, but in general they are not willing to act independently of government leadership. A.T.&T., with Telstar, and the Communication Satellite Corporation are exceptions, at least in part.

Nevertheless, though virtually everyone takes it for granted that the space program belongs in the public sector (at least for the time being), the situation causes concern, both outside and inside the government, as relationships between NASA and private enterprise are worked out.

Gilbert Burck, in a *Fortune* article, cites some reasons for some of the uneasiness that he thinks exists:

This decade's [space] program alone, which may be only preliminary, could impose unpalatable if not severe burdens on the nation. It will very likely kill all chances of reducing in our time the government's share of the economy. It will change, strain, and probably distort the distribution of the nation's resources. With all its emphasis on planning, both national and international, it could ultimately do violence to private enterprise itself.[1]

Mr. Burck goes on to say that the space program "is boosting the ardor and ambition of those who believe the world is headed for

---

[1] Gilbert Burck, "Hitching the Economy to the Infinite," *Fortune,* 65 (June, 1962), 124.

more state planning. . . . For them the great implication of space is that it will somehow free man from his preoccupation with profits and losses."

Ralph J. Cordiner, Chairman of the Board of the General Electric Company, is also somewhat fearful of the possible effects of a governmentally managed and financed space program. Decentralized power is to him a basic principle of the American system. "There are many competing points of initiative, risk, and decision —and that is the secret of this nation's drive and creativity." But to add to the public sector is to go toward centralization. "As we step up our activities on the space frontier, many companies, universities, and individual citizens will become increasingly dependent on the political whims and necessities of the federal government. And if that drift continues without check, the United States may find itself becoming the very kind of society that it is struggling against—a regimented society whose people and institutions are dominated by a central government." [2]

Mr. Cordiner's prescription is that once government has selected the objectives to be attained, it should turn their achievement over to "the private firms that have the managerial and technical capacity to get the work done—using competition and profit-or-loss incentives to the maximum." He thinks that freedom and progress will both be best served "if competitive private enterprise does just as much of the nation's scientific and technical work as possible —and government provides the legal and policy framework to stimulate outstanding performance." He sees three overlapping stages of the venture into space, with the emphasis shifting successively from exploration to economic development to mature economic operation; and he wants a concurrent shift of emphasis toward private enterprise. In the exploratory stage he mentions, in addition to communications satellites, the possibility of a privately owned launching service and privately owned laboratories both on earth and in space. As areas of activity for private firms in the second stage he adds a weather forecasting service and transportation by rocket between different points on earth. And for the stage of mature economic operation he envisages also the exploitation of the raw material resources of outer space along with other activities now unpredictable.

---

[2] Ralph J. Cordiner, "Competitive Private Enterprise in Space," in Simon Ramo, ed., *Peacetime Uses of Outer Space* (New York: McGraw-Hill, 1961), p. 222.

Though somewhat fearful of the possible consequences of the space program, Mr. Cordiner is not hostile to it. On the contrary, he speaks of the "inevitable partnership" of business and government in a "lengthy enterprise." I do not know what the relationship is between this outlook and the fact that General Electric is an important NASA contractor.

Information about the attitudes of businessmen in general is quite incomplete, but the indications are that they welcome the space program. Raymond A. Bauer thinks that many of them do so for a rather surprising reason: it gives them an excuse "for supporting governmental economic policies which in another garb would be fixed by these same men as dangerously radical." Rejecting Keynes, rejecting an active role for government in promoting welfare, yet sensing that their position may not make for rapid economic growth and prosperity, they need a cover under which to do the ideologically improper.

There are four ways in which this smuggling in of liberal economics occurs. Starting with a government-financed space program it is hoped that: (1) The government will develop opportunities which industry may later exploit. (2) Government financed scientific discoveries will evolve which will have practical applications. (3) There will be a direct application in our economy of many of the by-products of space research. (4) The money invested in the aero-space industry will "prime the pump." [3]

Actually, though in a formal sense space is an addition to the public sector, the point does not have as much significance as theoretically it might. As we noted in the last chapter, NASA relies very heavily on private concerns. Its most recent procurement report covers July to December, 1962.[4] In that period, of the money obligated in procurement actions of $25,000 and over, 63 per cent was committed directly to business firms, 23 per cent to other government agencies, 11 per cent to the Jet Propulsion Laboratory, and 3 per cent to educational and nonprofit organizations. In turn, the other government agencies and the Jet Propulsion Laboratory committed to business firms most of the money they got from NASA, permitting NASA to conclude that about 92 per cent of its procurement dollars went to private industry. The procurements covered not only hardware but also, as we will shortly see, man-

---

[3] Raymond A. Bauer, "Keynes via the Back Door," *Journal of Social Issues*, Vol. 17, No. 2 (1961), 50, 52.

[4] NASA, *Semiannual Procurement Report*, July 1, 1962, through December 31, 1962 (Washington, 1963).

agerial services and research and development. Almost half of NASA's contract awards to business (in terms of dollar value) went to only eight firms. In addition, there is some rotation of personnel from the business world into NASA and out again; the same man may be helping to plan and execute the space program on behalf of NASA one day and on behalf of a business firm the next day. Further, a high proportion of NASA's contracts, as we will see in a moment, call not for conventional items but for research and development; NASA does not simply place an order and then await delivery, but commonly works fairly closely with its contractors. This all means, inevitably, that the dividing line between the public and private sectors becomes somewhat blurred. NASA and its major contractors become interdependent, and who controls whom sometimes becomes a moot question. Mr. Cordiner spoke of a "partnership" between government and business, and the term is apt.

It is usually assumed that profits are the dominant or sole motive of business firms, and it is sometimes assumed that governmental programs are subversive of the profit system. The questions raised by these assumptions are much broader than the space program and will not be discussed here. It might be noted, however, that leaders in industry sometimes speak as if their motive in making contracts with NASA is not so much profits as service to the public good; and leaders in NASA repeatedly endorse the profit system, minimizing reliance on not-for-profit arrangements. How much hypocrisy there may be in these positions, if any, is for others to say.

PROCUREMENT POLICIES AND PROBLEMS

In NASA's procurements "the maximum practicable competition" is the declared goal.[5] But in the last half of 1962 only 5 per cent of the money committed directly to business firms was committed after formal advertising for bids. Another 51 per cent was committed on the basis of what NASA calls "competitive negotiation." This means that NASA describes its needs as clearly as it can to more than one firm, invites them to submit proposals, and then

[5] Robert C. Seamans, Jr., NASA News Release, November 13, 1962, p. 23. Cf. a letter from Mr. Webb to Senator Proxmire, in U.S. Congress, House, Committee on Science and Astronautics, *1963 NASA Authorization,* Hearings . . . on H. Res. 10100, 87th Cong., 2d Sess., 1962, Part 2, pp. 825-28 (hereafter cited as House Hearings, *1963 NASA Authorization*); Walter L. Lingle, Jr., NASA News Release, May 1, 1963.

selects the firm with which to negotiate a contract. The remainder, 44 per cent, was committed noncompetitively.

The principal reason for the limited extent of the competition is to be found in the nature of NASA's needs. As we noted immediately above, most of them are in the research and development category, meaning that what is wanted has never been done or produced before; so precise specifications cannot be written in advance. Thus the methods for selecting a contractor, and the criteria of selection, can scarcely be as simple and clear-cut as they ordinarily are when bidders with proven capabilities offer to produce more or less conventional items at a stated price. NASA maintains Source Evaluation Boards which evaluate potential contractors; presumably the Boards consider such factors as the quality of the personnel available to the contractor, his relevant experience, and his performance record, and they then report either to the NASA center that is to make the contract or to the Administrator, depending on the size of the procurement. Among the especially unusual criteria of choice is the fact that a contract may be awarded to a company not because it already has the needed capability but in order to help it develop the capability. Thus Mr. Webb says that "one of the principal factors cited in the selection of the Douglas Aircraft Co. [for the development of the second stage of the Saturn] was that the addition of the company would broaden the industrial base in the hydrogen technology field." And he speaks of using contract awards as a means of "expanding the industrial sources NASA can turn to for competition in the future." [6] It perhaps should be recognized that Douglas Aircraft had had considerable experience in missile and space work, even if not specifically in hydrogen technology. But the notable fact is that winners of contracts may be chosen not on the basis of prices or other ordinary objective considerations but on the basis of a considerable admixture of subjective judgment. As one author puts it, it is sometimes "necessary to determine by administrative judgment of the public interest those things that were once decided by the operation of the market." [7]

Perhaps I should note NASA's statement about its noncompeti-

---

[6] House Hearings, *1963 NASA Authorization*, Part 2, pp. 825, 826.

[7] Carl F. Stover, "The Government Contract System as a Problem in Public Policy," in Stanford Research Institute, *The Industry-Government Aerospace Relationship*, prepared for Aerospace Industries Association of America (Menlo Park, 1963), Vol. 2, Appendix A, p. 13.

tive procurements. "These include contracts for the acquisition and installation of facilities required at contractors' plants for the performance of their NASA research and development contracts; contracts arising from unsolicited proposals offering new ideas and concepts; contracts employing unique capabilities; and procurements of sole source items." They also include "follow-on contracts (contracts for additional or closely related work), placed with the same contractor who was originally selected on a competitive basis. . . ." [8]

In the last six months of 1962, considering all procurements of $25,000 and over, 77 per cent of NASA's contracts with business concerns (by dollar value) were on a cost-plus-fixed-fee basis, 6 per cent were on a cost-plus-incentive-fee basis, 12 per cent on a firm-fixed-price basis, and 5 per cent on an "other" basis. There is dissatisfaction with the cost-plus-fixed-fee arrangement both in NASA and among contractors. For the firms operating under such a contract, "outstanding performance or economy offers little immediate reward," [9] and for the government costs tend to go up. A Budget Bureau report in 1962 urged that the arrangement be abandoned wherever possible, preferably in favor of fixed-price contracting. But where cost reimbursement had to be retained, the Bureau recommended the incentive fee plan: an "arrangement under which the fee would not be fixed, but would vary according to a predetermined standard which would relate larger fees to lower costs, superior performance, and shorter delivery times. . . . Where the nature of the task permits, it may be desirable to include in the contract penalty provisions for inadequate performance." [10]

As the law requires, NASA is concerned about the impact of the space program on small business. Evidence on the impact is inconclusive. Of all of NASA's direct awards to business firms in the last six months of 1962, only 9 per cent (by value) went to "small business"; but of the 100 contractors receiving the largest dollar value of NASA's direct awards to business 27 were "small." Reports received by NASA in the last six months of 1962 from 32

[8] NASA, *Semiannual Procurement Report,* July 1, 1962, through December 31, 1962, p. 6.

[9] Cordiner, *loc. cit.,* p. 236.

[10] U.S. Congress, Senate, Committee on Government Operations, *Report to the President on Government Contracting for Research and Development,* prepared by the Bureau of the Budget, S. Doc. No. 94, 87th Cong., 2d Sess., 1962, p. 17 (hereafter cited as Senate, *Contracting for R&D,* 1962).

of its prime contractors indicated that they had passed 43 per cent of their NASA dollars on to subcontractors—17 per cent to "small" business and 26 per cent to "large." NASA encourages such sub-contracting. According to Mr. Webb, "Beginning January 1961, we have prescribed the use of a small business program clause in contracts over $1 million which offer substantial subcontracting possibilities. This program clause requires contractors to have an active small business subcontracting program. . . ."[11] Mr. Webb also speaks of a policy that is not designed entirely to benefit small business, but that would surely have this effect to some extent. "As a policy in making prime contract awards, we are steadily moving in the direction of insisting that prime contractors make strong efforts to seek out superior subcontract skills, among companies of proven performance wherever located, rather than risk failure or increased costs by trying to develop internal or new sources of competence to perform these tasks."[12] Congressional inquiries into NASA's treatment of small business have led to praise. A House study in 1961 concluded that NASA was "doing an outstanding job to assist small business in obtaining their fair share of the research and development dollar,"[13] and a Senate Select Committee on Small Business held NASA up as an example to DOD, recommending that the Department consult with NASA on ways of improving its practices.[14] I do not have data on the net effect of the space program on tendencies toward economic concentration. It is Ralph J. Cordiner's view that the program "is encouraging the creation of more businesses of all sizes." "To those who insist that small business is declining, I only ask that you leaf through the advertisements in the technical magazines to see how many thousands of new businesses have sprung up to handle the requirements of modern technology. Most of them are suppliers of specialty equipment. . . ."[15]

In Chapter 10 we noted considerable concern in Congress over the geographical distribution of NASA's contracting. In the last six months of 1962, considering prime contracts worth $25,000 and over

---

[11] House Hearings, *1963 NASA Authorization*, Part 2, p. 828.

[12] James E. Webb, address of March 27, 1963, NASA News Release, p. 6.

[13] U.S. Congress, House, Committee on Science and Astronautics, *Small Business Participation in the NASA Research and Development Programs*, Staff Study, 87th Cong., 1st Sess., 1961, p. 14.

[14] U.S. Congress, Senate, Select Committee on Small Business, *The Role of Small Business in Government Procurement—1961*, S. Rpt. No. 355, 87th Cong., 1st Sess., 1961, p. 10.

[15] Cordiner, *loc. cit.*, p. 219.

placed directly with business concerns, 48 per cent by value went to California. Following after California, other states ranked as follows: Missouri, 11 per cent; Louisiana, 9 per cent; New York, 5 per cent; Alabama, 5 per cent; Florida, 4 per cent; New Jersey, 3 per cent. Two states thus got 59 per cent of the awards; three got 68 per cent; and the seven got 85 per cent. The next five (including the District of Columbia) got a total of 9 per cent, leaving about 6 per cent for the remaining 39 states. Subcontracting brought slightly greater diffusion. For the period of January 1, 1962, to February 28, 1963—thus a different period from the one reported on above—twelve of NASA's major prime contractors did 83 per cent of this subcontracting (by dollar value) in seven states, but four of the seven are not on the above list. California is again in an exceptionally favored position, with 49 per cent of the dollar value of the subcontracts.

NASA's position on this matter is that its prime duty is "to carry out the civil space program in a timely, efficient, and economical manner."

It is the judgment of management throughout NASA that the ultimate success of the program depends to a large extent on placing contracts with companies which are found best qualified to perform the work. It should be recognized that certain companies have successfully performed similar work and have acquired unique technical experience, facilities, and equipment, which would cost hundreds of millions of dollars to duplicate. It is technically and economically advisable to utilize the services of such companies wherever they are located or whatever their size.[16]

It turns out, of course, that the best qualified companies are located in very few states.

I have no serious doubt that political considerations have been among those influencing the choice of sites for NASA installations—whether the original choice was by one of the armed services (as in the location of an army installation at Huntsville, Alabama) or by NASA itself; and to some extent the location of the installations influences the geographical distribution of contracts. Whether or not political considerations have directly influenced the placing of contracts in the past, many congressmen are exerting great pressures for the future. Representative Roudebush expressed a view widely shared by his colleagues when he said, "I think more effort must be expended to split these space contract dollars—of course,

---

[16] U.S. Congress, House, Committee on Science and Astronautics, *1964 NASA Authorization*, Hearings, 88th Cong., 1st Sess., 1963, Part 4, p. 3340 (hereafter cited as House Hearings, *1964 NASA Authorization*).

to competent firms—among the various states." [17] And, in a way, NASA is responding. It does not stick strictly to the position that the geographical distribution of its dollars is an irrelevant consideration. It provides statistics on the question, and its spokesmen before congressional committees frequently respond to complaints by citing states in addition to California that are receiving dollar benefits. NASA is handling its sustaining university program, to be described shortly, in such a way as to avoid a geographical concentration. And it has contracts with various research institutes (e.g., the Midwest Research Institute) and arrangements with a number of universities (e.g., with Indiana University and its Aerospace Research Application Center) designed to find ways to bring benefits from the space program to the various parts of the country. How much more it will do remains to be seen. Congress is in an invidious position on the problem, for if it insists—formally or informally—on a greater geographical dispersion of NASA's dollars it runs some risk—as NASA spokesmen implicitly indicate—of impairing the speed and efficiency with which the program is executed. In short, we have here an illustration of an administrative and political problem created by some degree of incompatibility between the purposes pursued through the space program.

PATENT POLICIES

Probably the most intensely debated provision of the Space Act of 1958 relates to patent policy, on which there were contradictory precedents. The long-established policy of DOD is to permit business firms working under contract to patent their inventions, provided that the government is assured free use of them. In contrast, legislation establishing the Atomic Energy Commission requires it to take title to patentable inventions developed with government funds, and this is the precedent that prevailed when the Space Act was passed. NASA is required to take title to inventions made in connection with work on its contracts unless the Administrator finds that a waiver would serve the interests of the United States, in which case the contractor may patent the invention, assuring free use of it to the government.

The provision has been defended and attacked ever since. The main justification for it is the principle that if the use of public funds leads to an invention, the public should get the benefit without having to give a special reward to the private contractor. Vari-

---

[17] *Ibid.*, Part 2, p. 456.

ous arguments are advanced on the other side. One is that the source of contract funds is far from being the only relevant factor—that inventions often stem from a staff and an innovative spirit built up over the years, and that private firms should be rewarded for these assets even if they are using public funds at the time an invention is made. Another is the practical argument—extremely difficult to establish or refute—that firms are not as likely to seek NASA contracts or to assign their best personnel to work under them if they are denied patent rights. Still another is that private owners of inventions are more likely than the government to see to it that an invention is exploited quickly and effectively. And still another is that the existing arrangement tends "to undermine our traditional patent system and to establish a dangerous precedent for government ownership of inventions developed in private laboratories and plants." [18]

True to the requirements of the law, NASA in 1959 issued a regulation requiring contractors to report inventions, innovations, improvements, and discoveries made in the course of their work, and the normal expectation was that NASA would patent whatever was patentable. The Administrator was reluctant to waive NASA's rights. But experience under the arrangement was discouraging. "The number of inventions, innovations, improvements and discoveries that were reported . . . appears to fall short of what might reasonably be expected." [19] As we have noted in Chapter 6, this fact has been cited to support the view that the space program does relatively little to stimulate technological development. But this is a point of view that NASA can scarcely accept. It obviously hopes that the explanation of the shortfall in reported innovations lies in the patent policies pursued. And in the fall of 1962 it proposed new regulations suggesting a more liberal policy in granting waivers, permitting private contractors to acquire patent rights.[20] Moreover, it shifted its position on the question of formally amending the provisions of the law and sought amendments calling for patent policies like those of DOD.[21]

---

[18] Representative Emilio Q. Daddario, "Problems in Space Policy," *Data* (The Magazine of Defense Marketing), 7 (June, 1962), 23.

[19] G. D. O'Brien, "NASA Patent Policy and Procedure," in NASA, Office of Scientific and Technical Information, *Proceedings of the Second NASA-Industry Conference*, Washington, D.C., February 11-12, 1963 (Washington, 1963), p. 203.

[20] *Ibid.*, p. 205-6.

[21] Elinor Langer, "Patents: Proposal to Change NASA Regulations Draws Attack from Senate Small Business Committee," *Science*, 139 (March 22, 1963), 1188.

Arrangements for Special Services

DOD, and especially the Air Force, has led the way since World War II in developing novel arrangements with private organizations for special services, and NASA—along with a considerable number of other government agencies—has been going along the same general path.

The RAND Corporation, established after World War II under Air Force sponsorship, is the best known of the special service organizations. Its primary assignment at first was to study the idea of launching reconnaissance satellites, but it quickly took up additional subjects as well, and has come to engage rather broadly in research on questions of policy relating to national defense. Subsequently a great many additional organizations have been created —some to engage, like RAND, in policy and operations research, some to provide engineering, technical, or managerial services, and some to engage in a combination of such activities. They all have to do with research and development primarily as distinguished from the production of hardware. Most of them would disappear if they lost federal patronage. Most of them are not for profit.

The Jet Propulsion Laboratory, owned by the government and managed by Caltech, is the principal research and development organization operating under a NASA contract; about 10 per cent of NASA's procurement dollars have been going to it. Apart from the Jet Propulsion Laboratory, inherited from the Army, NASA has tended to seek its special services from private industry, or from organizations associated with private industry and operated for profit. Bellcomm illustrates the fact. With the reorganization of NASA after the acceleration of the program in 1961 the Office of Manned Space Flight was created, and within it the Office of Systems. Apparently the expectation was that it would build up the necessary staff to manage the program, but the expectation was not realized. A.T.&T. was then asked to provide the needed personnel, and the result was the establishment of an A.T.&T. subsidiary, Bellcomm, devoted entirely to service to NASA.[22] The magnitude of the tasks turned over to Bellcomm is suggested by the fact that the cost and fee for FY1964 is estimated at $12 million.[23]

---

[22] U.S. Congress, House, Committee on Science and Astronautics, *Space Posture*, Hearings, 88th Cong., 1st Sess., 1963, pp. 172-73 (hereafter cited as House Hearings, *Space Posture*, 1963). Cf. *Aviation Week*, 77 (July 2, 1962), 76; 79 (March 11, 1963), 115.

[23] House Hearings, *1964 NASA Authorization*, Part 1, p. 103. Cf. *ibid.*, Part 2, pp. 144, 146, 371 ff.

Later NASA made a contract for special services with General Electric, this time not arranging the establishment of a special corporation. General Electric "is performing design studies and engineering services to assist the Office of Manned Space Flight and related NASA centers in the areas of integration, reliability, and checkout for Project Apollo." The cost and fee for FY1964 is estimated at $143 million. The contract is for services only, and General Electric is barred from serving as a contractor or supplier in certain other areas where its privileged relationship to the Apollo program gives it a special advantage.[24] The Air Force once had a similar arrangement with Ramo-Wooldridge and later with Space Technology Laboratories, a Ramo-Wooldridge subsidiary. It led to considerable controversy, for a variety of reasons; among other things, companies subordinated to the "systems management and technical direction" of Ramo-Wooldridge objected that its privileged access to their own proprietary information and to governmental information gave it an unfair competitive advantage.[25] Some frictions have apparently developed in connection with the Bellcomm and GE contracts, but it remains to be seen how serious they will be.

Apart from the attitudes of private firms toward subordination to other private organizations, there has also been debate both in and outside the government over the wisdom of contracting to private agencies for services that might be performed in-house.[26] A Budget Bureau study of 1962, in which DOD, NASA, and other interested agencies participated and concur, staunchly defends and advocates the practice.[27] It points to the vast increase in federal research and development expenditures—from about $1.1 billion in 1950 to over $12 billion in 1963—and it indicates that "public purposes will continue to require larger and larger scientific and technological efforts for as far ahead as we can see." Already "the federal budget finances about 65% of the total national expenditure for research and development, [and] the federal share is rising." Of the total federal expenditures for research and development,

---

[24] *Ibid.*, Part 4, p. 3251.

[25] U.S. Congress, House, Committee on Science and Astronautics, *Independent Nonprofit Federal Research Contractors*, Staff Study, 87th Cong., 2d Sess., 1962, pp. 1-2.

[26] Victor K. Heyman, "Government by Contract: Boon or Boner?" *Public Administration Review*, 21 (Spring, 1961), 59-64; Don K. Price, J. Stefan Dupre, W. Eric Gustafson, "Current Trends in Science Policy in the United States," *Impact of Science on Society*, Vol. 10, No. 3 (1960), 194-95.

[27] Senate, *Contracting for R&D*, 1962.

about 80 per cent are today made through nonfederal institutions. And, while "the Government's capabilities for direct operations in research and development need to be substantially strengthened, there is no doubt that the Government must continue to rely on the private sector for the major share of the scientific and technical work which it requires."

A basic premise of the Budget Bureau report is that the government must have sufficient in-house capabilities to make policy decisions. Given such in-house capability, the report endorses various kinds of arrangements that have already been tried for obtaining, through contract, the scientific and technical services needed to accomplish public purposes; and it encourages further innovation. Research and development assignments should go to in-house facilities or to a private agency, depending on where the job "can be done most effectively and efficiently, with due regard to the strengthening of institutional resources as well as to the immediate execution of projects." Conflicts of interest are to be avoided, of course.

Various kinds of advantages encourage the assignment of research and development tasks to private agencies through contract rather than keeping them within the government. Sometimes speed is a major consideration; the private agency may be able to get the job done more quickly than it could be done in-house, either because it has the personnel and facilities already available or because it can get them in hand more quickly than a government agency could. This was apparently the major factor in the Bellcomm arrangement, cited above. Sometimes flexibility is the principal advantage; the government can get short-term projects done without getting caught in bureaucratic problems relating to the creation and abolition of offices and the recruitment and dismissal of personnel.

Speed and flexibility are both related to salary levels and the working environment. Private agencies are not restricted to civil service salary levels, and so can pay more than the government does. This leads into the odd fact that resort to private contracting agencies is a device by which the government can circumvent its own salary restrictions; having fixed civil service salaries at too low a level, it sponsors the creation of private agencies that then pay more—and make it all the harder for the government to recruit personnel needed for in-house purposes.[28] Moreover, there have been abuses, officials in not-for-profit agencies obtaining salaries

---

[28] *Ibid.*, pp. 47-49.

that make the arrangement highly profitable to them. The Budget Bureau report suggests that "the basic standard for reimbursement of salaries and related benefits should be one of comparability to compensation of persons doing similar work in the private economy." Quite apart from the question of salary levels, a considerable number of people for quite a variety of reasons find private employment more attractive than employment in the government bureaucracy.

Political expediency and philosophic principle may also enter into decisions to assign research and development tasks to private agencies. As noted in the preceding chapter, the letting of contracts tends to build up a supportive political constituency and to find favor in Congress; and it permits the job to be done without direct and overt additions to the government, which in principle should do something to appease those who are against "big government" and "creeping socialism." At the same time, the ambiguity of the situation should be noted. Is an agency really "private" when it was created for the specific purpose of providing services to the government and when its very existence depends on government contracts? And what is the relationship between reliance on nonprofit organizations and endorsement of the principle of competitive free enterprise? Ralph J. Cordiner finds it "disturbing" that the government sometimes sponsors "so-called nonprofit organizations which are totally dependent on government contracts." "However generous their motives, these nonprofit organizations are usurping a field traditionally served by private consulting firms and producer companies, and hence are little more than a blind for nationalized industry competing directly with private enterprise—on a subsidized, non-tax-paying basis." [29] NASA is apparently influenced by this kind of consideration, for its research and development contracts go more to profit-seeking than to not-for-profit organizations. Mr. Webb was pleased to report that NASA had "resisted every impulse" to make the arrangements with Bellcomm and General Electric on a nonprofit basis.

NASA and the Universities

Implicit in the above is the fact that intellectual resources are crucial to the space program, as they are to every difficult and purposeful activity. The knowledge produced by research is vital.

---

[29] Cordiner, loc. cit., p. 221.

Almost automatically this raises the question of the kind of relationship that exists, or should exist, between NASA and the universities, both in terms of tapping existing talent and in terms of the problem of developing new talent for the future.

One of the early reactions to Sputnik was an intensification and acceleration of an appraisal of the quality of American education at all levels that was already under way. The fear was that the breakaway lead of the Soviet Union in space reflected a superiority in the Soviet educational system that might have enduring and pervasive effect, and the question was what kind of a response ought to be made. Estimates of the nature of the Soviet challenge are indicated by the following report of NASA Administrator Glennan after a trip to Russia in 1959. "The Russians are totally engaged in a drive to employ the educational process to win world leadership in technology, and thus to win world leadership in all other matters. Theirs is the fervor of the Crusades. As John Turkevitch, a great chemist and a great teacher at Princeton has said, 'The Russian today has greater faith in the Soviet destiny through science that through Marxism.'" [30] Reports of this sort continue to be issued, along with warnings of the urgent need of educational improvement in the United States.

The first major step in response to the Soviet challenge was the enactment of the National Defense Education Act in 1958 for strengthening graduate education in fields having to do with national defense—a purpose that the Office of Education, which administers the act, has construed in a broad and liberal way. NASA's own response was very much slower. For several years its relationships with the universities aimed at exploiting existing talent for immediate purposes through contracts and grants designed to get specific research projects under way. There were no efforts specifically designed to develop new talent—no fellowships, or any arrangement for assisting the universities to acquire the facilities needed for space research. In 1960 the House Committee on Science and Astronautics created a panel of scientists with which it has met once or twice a year ever since, and members of the panel made the needs known. At a meeting in 1960 Dr. Van Allen noted that for FY1961 about $123 million were contemplated for constructing and equipping federal laboratories, but he was "unable

---

[30] T. Keith Glennan, address to the National Press Club, November 19, 1959, NASA News Release, mimeo.

to discover as much as $25 for a workbench at a university, from which the expert talent to staff these facilities must come." He described the universities as "the poor cousins of American society."[31]

Subsequent congressional actions, occurring after the expansion of the space program in 1961, have changed the situation markedly. NASA now has a very extensive and expanding university program.

Basic to the program is the recognition of a need. Dr. Killian's statement is that "dollar expenditure, including public and private, for research and development is rising about 15% each year, but our pool of technical manpower is growing only 6% a year."[32] Earlier the National Science Foundation had coupled the statement that the supply of scientists and engineers was growing at 6 per cent a year with the statement that the number engaged in research and development was growing at 10 per cent.[33] Such figures obviously suggest that demand may outrun supply—an outcome that can be avoided only by reducing the demand or increasing the supply or doing some of each. Dr. Killian's clear inclination is to reduce the demand, especially insofar as it is created by the lunar program. But the Administration, and particularly NASA, can scarcely accept this choice. They must try to increase the supply. "The task of developing our manpower resources in sufficient quality and quantity to keep pace with the expanding research and development effort is a matter of great urgency."[34] Moreover, the Panel on Scientific and Technical Manpower of the President's Science Advisory Committee (PSAC) has endorsed the view that proper measures will bring about an "abrupt increase" in the number taking graduate work in engineering, mathematics, and the physical sciences "without a diversion of bright people from other fields." And it recommends a program designed to bring this about. The declared aim is to increase the number of doctor's degrees awarded each year in engineering, mathematics, and the physical sciences to reach 7,500 in 1970 (as compared to 3,000 in 1960); to increase the number completing a year of graduate work in these fields to 30,000 in 1970; and to improve the quality and bring about a wider

---

[31] U.S. Congress, House, Committee on Science and Astronautics, *Panel on Science and Technology. Second Meeting*, H. Rpt. No. 2226, 86th Cong., 2d Sess., 1960, p. 62.

[32] James R. Killian, Jr., "The Crisis in Research," *Atlantic Monthly*, 211 (March, 1963), 69.

[33] Senate, *Contracting for R&D*, 1962, p. 4.

[34] *Ibid.*

geographic distribution of "centers of educational excellence." [35]
In a sense, NASA's university program anticipated such recommendations.

Universities contribute to social needs in the normal course of events; this is their *raison d'être*. Dr. Hugh L. Dryden, Deputy Administrator of NASA, stresses this in saying that the university "has an inherent responsibility entirely apart from any thought of governmental support" to contribute to the exploration of space.[36] Nevertheless, NASA assumes an obligation too, both to see to it that its own future needs can be met and to see to it that other needs do not suffer unduly as a result. NASA feels "a strong responsibility to stimulate the training of the personnel that will be required to carry out the space program," [37] and "like the logger who has responsibility of replacing for the future the trees which he harvests, NASA, as a user of university-trained talent, has an obligation to carry a fair share of the load of replacing the resources consumed. . . . NASA stands ready to invest substantial resources in partnership with the university." [38]

The "Sustaining University Program" to which these considerations have led provides for action in several categories. There are training grants. Beginning with 10 predoctoral traineeships at each of 10 universities in 1962-63, the suggested goal is "support of about 4,000 graduate students per year in 150 qualified universities, to yield an annual output of about 1,000 new Ph.D.'s in space-related fields." [39] This would mean a program for the space sciences of about the same size as the 1962-63 program under Title IV of the National Defense Education Act, which covers the space sciences and many other fields as well. In addition to its training

---

[35] President's Science Advisory Committee, *Meeting Manpower Needs in Science and Technology. Report Number One: Graduate Training in Engineering, Mathematics, and Physical Sciences,* December 12, 1962 (hereafter cited as PSAC, *Meeting Manpower Needs*).

[36] Hugh L. Dryden, "The Role of the University in Meeting National Goals in Space Exploration," in NASA, Office of Scientific and Technical Information, *Proceedings of the NASA-University Conference on the Science and Technology of Space Exploration,* Chicago, Illinois, November 1-3, 1962 (Washington, 1962), I, 88 (hereafter cited as *NASA-University Conference Proceedings*).

[37] Thomas L. K. Smull, "NASA-University Relationships," in *NASA-University Conference Proceedings,* I, 55.

[38] Dryden, *loc. cit.,* p. 90.

[39] *Ibid.;* D. S. Greenberg, "NASA: New Fellowship Program Will Make Space Agency Biggest in Graduate Aid," *Science,* 139 (January 4, 1963), 23-24.

grants, NASA also has other educational programs: postdoctoral "associateships" for study at a NASA center or at a university; international fellowships, for foreign students sponsored by their home governments; and experimental summer programs designed to interest and instruct undergraduates in the space sciences. Further, NASA makes grants for the construction of buildings and laboratories, and it continues to make research contracts and grants. The amount committed to the universities in 1962-63 was in the neighborhood of $100 million.[40]

Underlying the university program is the principle that research is to be supported in such a way as to strengthen rather than weaken the existing university structure. "While we are anxious to reap the benefits of the research potential in the universities, we want to support research in the traditional atmosphere of instruction and learning from research that results from keeping the research activity surrounded by students. For example, we are not interested in the creation of institutes that tend to draw university faculties away from the educational aspects of their research." [41] Degree programs remain entirely under the control of the university, which means that the training given can be broad; and those who receive training may later accept employment wherever they please.

To what extent PSAC and NASA are right in expecting that the traineeships will draw additional students into engineering, mathematics, and the space sciences—and to what extent those drawn in are net additions to graduate work rather than transfers from other fields—remains to be seen. Complex factors are at work in motivating students to go on to graduate school, and to choose among available degree programs. The number taking graduate work in these fields has been declining some in recent years despite the fact that the amount of money available for their support has been increasing; the social sciences have done better in attracting increasing numbers.[42] Some members of the Panel on Science and

---

[40] National Academy of Sciences, Space Science Board, *A Review of Space Research*, report of a summer study conducted at the State University of Iowa, Iowa City, June 17–August 10, 1962, Publication 1079 (Washington: National Academy of Sciences—National Research Council, 1962), Ch. 12, p. 3 (hereafter cited as NAS, *A Review of Space Research*).

[41] Smull, *loc. cit.*, pp. 52-53.

[42] Cf. Harold Orlans, *The Effects of Federal Programs on Higher Education* (Washington: The Brookings Institution, 1962), pp. 36-38; PSAC, *Meeting Manpower Needs*, p. 18.

Technology of the House space committee have challenged the view that more graduate fellowships will accomplish the intended results.[43] The test is yet to come.

NASA is also seeking additional ways to relate its program to the universities and to utilize the universities. It has retained the Midwest Research Institute "to study in depth the fifteen leading universities of six midwestern states . . . to determine how their participation in this new age can be intensified." [44] And it has begun inserting in contracts with universities a requirement that they encourage research on the practical applications of space science and technology and on the economic and social impact of the exploration of space. Further, as Mr. Webb describes it, each university undertakes "in an energetic and organized manner . . . to explore mechanisms whereby the progress and research results achieved in space science and technology may be fed into the industries and segments of the economy with which the university normally has close relations."[45]

The reaction within university communities to the requirement that practical applications be promoted is sure to be mixed. But other features of the university program are likely to be very generally endorsed.[46]

Concluding Comments

In some degree the space program is modifying governmental relations with business, the government's own practices, and its relations with the universities.

Big as the space program is, its budget is still small when compared, say, to that of DOD. The impact of DOD on government-business relationships is much greater. Nevertheless, NASA's operations add significantly to the involvement of the federal government in the economy as a whole as well as in the economic well-being of particular sections of the country and particular business concerns. They make for "big government," and they raise questions about the relevance of the principle of competitive free enterprise. At the

---

[43] U.S. Congress, House, Committee on Science and Astronautics, *Panel on Science and Technology. Fifth Meeting,* 88th Cong., 1st Sess., 1963, esp. pp. 59, 62, 93.

[44] James E. Webb, address to Associates of the University of Kansas City, December 6, 1962, NASA News Release, p. 9.

[45] James E. Webb, address of January 30, 1963, NASA News Release, p. 9.

[46] NAS, *A Review of Space Research,* Ch. 12, p. 6.

same time, NASA has deliberately sought to conduct its program compatibly with the principles of competitive profit-seeking. There are urgent complaints, mainly from Congress, about the geographical concentration of NASA's contracting, but it generally seems to be taken for granted that NASA has been effective in getting the support and services it needs to execute its program.

The principal modification of governmental practices associated with the space program is in the utilization of private concerns not only for research and development but also for managerial services. The practice accentuates the "partnership."

So far as NASA's relationships with the universities are concerned, perhaps the most notable fact is that they are developing on a considerable scale. The desire to increase educational opportunities and to improve the American educational system is not among the reasons commonly cited to justify the space program. Nevertheless, these results are being achieved. Whether credit for the benefits should go to the space program or to Soviet competition is a matter for choice.

INTERNATIONAL COOPERATION

14

When the House select committee reported on space legislation in 1958 it took a vigorous stand in favor of international cooperation. "It is necessary to make real, aggressive efforts at forming international programs, at developing the purely international frame of mind in which lies this earth's only ultimate stability. Everyone agrees . . . that the internationalization of the space effort is good." The committee declared that the proposed space agency "must be organized first as an active agent of international cooperation and ultimately as the basis for an international organization." The Senate special committee took a similar view; among its four or five major concerns was the question whether the bill under consideration provided adequately for international cooperation. While space legislation was pending, in the summer of 1958, both houses adopted a resolution declaring "that the United States should seek through the United Nations or such other means as may be most appropriate an international agreement providing for joint exploration of outer space." [1] As enacted, the Space Act listed "cooperation by the United States with other nations and groups of nations" among the objectives to be pursued; and later the Senate special committee formally commended NASA for establishing an Office of International Programs, declaring that Congress considered international cooperation "to be one of the most essential

---

[1] U.S. Congress, Senate, Special Committee on Space and Astronautics, *Final Report* . . . Pursuant to S. Res. 256 of the 85th Congress, S. Rpt. No. 100, 86th Cong., 1st Sess., 1959, p. 17.

functions" of the organization.[2] The Wiesner Ad Hoc Committee on Space, listing the goals of space activities for President-elect Kennedy in January, 1961, spoke of the "exciting possibilities for international cooperation"; and the new President, in his first State of the Union message, said that his administration intended "to explore promptly all possible areas of cooperation with the Soviet Union and other nations" in space matters. It is perhaps needless to say that the natural scientists associated with the IGY were proud of the cooperation that it involved, and that they sought its continuation. In general, sentiment in favor of the principle of international cooperation in space matters was and remains strong and virtually unanimous, though, as we will see, some have doubts and reservations about cooperation with the Soviet Union and other Communist states.

Why is there so much support for cooperation in this field? What are its alleged purposes and advantages? On the basis of what kinds of principles does it occur, and how sensible do they seem to be? What kinds of cooperation are attempted, on what scale, and through what organizational arrangements? What role do the United Nations and other international organizations play in relation to the cooperation?

In dealing with these questions our focus will be on the cooperative activities and policies of the U.S. government. We will deal with the international cooperation of private persons and organizations only insofar as it relates to the governmental program.

The Reasons for International Cooperation

The circumstances in which the space age was inaugurated set the stage for cooperation. Though the rockets that launched Sputnik I and Explorer I into orbit were developed to serve the military purposes of states locked in struggle, the satellites went into orbit in connection with the IGY, which joined scientists from all over the world in a cooperative undertaking. Moreover, both because of the spectacular achievements in space and for other reasons, the IGY was very generally regarded as a great success, fixing a precedent that at least had to be taken into account. The Director of NASA's Office of International Programs, Arnold W. Frutkin, said in 1960 that "the IGY operation . . . achieved a dynamism which

---

[2] *Ibid.*, p. 30.

almost demands that we continue to work within the same sort of framework." [3]

But quite apart from the precedent as such, the reasons that led to cooperation during the IGY continue to be cogent, and others have developed. They relate to the various motives of the space program described in the chapters of Part II.

We have already noted in Chapter 5 that some call for cooperation in the name of security and peace. In fact the desire to demonstrate concern for peace—and, more generally, for international relationships of mutual benefit—is stressed more than any other in connection with space cooperation. "In the broadest sense," says Mr. Frutkin,

we are seeking to reduce international tensions, to transmute dangerous rivalries and ambitions into constructive competition, to build communities of interest—in Europe, Latin America, and elsewhere, and to establish patterns of cooperation in the world. . . . There has been a tremendous amount of sentiment here and abroad—and especially in the small nations—for international cooperation in exploring space in the hope that this might reduce, rather than expand, the dimensions of the cold war. [4]

Space cooperation is also endorsed as a means of contributing to the objective discussed in Chapter 6: promoting progress in science and technology. And some kinds of cooperation are virtually imperative for the success of the U.S. program. NASA faces a very practical need for stations around the world for tracking satellites and receiving data telemetered from them; it is making use of 27 such stations in 19 different foreign political entities. The Minitrack network—primarily for use in connection with unmanned satellites and space probes—comprises eight stations abroad and five in the United States. The Deep Space Instrumentation Facility—for spacecraft traveling to the moon and beyond—includes two stations abroad (at Johannesburg and Woomera) and one in the United States (at Goldstone). The Manned Space Flight network, developed in connection with the Mercury program, includes eight stations abroad, eight in the United States, plus U.S. ships at sea. And the Baker-Nunn network, for optical tracking with telescopic

[3] U.S. Congress, Senate, Committee on Aeronautical and Space Sciences, *Documents on International Aspects of the Exploration and Use of Outer Space, 1954-1962*, Staff Report, S. Doc. No. 18, 88th Cong., 1st Sess., 1963, p. 168 (hereafter cited as Senate, *Documents on International Aspects*, 1963).

[4] Arnold W. Frutkin, "International Cooperation in Space Exploration," address at the Third National Conference on the Peaceful Uses of Space, Chicago, Illinois, May 7, 1963, pp. 2-3.

cameras, includes facilities in nine foreign political entities.[5] The use of these stations suggests another need too: for international agreements designed to minimize interference by one state in the legitimate activities of others—in particular, on the wavelengths to use in space telemetry. Further, if a communications satellite system is to be developed, cooperation is an obvious imperative, for the system will depend upon ground terminals providing connections with local networks; and in the long view it may be highly desirable to keep at a minimum any incentive that other countries might have to establish a competitive system. Similarly, cooperation is also of obvious advantage in connection with the meteorological satellite program and in various other specific undertakings, such as the projected geomagnetic survey, calling for coordinated observations throughout the world. Considerable stress is placed, too, on the point that we cooperate in order "to tap a rich pool of scientific talent in other countries"—"to enlist the constructive participation of scientists of other countries in the immense task of advancing man's knowledge and use of his spatial environment." [6] Further, as Mr. Webb says, through international cooperation "a means is provided for the developed and the undeveloped country both to stimulate their young people to take their place in the modern world, to keep abreast of the new technologies, to keep the technological gap from growing so great that it will create an unbridgeable chasm between nations." [7]

Curiously enough, though some advocates of the space program contend that it will pay off for us ("for every nickel we put into it, we get a dime back"), the economic argument is different when the question concerns international cooperation. In this context the emphasis is on the desirability of having other countries share the burdens, now or later. Thus a report of the House select committee in 1959 envisaged space projects of the future "so extensive as to make their undertaking by a single nation impracticable." It spoke of "spreading the costs of certain phases of space exploration over a wide portion of the Western World," and it favored building up a

[5] NASA News Release No. 63-10, January 27, 1963.

[6] U.S. Congress, House, Select Committee on Astronautics and Space Exploration, *The United States and Outer Space*, H. Rpt. No. 2710, 85th Cong., 2d Sess., 1959, p. 15 (hereafter cited as House, *U.S. and Outer Space*, 1959); Arnold W. Frutkin, "U.S. Cooperation in Space Research," address of June 28, 1961, NASA News Release No. 61-143, p. 3.

[7] James E. Webb, address of March 27, 1963, NASA News Release, p. 16.

pattern of cooperation against the day when "the cost or extent of such ventures [in space] begins to assume excessive proportions." [8] And Hugh L. Dryden once declared: "We in NASA are convinced that every possible effort should be made to secure the cooperation of other nations. The task of space exploration is global in nature; it requires large resources; and its needs are better matched by the resources of the whole world than by those of one nation." [9] Actually, the two lines of thought—that space ventures will pay but that costs should be shared—are not necessarily incompatible. In principle, an economically profitable venture often requires greater resources than one investor is able or willing to supply. But whether a net profit will ever be forthcoming from space activities remains to be seen.

Prestige and pride also figure among the justifications of international cooperation. Mr. Webb speaks of the "effort to project the image of the United States as a nation wanting to work with other nations to develop science and technology, the image of a nation leading in this field and willing to share this knowledge with other nations." [10] The Ad Hoc PSAC Panel on Meteorological Satellites reported in 1961 that "the impact of the proposed satellite program upon U.S. prestige abroad will be greatly enhanced if it is a part of an international cooperative program in atmospheric science and technology." [11] No one says, of course, that we cooperate to have a basis for pride, but to the extent that we cooperate with others in order to beat the Russians more surely or quickly, or in order to achieve preeminence, pride is certainly involved as an objective. Perhaps it is more significant to note, however, that concern for prestige and pride works against cooperation with the Russians. Where our object is to beat them and their object is to beat us, any plan for extensive cooperation is out of the question. (This does not deny that humanitarian considerations or a spirit of good sports-

[8] U.S. Congress, House, Select Committee on Astronautics and Space Exploration, *International Cooperation in the Exploration of Space*, H. Rpt. No. 2709, 85th Cong., 2d Sess., 1959, p. 12.

[9] Hugh L. Dryden, "Prospects for Space Travel," address of April 21, 1960, mimeo., p. 35.

[10] U.S. Congress, House, Committee on Appropriations, *Independent Offices Appropriations for 1963*, Hearings Before a Subcommittee . . ., 87th Cong., 2d Sess., 1962, Part 3, pp. 418-19 (hereafter cited as House Hearings, *Independent Offices Appropriations for 1963*).

[11] U.S. Congress, Senate, Committee on Aeronautical and Space Sciences, *Meteorological Satellites*, Staff Report . . . Prepared by the Library of Congress, March 29, 1962, 87th Cong., 2d Sess., p. 174.

manship might in exceptional circumstances lead either side to lend aid to its rival.)

Organizational Arrangements for Cooperation

Within NASA, the Office of International Programs is responsible for international cooperative activities. Its function is to generate proposals for cooperation of various types, to consider proposals for cooperation received from other NASA offices, from other U.S. sources, and from abroad, to work with the Department of State in negotiating formal international agreements for cooperation, to provide various supporting services for NASA's international activities, and to maintain appropriate liaison with other governmental and nongovernmental agencies.

Within the Department of State, matters pertaining to space are handled principally in the Office of International Scientific Affairs and in the Office of the Assistant Secretary for International Organization Affairs. The Office of International Scientific Affairs includes an Outer Space Section, whose Chief is in a focal position. He works with NASA's Office of International Programs, and for some purposes maintains liaison with a variety of other governmental agencies, e.g., the Weather Bureau and the Federal Communications Commission. He assists other State Department personnel in negotiating (or renegotiating) agreements concerning tracking and data-acquisition stations in other countries. And he works with those in the Office of the Assistant Secretary for International Organization Affairs who deal with space problems. The principal person in point is a Deputy Assistant Secretary as well as the Deputy U.S. representative to the UN Committee on the Peaceful Uses of Outer Space. It is the Department of State that concludes the more formal and important international agreements on space cooperation, even if NASA personnel have done the negotiating. For less formal or important purposes, representatives of NASA come to a direct understanding with their counterparts from other countries.

The National Academy of Sciences, and more particularly its Space Science Board, should also be mentioned. They are sources of advice to NASA and to the Department of State on questions pertaining to international cooperation; they serve as a channel of communication between NASA and the Department of State, on the one hand, and the organized nongovernmental scientific community in this country and abroad, on the other; and they assist in the actual administration of the personnel exchange program.

Within the United Nations the General Assembly is the major agency having to do with space activities. More particularly, questions pertaining to space come under the jurisdiction of Committee I of the General Assembly, to which political and security matters are referred. In 1958 the General Assembly established an Ad Hoc Committee on the Peaceful Uses of Outer Space, but a dispute concerning its composition impaired its usefulness. The Soviet Union insisted on the equal representation of the two sides—East and West—plus some representation of neutralist states. The United States rejected the principle underlying the Soviet demand, insisting that the usual rule be followed, giving representation to the various regional groups into which the members of the General Assembly were informally divided. In a technical sense, the American view prevailed, but then 5 of the 18 members (the Soviet Union, Czechoslovakia, Poland, India, and the United Arab Republic) boycotted the sessions of the committee. A new, enlarged committee was agreed upon for the following year, but it took two more years to work out an agreement concerning its officers and voting rules.[12] Finally, the committee met briefly in the fall of 1961, and has been holding periodic meetings ever since. It consists of 28 members, and conducts its business without voting—meaning that objection by any member blocks action.

The United States is also a member of various other international agencies having space within their purview, e.g., the World Meteorological Organization, the International Telecommunication Union, and UNESCO.

Principles Guiding the Development of International Programs

NASA has different sorts of international programs. It is willing to launch individual scientific instruments or whole satellites provided by foreign scientists, and for certain purposes (e.g., meteorological purposes) it expects to arrange with the Soviet Union for coordinated launchings. It coordinates sounding rocket launches internationally, and participates in programs calling for various activities on the ground relating to space experiments, such as ac-

---

[12] Lincoln P. Bloomfield, "The Prospects for Law and Order," in Lincoln P. Bloomfield, ed., *Outer Space. Prospects for Man and Society*, The American Assembly (Englewood Cliffs: Prentice-Hall, 1962), p. 167.

tivities having to do with meteorology, communications, tracking, and data acquisition. And it joins with foreign organizations in exchanging information and personnel.

Cooperative, or at least international, activities of other sorts are identified more fully with other agencies. The Department of State leads in international discussions of the law of outer space and of the role of the United Nations in space. The Weather Bureau and the Federal Communications Commission are the principals in certain international activities relating to their special spheres of activity. The military uses of space have not yet developed enough to lead DOD to establish anything that it calls an international program, though it has ground installations in various foreign territories.

The Director of NASA's Office of International Programs, Mr. Frutkin, states a number of "guidelines" for international space cooperation.[13] He describes NASA as "a technical agency . . . interested in sound programs with valid scientific objectives." Programs should be "substantive in character." They should "grow out of, or be capable of integration with, NASA's own operating and research programs." Hopefully, they should call for "projects which we ourselves would wish to carry out if they were not to be done jointly." In addition, Mr. Frutkin wants to "deal, for most purposes, with a single agency or group in a given country"— usually government-sponsored or supported. Among other reasons, this is to avoid the political embarrassment to the United States that might follow if NASA became involved in domestic struggles in other countries among different elements with interests in space. Prior to formal agreements for cooperation, Mr. Frutkin wants full discussions with technical personnel in the other country to maximize common understanding and to maximize the prospect that the cooperative program worked out is one that can be effectively implemented. Agreements for cooperation are not to call for an exchange of funds. Each party finances its own share of the program. But, though the other side must make a significant contribution, committing important resources, it is not required to match the American contribution; in fact, the contributions may be very unequal. And the rule against exchanging funds does not preclude

---

[13] Arnold W. Frutkin, "U.S. Cooperation in Space Research," address of June 28, 1961, NASA News Release No. 61-143, pp. 3-5; Senate, *Documents on International Aspects*, 1963, pp. 168-75.

loans of expensive hardware. The guidelines also include the principle that the results of joint projects are to be made generally available to the scientific community.

Though NASA is a "technical agency" with scientific objectives, it is also a political agency with political objectives. The desire to reduce international tensions and contribute to peace, for example, reflects a political choice. Obviously a U.S. governmental agency engaged in international activities must support U.S. foreign policies and stay within the limits that they fix. It is not enough to say that the implementation of a sound scientific program is good politics. In some cases, politics overrides science.

Perhaps the sharpest illustration of the effect of political considerations occurred in connection with the world meteorological workshop that NASA sponsored in the fall of 1961. Since the U.S. government does not recognize the governments of East Germany and Communist China, delegates from these areas could not be invited. Political considerations are also in evidence when Soviet scientists visit the United States, for the State Department's rule must be observed that Soviet visitors are to be under restrictions comparable to those imposed on Americans who go to the Soviet Union. More importantly, the question has arisen whether NASA should assist the European Launch Development Organization (ELDO), which, as the name implies, aims to develop launching vehicles. Such vehicles, though designed to launch satellites, might also be used to launch missiles—perhaps with nuclear warheads. In this situation, the principle that NASA is "interested in sound programs with valid scientific objectives" obviously gives inadequate guidance. As Mr. Frutkin says, "the heavy military implications of launch vehicle development" must be "a governing consideration for the foreseeable future." [14] The question of space cooperation thus gets mixed up with various questions of high policy toward our NATO allies and toward the Soviet Union regarding the spread of nuclear capabilities; and it becomes a question not only for NASA but also for the Department of State, DOD, and the National Security Council. Mr. Frutkin suggests, incidentally, that the political considerations may permit "limited collaboration." "It is our belief that there are some technical prob-

[14] Arnold W. Frutkin, "Progress in International Cooperation in Space Research," address at the Third European Space Flight Symposium, Stuttgart, May 23, 1963, NASA News Release, pp. 12-14; James E. Webb, in House, *Independent Offices Appropriations for 1963*, p. 418.

lems and developments in the launcher field which are largely, if
not exclusively, of application to space research purposes rather
than to military objectives." Where such problems are of "mutual
interest," cooperation may occur. Political considerations also obviously influence NASA's "preference to deal exclusively through
ELDO in connection with civil applications of vehicle technology"
rather than to deal with the individual governments or industrial
firms.

It seems likely that NASA will face other problems of this general
type. The national space committees that have been formed in some
two dozen countries—in part because NASA prefers to deal with
only one agency—commonly include a military element. Thus
NASA might be asked to cooperate in projects in which the military
is involved, and this suggests problems. As a civilian agency that
cooperates with the American military, NASA would presumably
accept a comparable arrangement abroad. Suppose, though, that
a foreign space project is scientific in character and purpose, but
under military management. Or suppose that a project (other
than the development of a launching vehicle) is under civilian
management, but has clear and significant military implications.
What would and should NASA do? How far do we want to go in
seeking to avert the militarization of space activities? If cooperation
is to occur with a foreign military agency, should it be through
DOD rather than through NASA? The test of scientific validity
might contribute toward the answer, but as in the case of ELDO
it is not the only test to be applied.

Political influences show up in other ways. On one occasion when
NASA's technical purposes could be served equally well by locating
a ground installation in any of a number of countries in a given
region, the deciding factor was political. Apparently, too, political
considerations are dictating that a location outside of South Africa
be sought for an installation authorized for the same longitude as
Johannesburg.[15] As we will see in the next chapter, NASA pursues
political objectives very actively in contributing to the efforts of
the USIA to disseminate information abroad concerning the space
program. The most interesting question along this line is not
whether political goals are pursued but whether NASA does or
should enter into a cooperative space project solely or largely for

---

[15] U.S. Congress, House, Committee on Science and Astronautics, Subcommittee on Applications and Tracking and Data Acquisition, *1964 NASA
Authorization*, Hearings, 88th Cong., 1st Sess., 1963, Part 4, p. 2850.

the anticipated political effect, regardless of the prospective scientific returns. Those managing NASA's international programs are saying no. This puts them in a different category from those managing the programs of economic and military aid abroad, who have concluded that in some circumstances the answer, for them, must be yes. They must sometimes give aid not really for economic or military reasons but for political reasons—e.g., to shore up a government or win its support. So far, NASA's different course has apparently not led to problems. State Department spokesmen indicate that they have never yet felt it desirable to urge NASA to engage in a cooperative program that was not "substantive" and "scientifically valid." This is stated as a fact, not implying a prediction.

We might note that under one of NASA's international programs Pakistan receives assistance for launching sounding rockets. Reporting this, Dr. Hugh L. Dryden cited a Pakistan newspaper which described the launching of a rocket as an achievement in which every Pakistani could take legitimate pride. And Dr. Dryden commented that sometimes "relatively small expenditures bring a return in international good will and cooperation far beyond the amounts expended." [16]

Despite the possibilities that this suggests, it may be NASA's best political strategy to minimize the political aspects and aims of its international programs. The scientific community both at home and abroad may respond better on this basis. Moreover, NASA would risk some support if members of Congress came to put the international space program in the same category as foreign aid. And there would be questions if, instead of insisting on programs "substantive in character" (which presumably means "seriously designed to enhance scientific knowledge"), NASA were to announce its willingness to undertake programs for political (and therefore insubstantial?) reasons.

The "guidelines" that the Department of State follows in its activities relating to space are unavoidably complex. For example, difficulties with the Soviet Union over the composition of the UN committees on the peaceful uses of space had to be handled in the broad political context in which they occurred, and in such a way as not to undermine the American position on similar kinds of problems. Further, the stands that the Department of State takes

---

[16] U.S. Congress, Senate, Committee on Aeronautical and Space Sciences, *NASA Authorization for Fiscal Year 1963*, Hearings, 87th Cong., 2d Sess., 1962, p. 61.

in the effort to develop agreement on the law of outer space must be in substantial accord with the stands taken on comparable problems in other fields. More specific statements would require too extensive a review of American foreign policies to be attempted here.

The Extent of Space Cooperation Outside the United Nations

By the end of 1962 the United States had made arrangements for some kind of space cooperation with a total of 61 political entities.[17]

As indicated above, the arrangements fall into various categories. In 1962 NASA launched two "international satellites"—one in cooperation with Canada and the other in cooperation with Great Britain. Through 1962 sounding rockets had been launched, mainly abroad, in cooperation with nine countries; the number launched in 1962 was 21. Forty political entities have taken part in projects supporting the weather and communications satellite programs. As indicated above, 19 provide the sites for the 27 ground installations used by NASA abroad. Mr. Frutkin reports that "well over half" of these installations "are operated wholly or in part by local technicians, and additional participation may be expected as a result of continued training programs. British, Canadian, and Australian agencies actually defray all or a significant part of the operating costs of stations located in their territories."[18] Some 19 countries have sent personnel to the United States to participate in the various training programs that NASA sponsors. One is for senior foreign scientists who come for work at one of the NASA centers; 38 participated in the program in 1962, obtaining stipends from NASA via the National Academy of Sciences, which administers the program. Other training programs are for graduate students who come to study for a year or two in American universities having space science programs, and for technicians who obtain on-the-job training in NASA laboratories and the launching station at Wallops Island, or who obtain training (in this country

[17] U.S. President, Report to the Congress, *United States Aeronautics and Space Activities, 1962* (Washington: National Aeronautics and Space Council, 1963), pp. 29-30; Arnold W. Frutkin, "Progress in International Cooperation in Space Research," May 23, 1963, NASA News Release, p. 2; Arnold W. Frutkin, "International Programs of NASA," in Hugh Odishaw, ed., *The Challenges of Space* (Chicago: University of Chicago Press, 1962), p. 273.

[18] Arnold W. Frutkin, "International Cooperation in Space Research," *Astronautics and Aerospace Engineering*, 1 (March, 1963), 101.

and abroad) for the specific purpose of working in one of the NASA installations in their home country. Under the international fellowship program for graduate students, NASA provides "university costs and necessary travel expenses within the United States" and sponsoring institutions abroad defray "international travel costs and subsistence in the United States."[19] The personnel exchange program also provides for sending scientists from the United States to universities and NASA centers abroad for teaching purposes. NASA also has arrangements for the international dissemination of scientific data, e.g., through the National Academy of Sciences, COSPAR, and the World Data Centers for which COSPAR is responsible. (COSPAR is the Committee on Space Research of the International Council of Scientific Unions.) Cooperation with ESRO (European Space Research Organization) is anticipated.

The cooperative program in meteorology is especially noteworthy. As is well known, the program is based on satellites that take pictures of the cloud cover and transfer them to special ground stations. The program includes the issuance of storm warnings in special circumstances, the transmission of cloud analyses to other countries, arrangements for intensified observations in a number of countries, coordinated with the passage of a weather satellite overhead, and the holding of international workshops for meteorologists. Developments are planned to permit any country with the proper equipment to receive pictures from a weather satellite overhead and so obtain directly the data that it wants.

Cooperative arrangements for a global satellite communications system may become notable; at least, the principle of cooperation has been stressed from the first, and for obvious reasons. A report of the House space committee in 1961 indicated that communications satellite systems "by their very nature require international cooperation on an unprecedented scale." The committee favored arrangements making it "very clear to all other nations that it is to their benefit to cooperate." It foresaw a "new intimacy among the nations of the world [that] could help to bring about greater understanding and improved relations for all mankind." And it agreed with the President's proposal that the United States should strive for "a global system, not one which will serve only areas where profits are assured." "U.S. policy should make the system

[19] Frutkin, "International Programs of NASA," loc. cit., pp. 274-75; Arnold W. Frutkin, "Space and the Scientific Community," AIBS Bulletin, 12 (October, 1962), 69.

accessible to all nations, including those where prospective operations are predicted not to be immediately profitable." [20] The Communications Satellite Act of 1962 likewise called for international cooperation, and indicated a prospect that the Communication Satellite Corporation would be obliged to promote political purposes as well as to pursue profit. But neither the bill nor any subsequent pronouncement has made it clear what the bases might be for cooperation in this field. A State Department official denies any thought "that other countries will satisfy their interests in satellite communications by purchasing shares in the U.S. company," and suggests that, instead, the U.S. company may itself "participate in a truly international arrangement which would provide for broad ownership and participation on a world-wide basis." [21] But obviously the bases of international cooperation in this sphere remain to be worked out.[22]

One of the notable bilateral cooperative programs is with the Italian Space Committee. Apart from the launching of sounding rockets in cooperation with NASA, the Italian committee has developed the San Marco Project, calling for the launching of a satellite from a movable platform in the ocean off the east coast of Africa at the equator.

The Italian side is responsible for the concept, design, and construction of the satellite, for the launch platforms and instrumentation, and for much of the downrange tracking equipment. The Italian group will conduct the launching itself. NASA is responsible for technical training of many of the Italian team, for certain preliminary small rocket tests of the Italian satellite instrumentation, and for providing the Scout rocket vehicle which will be employed to place the Italian satellite in orbit.[23]

Still more notable, of course, is the cooperative arrangement made with the Soviet Union in 1962. Even prior to Sputnik, Soviet

[20] U.S. Congress, House, Committee on Science and Astronautics, *Commercial Applications of Space Communications Systems,* H. Rpt. No. 1279, 87th Cong., 1st Sess., 1961, pp. 21-22, 28.

[21] Richard N. Gardner, "Cooperation in Outer Space," *Foreign Affairs,* 41 (January, 1963), 355.

[22] Murray L. Schwartz and Joseph M. Goldsen, *Foreign Participation in Communications Satellite Systems: Implications of the Communications Satellite Act of 1962* (Santa Monica: RAND, 1963); Lincoln P. Bloomfield, "The Politics of Outer Space," *Bulletin of the Atomic Scientists,* 19 (May, 1963), 13.

[23] Arnold W. Frutkin, "International Cooperation in Space Exploration," address at the Third National Conference on the Peaceful Uses of Space, Chicago, Illinois, May 7, 1963, p. 8.

scientists had on numerous occasions suggested international cooperation in space efforts,[24] and the early Soviet satellites were sent up in connection with the IGY. In principle, Soviet endorsement of international cooperation continued, but as a practical matter the stress was on secretiveness. On the American side, there have also been endorsements of cooperation. T. Keith Glennan regarded space as "one of the most fruitful areas for agreement between ourselves and our principal international competitor," [25] and he offered the services of our tracking network when and if the Soviet Union undertook manned space flight—an offer that the Soviet Union did not accept.[26] For whatever reason, Soviet policy shifted in 1961-62.[27] In congratulating President Kennedy on the Glenn flight in February, 1962, Khrushchev included the statement that "if our countries pooled their efforts—scientific, technical, and material—to master the universe, this would be very beneficial for the advance of science and would be joyfully acclaimed by all peoples who would like to see scientific achievements benefit man and not be used for 'cold war' purposes and the arms race." Taking up the suggestion, Kennedy made concrete proposals of cooperation, and the exchange led in June, 1962, to an agreement envisaging cooperation in several fields.[28] The agreement is distinctive in that it calls only for coordinated, parallel action, and not for any very intimate relationship. The United States and the Soviet Union are to establish communication links adequate for the transfer of the data obtained from their meteorological satellites and are to exchange such data. They are to plan a world geomagnetic survey, coordinate the launching of suitably instrumented satellites, and exchange data. They are to conduct experiments in the field of communications, employing an Echo satellite; and in the future they are to consider experiments with active repeater satellites.

[24] U.S. Congress, House, Select Committee on Astronautics and Space Exploration, *The National Space Program*, H. Rpt. No. 1758, 85th Cong., 2d Sess., 1958, p. 206.

[25] U.S. Congress, House, Committee on Science and Astronautics, *To Amend the National Aeronautics and Space Act of 1958*, Hearings . . . on H. Res. 9675, 86th Cong., 2d Sess., 1960, p. 516.

[26] T. Keith Glennan, "Opportunities for International Cooperation in Space Exploration," *Department of State Bulletin*, 42 (January 11, 1960), 62.

[27] U.S. Senate, Committee on Aeronautical and Space Sciences, *Soviet Space Programs: Organization, Plans, Goals, and International Implications*, Staff Report, 87th Cong., 2d Sess., 1962, p. 243.

[28] Senate, *Documents on International Aspects*, 1963, pp. 273-77.

With each other and with other nations they are also to discuss a project for an experimental global system of space communications. In implementing the experiments already agreed upon, each side is to act quite separately from the other and then exchange results. No provision is made for visiting laboratories or launching sites, or for exchanging details about launching vehicles or instrumentation. As Khrushchev pointed out to Kennedy, "Until an agreement on general and complete disarmament is achieved, both our countries will . . . be limited in their abilities to cooperate. . . . The principles for designing and producing military rockets and space rockets are the same." [29]

Nevertheless, in the summer of 1963 Soviet spokesmen appeared to show interest in the possibility of a cooperative lunar program and, as we have seen, Kennedy responded by advancing the proposal publicly. The move brought a mixed response in the United States. There had always been considerable skepticism in Congress about the feasibility of cooperating with the Soviet Union, and some fear that if it occurred the Soviet Union would manage to get the best of the arrangement. James R. Kerr found in 1962 that about half the members of the House space committee took one or both of these views.[30] Moreover, in the fall of 1963 both houses of Congress attached amendments to NASA's appropriation bill for FY1964 that showed opposition to the Kennedy proposal. The House amendment flatly prohibited the use of any money for a manned lunar landing attempted jointly with a Communist country; and the Senate aimed to bar a joint effort with any other country without the consent of Congress.

It seems very unlikely that Kennedy himself expected that an agreement with the Soviet Union would actually be reached. For that matter, it is not clear how serious the Soviet Union had been. The President of the Soviet Academy of Sciences had reportedly suggested that the first step toward a cooperative program should be to agree on the reasons why a manned lunar landing was desirable, which may have been his way of attempting to undermine American motivation.[31] Reasons of an entirely noncompetitive sort might or might not be regarded as adequate.

---

[29] *Ibid.*, p. 251.

[30] James R. Kerr, *Congressmen as Overseers: Surveillance of the Space Program* (Ph.D. dissertation, Stanford University, 1963), p. 252.

[31] *Congressional Record*, Vol. 109, No. 123 (August 9, 1963), 13,903.

Space Cooperation in the United Nations

In the early years of the space age, UN discussions of the possibilities of international action regarding space got mixed up with discussions of disarmament. Eisenhower linked the subjects in his State of the Union message in January, 1957—prior to Sputnik—when he spoke of establishing international control of missile and satellite developments. Two days later a U.S. memorandum submitted to Committee I of the General Assembly endorsed "the objective of assuring that future developments in outer space would be devoted exclusively to peaceful and scientific purposes" and suggested the desirability of "international inspection and participation" in connection with the launching of objects into space.[32] Had the Soviet Union gone along with the American proposal, it would clearly have been the loser in terms of relative power position, for it would have given up the possibility of strikes against the United States with ICBMs while the United States retained the possibility of strikes against the Soviet Union with bombers or with shorter-range missiles launched from advanced bases. It is thus not surprising that the Soviet Union wanted to link the discussion of an agreement regarding the military uses of space with a discussion of the liquidation of American military bases abroad.[33] And so the discussions went on, fruitlessly. The Soviet delegate was certainly right in saying in 1962 that "the question of the prohibition of the use of outer space for military purposes . . . does not admit of a practical solution in isolation from a radical solution of the disarmament problem." [34]

But space is a divisible subject, and in effect the General Assembly divided it in December, 1958, establishing the Ad Hoc Committee on the Peaceful Uses of Outer Space and asking it to report on various topics that had no direct bearing on arms control: (1) the activities and resources of the various international agencies relating to the peaceful uses of outer space; (2) the kinds of cooperation that the United Nations might appropriately sponsor; (3) the appropriate organizational arrangements within the framework of the United Nations for facilitating the cooperation; and (4) legal problems. The committee reported in July, 1959, despite

---

[32] Senate, *Documents on International Aspects*, 1963, p. 38.

[33] *Department of State Bulletin*, 38 (May 19, 1958), 814; 39 (July 7, 1958), 19.

[34] Senate, *Documents on International Aspects*, p. 265.

the fact, noted above, that five members boycotted its sessions.[35] Subsequently, the General Assembly has maintained the division. Proposed restrictions on military activities in space are discussed in conjunction with the question of arms control or disarmament. And proposals concerning "peaceful uses" of space are considered by the enlarged committee. It is with the latter that we are here concerned.

One of the recommendations of the Ad Hoc Committee was that a census of orbiting objects be maintained, and the enlarged committee (the Committee on the Peaceful Uses of Outer Space) endorsed the idea. Subsequently, in December, 1961, the General Assembly enacted a resolution which, among other things, calls upon states launching objects into orbit or beyond to furnish information of an unspecified sort to the Secretary-General of the United Nations, who is to maintain a public registry of the information. Adlai Stevenson has characterized the registry as a "modest but important step toward openness in the conduct of space activities." [36] But it is not really clear what good, if any, it may do. Since each side makes some launches for secret military purposes, each has reason to supply only minimal information for registry. Obviously, the United States depends on its own resources, not on the registry, to keep track of Soviet space activities, and presumably the Soviet Union does the same. So far, the principal apparent result of the resolution is to raise questions about the good faith with which it is being observed. Adlai Stevenson itemizes six satellite launchings which the Soviet Union has failed to register. Various American spokesmen give unqualified assurance that the United States is observing the agreement in full good faith, despite Hungarian allegations to the contrary.[37]

Another General Assembly resolution stems from a recommendation of the Committee on the Peaceful Uses of Outer Space that member states might establish sounding rocket facilities on the geomagnetic equator, available to all members for scientific research. Sponsorship by the United Nations is provided for, the implication being that such sponsorship will make the host country more surely eligible for technical and other assistance from various

---

[35] For the text of the report see *ibid.*, pp. 101-52.

[36] *Department of State Bulletin*, 46 (January 29, 1962), 182.

[37] *New York Times*, December 5, 1962, 2:5; June 7, 1963, 10:3; June 16, 1963, 2:4. Cf. Gardner, *loc. cit.*, p. 349.

international agencies. India is in process of establishing the facility.[38] The United States will surely give assistance in its development and make use of it once it is completed. The extent to which it may become a focus of cooperative activity, e.g., on the part of the Soviet Union, remains to be seen.

The United Nations and its committees have been the principal forum for the discussion of legal issues relating to space. The Ad Hoc Committee, reflecting the view of the United States, concluded that it was neither desirable nor practicable to attempt to formulate a comprehensive code of space law; rather, that it was better to take smaller steps as problems arose and as experience was gained.[39] In December, 1961, the General Assembly unanimously adopted a resolution in which it

commends to states for their guidance . . . the following principles:

a. International law, including the United Nations Charter, applies to outer space and celestial bodies;

b. Outer space and celestial bodies are free for exploration and use by all states in conformity with international law, and are not subject to national appropriation.[40]

Stipulation "a" confirms what is to be expected; members of the United Nations could scarcely maintain that in their relationships with each other in space they are free from the law that they accept for relationships on earth. But for a great many questions the relevant terms of law are very uncertain. Stipulation "b" seemingly makes it clear that no state has a right to exclude another from space, though doubts will persist as long as agreement is lacking on what is and what is not "in conformity with international law." The rule against the "national appropriation" of celestial bodies is much more vague. Does it forbid the United States or the Soviet Union from capturing an asteroid, if this ever becomes possible, and bringing it into near-earth orbit so that its resources can be exploited? If either the United States or the Soviet Union should ever establish any kind of base or colony on the moon or a planet, will it not have at least squatter's rights over the area occupied—and perhaps over a hinterland? What is the difference between occupation and appropriation? Such questions may or may not ever become serious.

---

[38] Senate, *Documents on International Aspects,* 1963, p. 341; Gardner, *loc. cit.,* p. 350.

[39] Senate, *Documents on International Aspects,* 1963, p. 143.

[40] *Ibid.,* p. 226.

In October, 1963, the General Assembly adopted the resolution cited in Chapter 4 calling upon states not to place weapons of mass destruction in orbit, and additional agreements concerning space law seemed to be impending.

We should at least recall the fact, noted above, that the United States joins in international action through the World Meteorological Organization, calling not only for steps to improve weather forecasting but also for "a cooperative search for ways by which man can start modifying the weather." [41] The hope is that "by encouraging cooperation now we may reduce the risk that this power will eventually be used by one nation to achieve selfish military or economic advantage at the expense of others." [42] And cooperative action occurs through UNESCO and the International Telecommunication Union. The latter organization sponsored a conference in the fall of 1963 at which Soviet and American delegates joined others in a notable agreement concerning the allocation of frequencies for space communications.

Conclusion

Speaking to Committee I of the General Assembly in December, 1962, the U.S. delegate, Senator Gore, declared that "United States policy and United States programs for outer space are peaceful in intent, cooperative in practice, and beneficial in action." [43] The summer study of the space program at the University of Iowa led to findings along the same line: "The present level of emphasis by the United States on programs of international cooperation in space science seems to be amply justified by the results to date and by those expected in the future. . . . The NASA International Program is considered to be imaginative and effective in achieving the scientific objectives of international cooperation, and it should be continued under its present policies and guide lines." [44]

This chapter does not cover all the evidence leading to such

[41] Harlan Cleveland, "Four Popular Canards About the United Nations," *Department of State Bulletin,* 45 (November 13, 1961), 800.

[42] Richard N. Gardner, "Outer Space, the Atmospheric Sciences, and U.S. Foreign Policy," *Department of State Bulletin,* 47 (October 1, 1962), 498.

[43] Senate, *Documents on International Aspects,* 1963, p. 369.

[44] National Academy of Sciences, Space Science Board, *A Review of Space Research,* report of a summer study conducted at the State University of Iowa, Iowa City, June 17–August 10, 1962, Publication 1079 (Washington: National Academy of Sciences—National Research Council, 1962), Ch. 15, p. 6.

conclusions, but it offers substantial support for them. In some degree all of the objectives of cooperation, outlined at the beginning of the chapter, are being served. The contribution that can be made to security and peace through international space programs is necessarily marginal. And the same can be said of the contributions that can be made to the other objectives pursued. The space program, in its major aspects, is a national program, and its success or failure in serving the various purposes will depend largely on national action. At the same time, marginal contributions through international action may be helpful and significant.

INFORMATIONAL ACTIVITIES

15

Congress has frequently looked with a critical eye at the publicity efforts of executive agencies. To be sure, in the case of an agency engaged in scientific and exploratory work, there is, in general, no real question about the desirability of releasing and disseminating the results. And Congress and the voters obviously need substantial amounts of information about the activities and problems of governmental agencies if they are to participate at all effectively in the political process. But should Congress permit public funds to be used to shape public opinion? Should it permit them to be used to influence Congress itself? Should it provide funds that will be used for the glorification of executive officials and the achievements of their agencies? The line between the desirable and the undesirable in this general area has proved to be terribly difficult to draw.[1]

In the case of the space program the problem, so far, is only hypothetical. In a highly unusual if not unique legislative provision, the Space Act specifically enjoins NASA to "provide for the widest practicable and appropriate dissemination of information concerning its activities and the results thereof." Moreover, before the space age came along, Congress and the President had already established the U.S. Information Agency (USIA) to tend to the American image in other lands. The result is that both within the country and abroad, extensive informational activities concerning NASA

---

[1] Francis E. Rourke, *Secrecy and Publicity, Dilemmas of Democracy* (Baltimore: Johns Hopkins Press, 1961), pp. 183-97.

are carried on, with full congressional approval; and in one way or another all of the purposes described in the chapters of Part II are served, including some that I have labeled ulterior motives and special interests. Informational activities concerning DOD's part of the space program are much more restricted and will not be covered here.

NASA's Domestic Information Program

Like most aspects of the space effort, the domestic informational program is impressive in terms of its magnitude. It is comprehensive in the audiences it aims to reach, and thus also in the methods and the levels of discourse employed. Lay audiences get major attention. At the same time, NASA disseminates scientific and technical information to specialized audiences, both to facilitate work on the space program itself and to contribute to the development of maximum spin-off benefits.

The most general informational efforts are those of NASA's top leadership. Testimony given to congressional committees is in point here, and, as we have seen, it is voluminous. Though the immediate object is to inform Congress so as to help provide it with a basis for legislative action, the testimony is also available to the public. Virtually all of it is on record. Furthermore, the job of administering the space program includes a great deal of public speech-making. In 1962 Mr. Webb spoke to 49 audiences, and in the first six months of 1963 to 42. As the number of his engagements indicates, he does not wait until he has an important new pronouncement to make, but carries variations on the same themes to one audience after another. He is an open protagonist of the space program, both disseminating information and seeking to persuade. In however restrained a way, he responds to criticisms of the program, including criticisms by former President Eisenhower and Senator Hickenlooper.

Many others in NASA also do a substantial amount of public speaking, e.g., at conferences sponsored by NASA. Those below the top level tend to focus on the special subjects that go with their offices. No central records are kept of the speech-making activities of personnel in the various NASA centers over the country, but it is said to be extensive. And speeches are supplemented by articles that appear in various journals.

Below the top level in NASA, the Assistant Administrator for

Technology Utilization and Policy Planning is responsible for the informational program—which is much broader than his title suggests. The functions for which he is responsible can be described under five headings: (1) public services and information; (2) educational programs and services; (3) "program development"; (4) scientific and technical information; and (5) technology utilization. Depending on the outcome of a reorganization under way, these titles may or may not identify offices.

The first function—public services and information—relates mainly to journalists and their needs. The responsible office issues news releases—some 145 of them in the first six months of 1963— and photos. Every two weeks it sends a one-page Space Sheet, printed in newspaper style, to all newspapers that request it (as 540 have done). The information naturally concerns launchings, flights, and the results achieved, and in addition it concerns such subjects as the letting of contracts, personnel changes, etc. Special packets of material are distributed to the press in advance of the more notable space events, such as the Gordon Cooper shot. For the most part, the materials give particular rather than general facts—"bare facts" rather than interpretation. They depict NASA as a dynamic and successful organization, operating an "open" program and solicitous of the public interest. Film clips are made available for use on TV.

The second function—educational programs and services—is performed mainly through films, special lectures, and exhibits. The responsible office makes available a considerable array of films— most of them of general interest, but some technical—for use on TV or for showing to special audiences. For example, there are films of different lengths on the international satellites, the Mercury program, the Saturn rocket, the orbiting solar observatory, etc. There is a short film, "John Glenn Speaks to Young Americans"; a half-hour film, "The John Glenn Story"; and an hour-long color film, "Friendship 7"—the Glenn capsule. At the time of writing a film on the Gordon Cooper flight is being prepared. The films are widely shown. In addition, as of the summer of 1963, 15 "Space-mobiles" (panel trucks) are assigned to different parts of the country, and the plan is to increase their number. Each one carries two lecturers together with the equipment and materials that they use in lecture demonstrations before various kinds of audiences, e.g., school assemblies and adult education groups. In FY1963 NASA received 7,500 requests for the lecture demonstrations and responded to more than three-fourths of them—audiences totaling 2.5 million being reported; in addition, the Spacemobile lecturers gave 88 TV performances reaching an estimated total audience of 2.8 million. In circumstances considered appropriate, NASA responds to requests for exhibits, ranging from a panel of pictures to the display at the Seattle World's Fair. The Gordon Cooper capsule is scheduled to tour the country.

The third function—"program development"—is more heterogeneous. It includes coordinating NASA's efforts in connection with conferences that it sponsors. In each of three successive years NASA has joined with local sponsors in holding conferences on the peaceful uses of space—in Tulsa, Seattle, and Chicago; it provides the speakers, publishes the proceedings, and cooperates in other ways, leaving it to the local sponsors to make the physical arrangements and issue the invitations and publicity. Similarly, NASA has sponsored two "NASA-Industry Conferences"—in 1960 and 1963—designed to give both a broad understanding of the aims, organization, and activities of NASA and information of more special interest to prospective NASA contractors; and similar conferences have occurred at some of the NASA centers (e.g., the Marshall Space Flight Center). In the fall of 1962 there was a NASA-University Conference at which 300 institutions from all 50 states were represented by 920 professors and administrative officials, who attended without expense to NASA. NASA's purpose was both to impart general information about the space program and to stimulate interest in training and research activities that might be of mutual benefit. "Program development" also includes the undertaking of various socioeconomic studies and research projects.

Inevitably those conducting activities in the above three categories are helping to shape opinion. This automatically goes with the selection of information to present. But there apparently has been no central, high-level decision calling for a deliberate, coordinated, and self-conscious effort to shape opinion in a certain way. The initial selection of staff members—and no doubt their willingness to follow the leads given in public statements by Kennedy, Webb, and others—seems more crucial to the outcome than specific instructions to those on the job. Inquiries concerning themes stressed in NASA's public relations activities elicit only puzzlement. The attitude is that a story is here to be told in an interesting and informative way. Activities are described not in terms of publicity or public relations, or, still less, of propaganda, but rather in terms of an educational effort and in terms of doing a newspaper-type job (the implication being that it calls for the release of "straight" news, without an effort to "sell" anything). Whether so intended or not, this attitude is no doubt itself good public relations.

The fourth and fifth functions—having to do with scientific and technical information and with technology utilization—relate to specialized audiences. The Office of Scientific and Technical Information helps interested parties gain access to scientific and technical literature having to do with space. It distributes literature of this sort emanating from NASA itself and from NASA contractors, plus special publications of various kinds, e.g., the *Orbital Flight Handbook*. It issues the semimonthly *Scientific and Technical Aerospace Reports* (STAR) and supports *International Aerospace Abstracts;* together, these journals provide abstracts of reports and articles on space science appearing all over the world. The abstracts are thoroughly indexed both in print and on magnetic tape for computer-based retrieval. All items abstracted in STAR are reproduced on microforms. Most of these materials are distributed on an automatic basis to NASA centers, contractors, subcontractors, and grantees, to the major libraries, and to various other governmental and private agencies in this country and abroad. This means that STAR and the microforms go out, as of the summer of 1963, to 8,500 addresses. The object is to see to it that scientists and engineers engaged in activities pertaining to space have the fullest opportunity to find out what others have done relating to the problems on which they themselves are working, thus maximizing the prospect that duplication of effort can be avoided and cumulative development occur.[2]

The Office of Technology Utilization seeks to identify innovations —"means of accomplishing a work objective either more effectively than before, or for the first time"—and to find nonspace applications for them. The assertion is that "a really conscious and driving attempt" must be made to see how feasible it is to transfer

---

[2] U.S. Congress, House, Committee on Science and Astronautics, *1964 NASA Authorization*, Hearings, 88th Cong., 1st Sess., 1963, Part 3, pp. 1733-50; Part 4, pp. 3004-5 (hereafter cited as House Hearings, *1964 NASA Authorization*).

innovations from the space program to other fields of activity.[3] To assist in the effort, NASA has set up an Industrial Applications Advisory Committee consisting of high officials in some leading industrial concerns. Innovations that are reported are studied by specialists both within the Office of Technology Utilization and in various research organizations under contract with NASA, and these latter organizations are expected to maintain close contacts with industries in their regions. Though NASA spokesmen disclaim any intention to discriminate among regions, it happens that the distribution of the research institutes reverses the emphasis in the distribution of NASA contracts: four are in the Midwest, two in the South, and one each on the east and west coasts. Moreover, more than four times as many NASA dollars go to the Midwest Research Institute as to any other.[4] NASA also has contracts with a number of universities, calling upon them "to study ways and means to make the scientific community, as well as the industrial and business communities, aware of new opportunities for application of specific developments or processes stemming from the space program."[5] And again it happens that there is a special Midwest emphasis. Assisted by a grant from NASA, Indiana University has established an Aerospace Research Application Center. Thirty industries have joined the Center on a membership basis, each paying a fee of $5,000, thus matching NASA's grant. The Center and the member industries are exploring ways of solving the transfer problem.[6]

So far, the innovations identified have come mainly from NASA centers. Private contractors—through whom NASA says it spends about 92 per cent of its money—have reported very few; this fact was noted above in the chapter on economic development as a motive of the space effort and in the discussion of patent policy in Chapter 13. A change in patent policy is one attack on the problem. And a study of techniques of motivating contractors to report innovations is another; the study is being made by Westinghouse under contract with NASA.[7]

---

[3] *Ibid.*, Part 4, p. 3432.

[4] *Ibid.*, Part 4, p. 3192; Louis B. C. Fong, "The NASA Program of Industrial Applications," in NASA, Office of Scientific and Technical Information, *Proceedings of the Conference on Space-Age Planning*, Chicago, Illinois, May 6-9, 1963 (Washington, 1963), p. 187.

[5] Fong, *loc. cit.*, p. 11.

[6] House Hearings, *1964 NASA Authorization*, Part 4, p. 3191.

[7] Fong, *loc. cit.*, p. 10.

Reporting on the above, the Director of the Office of Technology Utilization says that in NASA's view "the results of its own R&D effort [constitute] a national resource which must be utilized for the benefit of all mankind." NASA "feels it has a responsibility to the civilian industrial community" to make information available concerning potential nonspace applications of scientific and technological developments.[8] The assumption is that the problem of transfer, of innovation, of research rests on a state of mind, and NASA is seeking to cultivate a favorable state of mind.[9] The outlook and the activities of NASA are somewhat similar to those that go with agricultural extension services. Government—and in this case it is the federal government exclusively—is employing the rough equivalent of county agents to visit industrial concerns rather than farmers, to instruct them on potentialities created by space activities.

The Information Program Abroad

The USIA has prime responsibility for informational activities abroad—and, of course, commercial and other news and information services operate, as they do within the United States. The USIA has some 239 offices, manned by 1,300 Agency officers, in 105 countries, as well as a headquarters in Washington. With the population of the world as its potential audience, its activities are extensive and varied. It supplies voluminous written and illustrative materials on many subjects and in many languages for use in newspapers and magazines abroad. It publishes four magazines in Washington for distribution abroad, and its posts overseas publish 62 more, plus other publications. It operates 182 libraries and 79 reading rooms abroad, and supports 154 binational centers. It distributes books, stages exhibits, sponsors cultural events, and assists in the selection of foreign leaders and students who come to the United States each year. It distributes films, kinescopes, and videotapes over the world for showing in theaters and over TV—documentaries, newsreels and clips, and short subjects. It operates the Voice of America, currently broadcasting by short wave 761 hours a week in 36 languages, and it provides taped radio programs to some 3,000 medium-wave stations in the free world. And it engages in various related activities.

---

[8] *Ibid.*, p. 4.

[9] House Hearings, *1964 NASA Authorization*, Part 4, p. 3434.

Necessarily, the USIA gives considerable attention to the space program, and it gets very substantial cooperation and financial support from NASA. To facilitate the cooperation and to assure full coverage of the space effort, the USIA assigns one of its officers to NASA headquarters full time. Informational efforts occur in all of the categories mentioned above, and the efforts become especially intense in connection with the more spectacular events. The USIA's Press and Publication Service obtains various kinds of materials from NASA—either in quantity or for reproduction in quantity—which it distributes abroad: articles for newspapers or journals, photos, pamphlets, books. Prior to such events as the Gordon Cooper flight it sends packets to USIA posts giving background materials of the sort that mass media might use. The Voice of America provides full coverage. For the Gordon Cooper flight it "employed the largest radio network ever put together, utilizing 55 transmitters at strategic points around the globe with a total output of 5,673,000 watts, equivalent to the aggregate power of the 170 top U.S. standard broadcast radio stations." [10] Special Voice of America teams, reporting in Russian, French, German, Spanish, and Malay, were at Cape Canaveral. The USIA's estimate is that the Cooper flight drew "the largest overseas radio audience in history—some 50 million listeners." "Twice as many stations abroad picked up and rebroadcast VOA's running account of the Cooper flight as did on the previous Glenn shoot. In Latin America alone, 230 stations . . . rebroadcast the Spanish and Portuguese newscasts." [11]

The USIA's TV service obtains clips from NASA which it makes available to stations abroad, and it coordinates foreign network coverage of NASA activities. Most of the material distributed by the USIA motion picture service is supplied by NASA. The following concerns coverage of the Glenn flight.

A dramatic 10-minute documentary film—"John Glenn Orbits the World" —was released within the week to 106 countries, narrated in 32 languages. The distribution totaled 1,300 prints, including 400 35mm prints shown in theaters in 86 countries and 900 16mm prints seen in non-theatrical and mobile unit programs sponsored by USIA, ministries of education, schools, universities, and civic organizations. . . .

It is estimated that overseas audiences totaling well over 200 million saw the film during the four months following the orbital flight.

---

[10] USIA, Office of Public Information, Release No. 20, May 15, 1963.

[11] USIA, *20th Review of Operations, January 1–June 30, 1963*, p. 13.

An hour-long color documentary, "Friendship 7," produced by NASA, was also widely distributed by the USIA abroad. A total of 225 English-language prints were distributed to 71 countries and other prints were narrated in French, Spanish, Arabic, Hausa, Swahili, Mandarin, Indonesian, Burmese, Hindi, and Portuguese for further distribution.[12]

A half-hour film went out before the Gordon Cooper flight, and shorter films were released for use on TV and in theaters shortly after the flight. Space activities are covered regularly in *Panorama Panamericano*, a TV show supplied by the USIA and used in 48 cities in Latin America. A number of the exhibits displayed by the USIA abroad come from NASA: posters, scale and full-scale models of various satellites, etc. Two thousand copies of a seven-panel full-color exhibit were shipped abroad prior to the Glenn flight. The capsule in which Glenn orbited the earth was put on display in some 23 countries—the American Air Force providing the necessary Globemaster, and NASA and the USIA each providing an escort to manage the display and give explanations. The Soviet Union rejected a proposal that the capsule be displayed in Leningrad. Two Spacemobiles, accompanied by USIA officers trained by NASA, are touring Africa; others are in Latin America, Europe, and India, and the plan is to send out more. Foreign journalists and science writers coming to the United States, as well as distinguished foreign visitors, get special attention and services. Considerable play is given to the Echo satellite, which can be seen relatively easily, and to the meteorological satellites—especially when they provide a basis for typhoon and hurricane warnings. Before Telstar I went into orbit in July, 1962, the USIA gave attention to the question of gaining maximum political benefit from its utilization; and among other things it arranged for an exchange of telephone calls via Telstar between officials of 23 American cities and their counterparts in 23 Western European cities. It also distributed a 20-minute TV program concerning communications satellites and their possibilities.

We might note that NASA not only assists the USIA but engages in some activities abroad itself. In principle, "scientific" tasks abroad relating to space belong to NASA. For example, as we noted in the preceding chapter, NASA's program of international cooperation includes sending personnel abroad to give scientific or technical instruction; and NASA personnel commonly attend appropriate international conferences of scientists. But the line

[12] USIA, *18th Report to Congress, January 1–June 30, 1962*, pp. 7-8.

between the scientific tasks of NASA and the informational and educational tasks of the USIA is sometimes difficult to draw, and questions arise that have to be settled on an *ad hoc* basis: e.g., should a Spacemobile be manned by an employee of NASA or an employee of USIA?

The presumption is that the purposes of the USIA in publicizing the space program fit within its more general purposes, described as follows by its Director, Edward R. Murrow: "Everywhere we seek to encourage constructive public support for what the President has described as 'a peaceful world community of free and independent states, free to choose their own future and their own system so long as it does not threaten the freedom of others.' We present the United States as a strong, democratic, dynamic nation qualified to lead world efforts toward this goal." [13] Another way of putting it is that, in general, the USIA aims to maximize the prospect that other societies will develop and behave in ways that are compatible with the kind of life that we want to lead within the United States; and its sole means to this end is the dissemination of information about the United States—its activities and its policies.

In July, 1961, Mr. Murrow issued a memorandum identifying topics and themes to be given special emphasis in USIA activities; they related to the question of a ban on nuclear testing, to U.S. support for Berlin and for security and freedom everywhere, to support for the United Nations, to the desire for "a world of free choice" instead of a "world of coercion," and to the principles that best assure the desirable modernization of newly developing nations. Space was not explicitly mentioned in the memorandum as a topic calling for special emphasis. Nevertheless it is obvious that the USIA has been making a very substantial effort abroad to capitalize on space achievements. The themes stressed are identified as follows in the President's report to Congress concerning U.S. space activities in 1962: (1) the space program is peaceful and co-operative; (2) space achievements are evidence of competence in science and technology; (3) the stand for peace is not incompatible with the development of a strong defensive capability; and (4) the U.S. program is "open."

My own reading of a sample of USIA materials—mainly press service packets, including the one sent out prior to the Gordon

---

[13] U.S. Congress, House, Committee on Foreign Affairs, Subcommittee on International Organizations and Movements, *Winning the Cold War: The U.S. Ideological Offensive,* Hearings, 88th Cong., 1st Sess., 1963, Part 1, p. 3.

Cooper flight—suggests a rather different set of themes. The articles seem designed to convey implicitly some such message as the following: The United States is responding to great challenges in space, striving to solve significant problems. In our striving we encounter severe difficulties, and we have some failures. But we are also mastering difficulties, solving problems, achieving, and seeking further improvement. Moreover, we are both bold and determined, resolutely confident that in all respects, now or later, outstanding success will be ours. Ingenious and highly motivated men can accomplish almost anything! In our striving for achievement and success, we are nevertheless responsible—concerned about the health and safety of individual men and taking pains to avoid harm to any person or project anywhere. In fact, what we are achieving is beneficial to all mankind, and we do it in the open for all to see. We lead in most respects, and we will lead in all respects! Our activities are thus worthy, inspiring, and destined to succeed. Identify with us! Join us, giving your help! The future is on our side!

USIA materials rarely refer to the military part of the American space program, no doubt because of security restrictions and because of a desire to put the stress on peaceful purposes. Moreover, there are very few explicit references to the Soviet Union.

Data on the impact of the space program and related informational activities on opinion abroad are quite incomplete. The USIA makes contracts with certain foreign organizations to conduct public opinion polls. The results are, of course, available to various officials in the Executive branch of the government and, on request, to the chairmen and ranking minority members of appropriate congressional committees; but they are not made public for one or two years, depending on circumstances. Those available at the time of writing extend only through July, 1961, i.e., through the Gagarin flight but not through the Glenn flight. Polls taken in the latter part of November, 1957 (more than a month after Sputnik), in Great Britain, West Germany, France, Italy, and Norway indicated a preponderant view, by wide margins, that the Soviet Union was ahead of the United States in scientific development; only West Germany gave the United States the lead, by a narrow margin.[14] The question had not been asked prior to Sputnik, so exact comparisons are not available, but surely the polls marked

---

[14] USIA, Office of Research and Analysis, Survey Research Studies, "The Impact of Sputnik on the Standing of the U.S. Versus the U.S.S.R.," WE-52, December, 1957.

a sharp decline in America's standing. The import of this is qualified by other questions revealing that most of the respondents did not really consider the Soviet Union "generally ahead," but only ahead in space, and that most of them attributed the space leadership to an exceptional effort rather than to a general superiority of the Soviet system.

The best that can be said of the polls of June-July, 1961, is that their outcome was slightly less unfavorable.[15] The West Germans again attributed scientific leadership to the United States by a wide margin (50 per cent for the United States, 19 per cent for the Soviet Union) and the Italians switched their position (36 per cent to 28 per cent), but the British and the French still thought the Russians ahead. Of the British respondents, 21 per cent named the United States and 52 per cent named the Soviet Union; and the corresponding figures for the French were 16 per cent and 49 per cent. Asked which country they expected to be ahead in scientific development in 10 years, the respondents took similar positions; the West Germans and the Italians preponderantly named the United States, and the British and French preponderantly named the Soviet Union. The respondents in all four countries thought that the Soviet Union was ahead of the United States in total military strength; the average was 19 per cent for the United States and 41 per cent for the Soviet Union. They assigned space leadership to the Soviet Union by much wider margins, and only the West Germans expected the United States to wrest space leadership from the Soviet Union within the decade.

Given the orbital flights by Glenn and the other astronauts subsequent to the above polls, it is reasonable to expect that American standing abroad has improved relatively, though, as indicated above, polling data are not publicly available to establish the point. I have, however, seen surveys of the foreign press prepared by USIA personnel, e.g., after the Gordon Cooper orbital flight. They suggest that the reaction abroad to the American space effort is overwhelmingly favorable. Occasional criticisms appear, e.g., that the talent and resources devoted to space would be better devoted to solving various problems on earth, but, according to reports sent to Washington, the criticisms are very much outnumbered by expressions of praise and by indications that people abroad feel that

[15] USIA, Research and Reference Service, Survey Research Studies, "The Image of U.S. Versus Soviet Science in West European Public Opinion. A Survey in Four West European Countries," WE-3, October, 1961.

the space effort, rather than being American, is an effort of man (or of the free world)—an effort in which they therefore share. Wishes and hopes—and even demands—are expressed that the sharing might be more concrete and extensive. Responses to the manned flights are, of course, especially fulsome. One USIA officer reports that "every spaceman becomes a citizen of the world in the eyes of the millions who follow his flight." Furthermore, interviews with USIA and State Department officials who have access to all available information about attitudes abroad reveal considerable satisfaction and optimism on their part concerning the impact of the space program—and of publicity about it—on attitudes abroad. The space program is said to inspire confidence in the future of the United States and of the free world.

PART **IV** CONCLUSION

CONCLUSION

16

The questions posed in Chapter 1 concerned the why and the how of the space program, and the rationality of the relevant decisions. I did not expect to prove that the space program is or is not justifiable, and I have not offered proof. In the first place, I have deliberately excluded some relevant questions about the means being employed to execute the program; and, in the second place, I have simply taken some values for granted. But even so I have aimed to contribute to thought on the question and to present a general, macroscopic analysis of decision-making concerning space.

Excluded Questions

The excluded questions fall into two principal categories: technological and administrative. The main technological question concerns the degree of probability that the lunar goal is achievable. What are the odds that the first, or second, or third effort to get a man to the moon and back will succeed? If disaster should overtake successive teams of astronauts attempting lunar landings, or attempting to get back to the earth, the question of the rationality of the effort will take on a very different hue. I have not examined this kind of possibility. I have simply proceeded on the assumption that the chance of success is great enough to make it sensible to talk about the justifiability of the program in other terms.

The main administrative question, excluded in part, is whether the effort can be managed in such a way as substantially to realize the technological possibilities. To get an answer to this question, much more would have to be done than is in fact done in the chapters of Part III. I have made no attempt to assess procedures for recruiting and assigning personnel, and no attempt to appraise the administrative skills of Mr. Webb, Dr. Dryden, and the dozens of others who share in making crucial managerial and technical decisions. The chapters of Part III take up organizational and administrative questions of a broader and more general kind. Human failures are always possible, even within a structure that in general is effectively organized. Again, however, I have proceeded on the assumption that the chance of successful management of the undertaking, vast and complex as it is, is great enough to make it sensible to talk about the justifiability of the program in other terms.

Values, and Lindblom's Analysis of Decision-Making

To take values for granted is, I think, inevitable. I share the view generically described as positivist that there is no way of proving that one or another goal value should or should not be pursued—that there is no scientific way of establishing what ought to be done for its own sake. Goal values are postulated or accepted on faith—perhaps after experience has demonstrated that they are instrumentally so useful. The goal values with which I have dealt—those commonly cited to justify the space program—are almost universally accepted in this country, though some may prefer to think of one or more of them as instrumental.

Not only are goal values postulated, but also the relative importance to be assigned to them. Usually a course of action promotes several values at once, but often, too, the promotion of one set of values occurs at the cost of another set, and to determine how much sacrifice of some values is justifiable in order to promote others more fully is a terribly difficult problem—made all the more complicated by the possibility that the sacrifices may be only temporary and that the values temporarily sacrificed may themselves in the long run be served. It is imaginable, in principle, that values could be precisely weighted, that costs of pursuing them could be predicted accurately, and that a computer could then be used to determine how to maximize the achievement of values. But in practice the problem, at least with major governmental decisions, is too complex to be handled in this way.

Charles E. Lindblom has analyzed the process of governmental decision-making, very cogently, in terms of two contrasting models.[1] On the one hand, he describes the "rational-comprehensive" way of making policy choices, calling for consideration of the whole range of possible ends or values and the deliberate selection and weighting of those to pursue, followed by consideration of the range of possible methods and selection from among them. As the label implies, the method, in principle, gives free rein to rationality and might lead to drastic new policies. On the other hand, he describes the "method of successive limited comparisons." The comparisons are between possible policies that will have different outcomes, and they are limited in several respects. They involve "attention to relatively few values and relatively few alternative policies among the countless alternatives that might be imagined." The alternative policies "differ in relatively small degree from policies presently in effect." Thus the different outcomes considered are marginal and incremental rather than fundamental and radical, and the focus is simply on the differences. The successive limited comparisons involve the simultaneous consideration of the ends and means that are immediately relevant to the differences, not the successive consideration of all the various possible ends and then of all the various possible means.

Obviously the method of successive limited comparisons is the more manageable of the two; and it comes far closer than the rational-comprehensive model in applying to the various decisions made in connection with the space program. At the same time, Lindblom's description of the method needs to be modified some if it is to apply without strain, especially to the decision of May, 1961, to aim at a lunar landing in this decade.

After indicating that the alternative policies "differ in relatively small degree from policies presently in effect," Lindblom goes on to say, "Democracies change their policies almost entirely through incremental adjustments. Policy does not move in leaps and bounds." Now a policy is a strategy comprehending ends, rules of behavior (guides) for promoting them, and actual courses of action for promoting them.[2] No doubt the first of these components—the ends—

---

[1] Charles E. Lindblom, "The Science of 'Muddling Through,'" *Public Administration Review*, 19 (Spring, 1959), 79-88.

[2] Richard C. Snyder, H. W. Bruck, and Burton Sapin, *Decision-Making as an Approach to the Study of International Politics* (Princeton: Princeton University, Organizational Behavior Section, 1954), p. 52.

do change incrementally; but if the assumption relates to the rules or, above all, to the means, as I suppose it must, then doubts arise. The doubts concern not so much the question whether the model focusing on limited comparisons and increments can be applied as on the question whether it is apt. In some sense, everything about human affairs is limited and everything that is new or additional is incremental. But though there is no problem about saying that if a gnat lands on an elephant its weight is incremental, what if the elephant lands on the gnat? To employ a political illustration, what if the choice is between continued formal peace and the onset (or the very serious risk) of unrestricted nuclear war? The unrestricted nuclear war might be fought in the name of the same ends as those pursued in peacetime, so in this respect the comparisons required would be very limited. But the rules of behavior and the methods of action would differ so much that it seems inappropriate, if not grotesque, to think of the change as incremental and to think of the choice as stemming from successive limited comparisons.

Associated with the method of successive limited comparisons is the assumption that interest groups will be calling relevant considerations to the attention of the decision-makers, and that this is a more reliable means of getting attention for them than "rational-comprehensive" analysis. The point is plausible. But it is very doubtful whether interest groups have much to do with many major choices involving potentially drastic and far-reaching change— change pretty much beyond their ken, or outside the immediate area of their concern. I am not saying that interest groups are completely silent on such issues, but they often play a minor role.[3]

No other historical or potential decisions are in the same category with a choice between peace and unrestricted nuclear war. But others raise the same kinds of questions about the notion of decision-making based on successive limited comparisons. I would nominate, for example, the decisions leading to the Truman Doctrine, the North Atlantic Treaty, intervention in Korea, nonintervention in Hungary, the condemnation of Britain and France at Suez, intervention in Lebanon, support for the regimes in Taiwan and Vietnam, and the confrontation with the Soviet Union over missile bases in Cuba in the fall of 1962. And I think that, in terms of the problem under scrutiny, the commitment of May, 1961, to

---

[3] Raymond A. Bauer, Ithiel de Sola Pool, and Lewis A. Dexter, *American Business and Public Policy: The Politics of Foreign Trade* (New York: Atherton Press, 1963), esp. Ch. 12.

the lunar program is in the same general category. These decisions, though leaving values pretty much unchanged, all had radical import either in identifying rules of behavior that we would follow or in initiating major action programs.

Decision-Making About Space

But if the process of reaching such decisions is not accurately or aptly described either in terms of "rational-comprehensive" analysis or in terms of incremental change following successive limited comparisons, what description is better? So far as the decision of May, 1961, is concerned, my reading of events suggests something like the following.

VALUES

We start with values—with all of those dealt with in the chapters of Part II, but particularly with national security, national prestige, and national pride. For the overwhelming majority of those who speak up on problems of space policy, these are goal values (independent interests, self-justifying ends). As goal values they are emotionally based, though the emotions may be tutored by experience. It is a matter of emotion, of will, that we should maintain security against external threat, that we should enjoy a position of prestige in the world, and that we should be able to credit ourselves with achievements of which we can be proud. We can argue about what will contribute effectively to security, prestige, and pride, but (except for the minority of whom these are instrumental values) we do not argue that they are desirable. It is unpatriotic, if not almost sacrilegious, to question the desirability of maintaining national security against external threat, totally unacceptable to be treated by others with derision, scorn, and contempt, and so unthinkable that we would fail to maintain a basis for pride that we do not in fact ordinarily think of it. We assume it as a part of the natural order of things that we should seek to maintain security, that we should occupy a position of prestige in the world, and that our status and achievements should be such as to make us proud.

Of the three values, in relation to Sputnik, I believe that the most important was pride. Security is vitally important, of course, but it was threatened not so much by Sputniks as by missiles. Prestige is important too, but people who think they have a legitimate basis for pride can live without prestige or can live in the hope and expectation that what leads to pride will also give them prestige in time. But we cannot live with ourselves without pride. We cannot tolerate humiliation without making as great an effort as is necessary to overcome it.

We have other values too. We want peace, we want to promote scientific knowledge and technological development, and we want economic progress. But these values are not in the same category as the others. Virtually all who make them goal values assign less urgency or importance to them than to security, prestige, and pride. And many make them instrumental values, to be assessed in terms of their usefulness in serving more important goals and supported accordingly. It is instructive that even many of the scientists who support the space program do so more in the name of pride-in-achievement than in the name of the scientific knowledge that can be gained.

Sputnik was very widely regarded in this country—above all in political circles in Washington—as a threat to American security and as a blow to national prestige; and, though other words were usually employed to express the fact, it was also taken as a sharp blow to pride. And the blow was all the more galling because it came from what had been regarded as a rather backward country with a regime that, though feared, was also despised. Eisenhower resisted these reactions to Sputnik; and it followed that he would keep the space program relatively restricted, as he did. There was no great emotional involvement in the matter as far as he was concerned. But others around him took a different view, especially so far as prestige and pride were concerned. And obviously Kennedy took a different view.

As I reconstruct the situation, there was no call for rational-comprehensive analysis, and not much call for a comparison of possible ends or values. A few values of very great importance were at stake, pride above all. It is exaggerating considerably to compare the situation to the one created by Pearl Harbor, but still the analogy is suggestive. Had we conceded to Japan's demands in the Pacific, we no doubt could have bought peace there for an indefinite period. Were Hawaii and the Philippines worth a war? The very question is shocking, and one of the major factors that make it shocking is that Pearl Harbor was not simply an attack on territory; it was an intolerable affront to pride. Once the attack occurred, very little else mattered. Despite Eisenhower, many others in Washington saw Sputnik in something like the same light, even if it was dimmer. This kind of attitude is not uncommon. We have several phrases suggestive of the pursuit of one goal, or a very restricted set of goals, almost regardless of the consequences in other respects. People get implacably determined to do things "come hell or high water." They take a course of action and "let the chips fall where they may." They "nail the flag to the mast." They resolve to achieve a given goal "or bust." They "throw caution to the winds." They proceed "come what may." They thrill to the principle, "Millions for defense, but not one cent for tribute," and some even glory in the order, "Damn the torpedoes! Full speed ahead!" Emotional commitments are obviously involved. Of all the historical political movements and achievements that we regard as great, I wonder whether a high proportion were not based on a certain degree of abandon. In seeking equality for themselves, are the Negroes applying either rational-comprehensive analysis or the method of successive limited comparisons?

It is clear that in Congress after Sputnik and in the Executive after Kennedy's inauguration, very great importance was attached to beating the Russians. The crucial problem for the new Kennedy Administration was to identify a spectacular space event in which we had a good chance of doing it. I am not contending that Kennedy and those involved in his decision concerned themselves solely with pride, or even with pride, prestige, and security. Neither am I alleging that they proceeded with the imprudence and recklessness suggested by the "damn the torpedoes" order. Many were no doubt moved by some other values, and some were probably moved more by other values, as was the case with the scientists who advised Eisenhower. They could have pressed for a different decision had their consideration of the matter called for one. Moreover, even those swayed primarily by the more obviously competitive considerations no doubt concluded, through cursory analysis or intuition, that some other values would be served and that none would be hopelessly compromised or even seriously jeopardized. Moreover, it is clear that there was checking of the technological possibilities. Whether or not the lunar landing and safe return prove to be feasible, the question was considered.

MEANS

If we start with values in explaining and appraising a decision, what is the next step? It must be consideration of the choice of means. Again I join Lindblom in rejecting the notion of a "rational-comprehensive" analysis in the choice of means, at least as he describes the process. Whether the "method of successive limited comparisons" is the one that was followed, or should be followed, is perhaps moot. Just as Sputnik called a limited set of crucial values into question, so it fixed limits, however vague, on the choice of means that could be used in response. If Soviet space power threatened American security, the means of defense to be considered had to relate to that space power, and not to Soviet tanks. If Sputnik undermined American prestige, the means of recouping the situation had to fall within an area that the various peoples of the world would regard as comparable. To respond to Sputnik by addressing ourselves to the problem of a low water table would have been absurd. Similarly, if Sputnik wounded American pride, the response had to be relevant to the reason for the wound. It is our habit to think of ourselves as the people with know-how, the people who are bold, innovative pioneers—first in the world in technological achievement. Sputnik challenged this image of ourselves and made it seem irrelevant to suggest that we should restore our pride through urban redevelopment and educational improvement. The prospect that the Soviet Union would send a man into space made it almost a foregone conclusion that we would do the same. Even Eisenhower found it desirable to approve this response.

In principle, we—the American people—might adhere to different values or pursue them in different ways. It is not inevitable—it is not naturally ordained—that we should postulate national pride, national prestige, and national security as values or place so much emphasis upon them. Neither is it inevitable that know-how and technological achievement should be so important as sources of pride. Other peoples find satisfactions in other instrumental and goal values and so, no doubt, could we. A major effort in popular persuasion might conceivably have altered our postulates and our conception of what matters. But in practice it was not attempted and is not being attempted on a significant scale. Eisenhower made some effort to do it, but not a major one; and not enough other people have been willing to join him to make the effort succeed.

LIMITED COMPARISONS

Given the values, and given the types of responses that the nature of the challenge required (and this means that a great deal is given!), the method of successive limited comparisons then becomes applicable. For example, Kennedy might have made something other than a lunar landing the key event. The goal might have been to establish an orbiting space laboratory and maintain it for a year, or it might have been a manned fly-by of Mars, or it might have been something else. Moreover, after selecting the lunar landing, Kennedy might have said something about the timing other than that the goal should be achieved in this decade. For that matter, all of the decisions concerning organizational arrangements, mobilizing resources, international cooperation, and the dissemination of information may well have reflected successive limited comparisons.

Perhaps the problem in all this is that Lindblom had in mind primarily decision-making at the administrative level whereas my concern is with high policy. He assumed that "policy does not move in leaps and bounds," whereas my concern is with situations in which it does precisely that, at least where rules of behavior and courses of action are concerned.

The Test of Agreement

Lindblom makes another comment that I should note, that the test of the goodness or correctness of a policy is not to be found in the ends selected or even in the means employed but simply in agreement. "For the method of successive limited comparisons, the test is agreement on policy, which remains possible even when agreement on values is not. . . . In an important sense, therefore, it is not irrational for an administrator to defend a policy as good without being able to specify what it is good for." James Reston accuses Kennedy of using this test, at least by anticipation, saying that he asked not what was good for the country but what was easiest to get through Congress. It is quite possible too that many congressmen have used the test: with what vote on space legislation would their constituents most fully agree? And, notwithstanding Reston's reproving tone, the test is not bad, though I would shift the emphasis from the one employed by Lindblom. The emphasis, I believe, should be on the point that agreement reflects either shared values or different values that can all be served by the same course of action. The space program, including the lunar program, passes this test handsomely; agreement has so far been overwhelming.

One difficulty with the test of agreement is the failure of people to know their own minds and the inconstancy of their purposes. Before Sputnik there was apathy about space, and afterward came what some called hysteria; subsequently, the more the United States has achieved in space the more signs there are of waning enthusiasm. Sputnik called values into our consciousness of which we previously were unaware, and now that the threat to these values is declining there is a tendency to forget about them again. The test of agreement necessarily goes with decision-making in a democracy, but detached observers can scarcely be satisfied to shift their judgments about policy along with the differing outcomes of successive tests.

INDEX

Abelson, Dr. Philip H., 91-92, 159
Advanced Research Projects Agency (ARPA): established, 17, 191; transfer of space functions, 18, 192
Aeronautics and Astronautics Coordinating Board (AACB), 202-3
Aerospace Research Application Center, 257
Air Force: von Karman report, 10; and missiles, 10, 11; and manned space flight, 43-46; Project Forecast, 69; its future role, 69, 171-72; considerations influencing its askings, 70-72. See also Department of Defense
Allen, George V., 124, 130
Almond, Gabriel, 137-38
American Rocket Society, 13
Anfuso, Representative Victor L., 148
Antarctica, 82
Apollo Project: lunar landing as goal, 3, 7, 146-47, 273-75; proposed, 25; costs, 26, 95-99, 106-9; military significance, 61, 176; scientific significance, 90-99
Armed Services Committee, House, 197
Arms control: inspection from space, 39; and space cooperation, 247

Army: and missiles, 11; seeks space role, 13-16 passim; and Explorer I, 16. See also Department of Defense
Army Ballistic Missile Agency: transferred in part to NASA, 43, 189
Asteroids: as source of wealth, 115-16; and national appropriation, 249
Atlas, 10
Atomic Energy Act of 1946, 18

Bambi, 47-49
Bauer, Raymond A.: on motives of space program, 138; on business attitudes toward NASA, 213
Bay of Pigs, 27, 166
Becker, Loftus, 51
Bell, Representative Alphonzo, 145
Bellcomm, 221, 224
Berkner, Dr. Lloyd V.: on early space proposals, 12-13; on scientific advice, 14-15; on science and the technological revolution, 100-101; on U.S. leadership, 151-52; on pride in achievement, 157
Bombardment from space, 49-51
Boston: and electronics center, 168
Brodie, Dr. Bernard, 58